Christian
Commitment
For the 1980s

Which Side Are We On?

by
The Inter-Religious Task Force for Social Analysis

A Study/Action Guide

Editorial Working Group

ROSE ANCONA
Methodist Federation for Social Action
New York, NY

JOHN BOONSTRA, No. Amer. Reg. Sec.,
World Student Christian Federation
Co-Editor, *Radical Religion*
Berkeley, CA

PEGGY CASE
Student, Political Activist
Pontiac, MI

SHEILA COLLINS
United Methodist Board of
Global Ministries
TIA Women's Project
New York, NY

ROBERT L. DeWITT, Episcopal Bishop
Editor, *THE WITNESS*
Pres., Church and Society Network
Ambler, PA

MARGARET FERRY
Church and Society Network
Bear Creek, PA

JOSEPH L. HARDEGREE, JR.
Co-Editor, *Radical Religion*
Palo Alto, CA

DAVID KALKE, Worker-pastor,
Lutheran Church in America
Theology In the Americas
N.Y. CIRCUS
New York, NY

KATHLEEN SCHULTZ, IHM
Nat. Exec. Sec., Christians
for Socialism
Detroit, MI

GEORGE McCLAIN, Minister
United Methodist Church
Exec. Sec., Methodist Federation for
Social Action
New York, NY

HARRY STRHARSKY
Investigative Resource Center
Oakland, CA

MARY LOU SUHOR
Managing Editor, *THE WITNESS*
Ambler, PA

SANDY WYLLIE
Carpet, Linoleum Installer
Co-Editor, *Radical Religion*
Oakland, CA

EDITOR, PROJECT COORDINATOR
Harry Strharsky

CO-EDITOR
Mary Lou Suhor

PRODUCTION MANAGER
Brian McNaught

ART, COVER
Enrique Picheta

Special Thanks to:

Kay Atwater
Bill Berkowitz
Community Press Features
Data Center Graphics
    Collection

Episcopal Church Pub. Co.
    Bd. of Directors
Don Eunson
Bruce Ewen
Lynda Ann Ewen
Fred Goff

Liberation News Service
Sarah Stewart
Loretta Strharsky
Donna Taylor
Xanadu Graphics

Library of Congress Catalog Card Number: 80-80580
ISBN 0-936476-02-8 (Volume 2)
ISBN 0-936476-00-1 (Set)

Published by the Inter-Religious Task Force for Social Analysis
464 19th St., Oakland, CA 94612
Printed and Bound in the U.S.A.

Contents

Orientation and Overview 5

SESSION 1
Understanding Political & Religious Ideology
Introduction 10
The Idolatry and Promise of the Church 12
    by George D. McClain
Declaration 16
    by Several Bishops of Chile
Response 18
    by Pablo Richard
Unmasking the Corporate Missionary 21
    by David J. Kalke
Apostles of Reaction 29
    by George D. McClain
Group Exercise
    Suspicion and Bible Reading 36

SESSION 2
Capitalism in Crisis
Introduction 40
What Makes It a Crisis? 42
    by The Union for
    Radical Political Economics
The Present Crisis and the Danger of War 48
    by *People's Tribune*
A Glossary for Political Economics 59
    by Peggy Case
Group Exercise
    Analyzing the News 61

SESSION 3
Class Struggle In Our Times
Introduction 64
Contradictions Within Finance Capital 67
    by Larry Mellman
The National Association of Manufacturers 71
    by Lennie Brody
The Right-Wing Offensive
and the Working Class 73
    by Johanna and Robert Brenner
Group Exercise
    Which Side Are We On? Role Play 85

SESSION 4
Exploring the Alternatives
Introduction 89
Overcoming the Myths:
    The Political Economy of Socialism 91
    by Kathleen Schultz, IHM
Illusionary Alternatives to Capitalism 98
    by Joseph L. Hardegree, Jr.

Group Exercise
    Ideological Role Play 110

SESSION 5
The Socialist Movement in U.S. History
Introduction 113
Left Political Parties in the United States:
    Some Historical Lessons 115
    by Joseph L. Hardegree, Jr.
Victory in West Virginia 128
    by Mary Harris "Mother" Jones
Solidarity on the Embarcadero 134
    by Richard O. Boyer and
    Herbert M. Morais
Group Exercise
    Labor Movement Oral History Project 139

SESSION 6
Christians and the Socialist Option
Introduction 141
People's Institute of Applied Religion 143
    by Bill Troy and Claude Williams
Rediscovering Winifred Chappell 150
    by Miriam J. Crist
The Church League for Industrial Democracy 155
    by Gordon Greathouse
On Being Christian and Socialist 160
    by Dorothy Sölle
Group Exercise
    Uncovering Our Hidden Christian History 167

SESSION 7
How Do We Organize?
Introduction 169
Christians for Socialism:
    U.S. History & Perspectives 172
    by Kathleen Schultz, IHM
Opposition to the Tax Revolt 175
    by David J. and Judith W. Snider
    and Hugh C. White
The Transformation of St. Mark's Church:
    A Profile of Radical Christian Education 178
    by George D. McClain
"City Life":
    Lessons of the First Five Years 181
    by Kathy McAfee
New Testament Letters and
Combat Liberalism:
    A Comparative Reading 190
Group Exercise
    Activism and Self-Criticism 192

Appendix 193

Orientation and Overview

During the early waves of migration to the United States, as the Statue of Liberty beckoned to the oppressed, "Give me your tired, your poor, your huddled masses yearning to be free," this country was referred to by some as a melting pot of hardworking people seeking to fulfill the "American dream." As we enter the 1980s, that "melting pot" is more like a seething cauldron.

In the intervening years, many people have participated in an historic and intensifying struggle between capitalism and socialism. As capitalism gained hegemony over the world in protracted imperialistic lunges, the economic crises at home and abroad deepened and resistance took many forms. The world has seen tremendous upheaval and momentous events; nation after nation has sought revolution.

Over this period of time, the people in the United States have seen their dreams deferred as the economic system of capitalism in which they worked treated them, in the words of Carl Sandburg, "as a child, to be pleased or fed; or again, a hoodlum you have to get tough with," but seldom as though they were "a cauldron and a reservoir of the human reserves that shape history."

In recent times, people felt they had burst into a new era. Freed from the restrictive atmosphere and loyalty oaths of the McCarthy period of the '50s, they participated in shaping the politics of the '60s. Riding the crests of waves made in struggles of Civil Rights, Anti-War, Poor People's and Feminist Movements, the people saw themselves on the move.

But the sobering '70s were a setback as working people, without strong leadership and organization, stood defenseless as the gains they had won were taken back again. The capitalist system proved a resilient and powerful opponent. Equal rights for women and affirmative action programs gave way as workers lost ground to inflation; right-to-work laws, the rise of the Ku Klux Klan, anti-busing, red-lining and runaway shops all took their toll. The people were numbed.

Negativism set in, exacerbated by the fact that the two-party system offered no real choices. Elections were determined by the amount of money candidates could pour into them, how they could influence opinion polls, and how they could impress audiences by their "TV images" as created by public relations firms. In a Nevada election, people's cynicism reached its zenith when the slot, "None of the above," received more votes than the candidates listed.

During the '70s it seemed as though people stopped to regroup — minds reeling after the decade of the '60s with its frenetic politics, marked by murder and assassinations — the Kennedys, Martin Luther King, Jr., Fred Hampton, Viola Liuzzo, the students of Jackson and Kent State, among them. And so it appeared that in the '70s the people were immobilized. "The mammoth," as Sandburg termed them, "rested between cyclonic dramas."

As we enter the decade of the '80s, the mass media has recorded a dramatic shift to the Right, but that is only half the story. Concomitant with that has been a dramatic, though unheralded, movement to the Left as well. People not only "rested" but also looked inward to draw upon a new reserve of strength. They analyzed and evaluated past experiences. They studied Marxism, as a method of analysis, and they reclaimed a proud history of Left tradition in this country once lost to public memory because of fear and '50s Cold War repression.

ORIENTATION & OVERVIEW

Today there is a simmering, growing, renewed readiness for activism. Movement is building slowly and subtly nationwide. It is not marked by the romantic fervor and heady idealism that characterized protest in the '60s. The movement of the '80s is rooted in a more deliberate and less spontaneous activism. The ardor and the short-fused anger of the '60s have been channeled into a deep commitment to long-term struggle.

Those experienced activists from previous decades who carry many physical and mental scars from the struggles against racism, sexism and imperialism have, upon reflection, come to a number of conclusions. One is that a system based on profit and greed cannot solve our major social problems. Secondly, attacking that system by focusing on single issues is not effective. The pervasive powerlessness now felt by racial minorities, women, gays, and others is the powerlessness resulting from fragmentation within a system which pits one division within the working class against another. Working people today have rediscovered the conviction that spurred previous generations of activists: Together we can take control of the forces that shape our lives.

As we enter a new "era of limits" and we recognize that U.S. influence in the world is on the decline, we can see that the middle ground is quickly eroding. People are moving off center to the Left, at the same time the Right is organizing a well-financed offensive. The nation is entering another period of worsening relations with the Soviet Union. SALT II is shelved. Detente is said to be dead. The armaments budget is skyrocketing while social services are declining. The Cold War is on again and threatening to become a hot one. A new imperial foreign policy, "the Carter Doctrine" has been formed. Draft registration is being reinstated. The military is making preparations to war over our oil addiction under the guise of "national security." The Soviets have invaded Afghanistan and paranoia shows signs of setting in for another long run. In part, this is the kind of environment that spawned McCarthyism 30 years ago. These dangerous times require courage and clear thinking. Strategy becomes very important and it can only be developed based on sound analysis. It is that fact, above all others, which motivated the formation of the Inter-Religious Task Force for Social Analysis and the production of this study guide, *Which Side Are We On?*

Equally motivating was the fact that the editors believed that for Christians, political consciousness-raising and ideological struggle within the churches go hand in hand. An analysis, therefore, which links the radical salvation history of the people of God to an understanding of the primacy of the economic system in determining the social health of the whole human family is essential.

A companion publication entitled, *Must We Choose Sides?*, is available from the address listed on the back cover ($5.95 plus $1 postage and handling) for those who find these readings and exercises too advanced for their constituencies, or who have not bought these two volumes as a set. That earlier edition tackles subjects at a more basic level, gives suggestions on how to form a study group, and provides details about the origin of this task force.

Let us merely repeat here that we initiated a collective editorial process, and our editorial working group consists of six women and seven men — people who are lay, ordained, or members of religious orders. Our religious affiliations are Roman Catholic, Lutheran, Methodist, Episcopal, Reformed Church of America and Disciples of Christ.

Readers of this guide will find no blueprint for revolution. As with the attempts to scale the heights of mountains, the trails leading to a better society are punctuated with the record of tragic failures. History is replete with accounts of counter-revolutions, coups, conquests and utopian experiments, many of which are recalled in this book. Some have been cynically cruel, some merely romantic, others hopelessly idealistic. Some, however, have been cogent, careful, constructive.

Some have plunged humankind into decades of decadence, others have opened new windows of hope for millions. But the quest goes on, as it must, because the unquenchable human spirit, reflecting its divine source, refuses to be daunted in its search for a society that is just and humane.

As editors of this book, we are not of one mind on the particulars of what that new society will look like, nor are we of one mind on the point of view expressed by all the readings in this book. We are, however, unified in the endorsement of the contents of this volume as a serious and considered effort to make a contribution to the struggle for our future.

We also feel it important to stress that we have been taught to resist socialist ideas in this country, especially by the class-controlled media. This book is an attempt to shake us loose from the one-sided information we have been given since youth, into a liberating experience of discovery of both our radical heritage and an understanding of the present forces that will shape our future. Into that search we are drawn by the fact that our existence is inescapably, and crucially, a social existence. The texture of our economic life with others and the quality of our society determines our humanity, as the pages of this book seek to make clear.

Session 1: Understanding Political & Religious Ideology

In this first session we are invited to examine the fact that theology has never been neutral nor have ideologies ever been "objective." As theologian Juan Luis Segundo explains it, any attempt to put through a radical change in the existing structures must present itself as an ideology. But, any attempt to support the status quo reflects an ideology as well. In this way, theology and ideology have always taken sides in class struggle.

Along these lines, we have heard, perhaps, of "Christians for Socialism," but not of "Christians for Capitalism." While people do not organize under that rubric, many are wittingly and unwittingly joined to carry out a strategy of exploitation against the workers and the poor. The exercise in this session helps us to "unmask" our own political and religious ideology.

Session 2: Capitalism in Crisis

Working people — or the eight million unemployed — do not need a long litany of facts

and figures to prove to them that capitalism is in crisis. They awake every morning to news of rising costs and shortages, and experience the consequences in sacrifice and suffering. But key to proposing solutions for change is the *way* we analyze the crisis, which, in turn, is influenced by the ideological perspective from which we approach it.

This session employs an ideology committed to the interests of the working class and the poor. Its purpose is not only to understand the crisis, but to change the economic system which spawns it. The exercise asks us to analyze the role of the media in undergirding the capitalist ideology and fragmenting our view of the news.

Session 3: Class Struggle in Our Times

We live in a society that is divided into classes. That observation seems simple enough. But when we try to analyze the concept of class struggle, our task becomes far more complicated. The struggle is not so simplistic as the workers and the poor vs. the owners and the rich. Contradictions abound among the workers themselves, and the

owners as well, as each class tries to organize in its own interest.

And, of course, it is always to the advantage of the capitalist class to exacerbate conflict amongst the workers, to keep them off balance and disorganized in ethnic and sexist disputes; so much so that capitalists have financed a right-wing offensive against workers. This session initiates exploration of all the above aspects of the class struggle.

Session 4: Exploring the Alternatives

First, we test the validity of a number of myths we have heard all our lives about socialism — myths mostly propagated by that class

which controls the educational institutions and dominates the media. Then, on a positive note, we take on a study of the political economy of socialism, examining four components: Social ownership, working people's power, laws of socialist economy, and socialist values in everyday life.

Finally, this session provides an ambitious overview of illusionary alternatives to capitalism. Included is a critique of various individualistic, incremental, and structural change alternatives (pietistic religion, human potential movements, pacifism, liberal reform, populist and social democratic movements, and fascism).

Session 5: The Socialist Movement in U.S. History

History as written from the "top" — or dominating class — is quite different from history as lived from the "bottom" — or the exploited. This session recaptures for us those lost moments of a proud history which we must know to strategize for the future. We live through workers struggles as seen through the eyes of Mother Jones, and striking dockworkers in San Francisco.

Mother Jones

Ironically, many U.S. citizens know more about the history of the Left in other countries such as the Soviet Union or China than they do about the Left in their own. Further, as this book is written, no one party has emerged to attract the imagination of the masses here. Since real success for such an organization depends on an analysis of why past attempts have failed, this session is crucial to our political future.

Session 6: Christians and the Socialist Option

In this session we become acquainted with a number of Christians whose lives reflected

that they had successfully dealt with the relationship between faith and politics. As theologian Gustavo Gutierrez points out, "human reason has become political reason. For the contemporary historical consciousness, things political are not only those which one attends to during the free time afforded by one's private life; nor are they a well-defined area of human existence. It is the sphere for the exercise of a critical freedom which is won through history. It is the universal determinant and the collective arena for human fulfillment. Nothing lies outside the political sphere understood in this way."

In a world where politics is the fundamental human dimension, then, Christian love can hardly be apolitical, as proven in the lives of those described in this session. Needless to say, socialist Christian history has been ignored, as has socialist history, in this country, especially in the wake of the McCarthy period. In that regard, we are also reminded that "the cross" will always be part of class struggle.

Session 7: How Do We Organize?

Now comes the hard part. Having taken a class stand, where do we go, what political entity will guarantee the rule of the working class majority, who are our allies, where are the resources, what is the strategy? Hard questions, these, only some of which we can help to answer in this book. To offer a blueprint would be naive and utopian. But there are some vital steps we can take at this point.

This session helps us to develop a method for evaluating our own political action, to distinguish between substantive reform and reformism, and to build upon our strengths. The *appendix* that completes this book lists extensive resources for continued study and action.

∎

Picheta

Understanding Political & Religious Ideology

In the old Disney comic strips, when cartoon characters such as Donald Duck or Mickey Mouse get a bright idea, a light bulb appears in a balloon next to the character, with the word, "click!"

In this first session, our task is to examine the nature of that "click," asking the question, "Where do ideas come from?" And not only ideas — but also the values, beliefs, norms, attitudes which together with ideas meet in a nexus to form our *ideology*. "Ideology," for many, has become a pejorative term, and "ideologues" to be avoided at all costs. But everyone has an ideology, whether he or she recognizes it or not. It informs our faith, our politics, our philosophy, our commitments.

Ideologies are rooted in perspectives based on either idealistic or materialistic interpretations of history. These will be examined in detail as our readings graphically illustrate how ideas are promoted in the interest of social classes — the capitalist ruling class, petit-bourgeois (middle) class, or working class.

As a matter of fact, even Donald Duck has an ideology. He is not simply an innocuous, little cartoon character. His "ideas," when analyzed from a Third World viewpoint (in *Para Leer al Pato Donald* by Dorfman and Mattelart) expose him as a bearer of capitalist propaganda and a purveyor of cultural imperialism. Remember his rich capitalist uncle, Scrooge McDuck? Even lovable Little Orphan Annie has her powerful Daddy Warbucks, a name remarkably explicit in its message.

It should be reiterated that ideology, as we are employing the concept, is not to be condemned as something that only other people have or something from which we should strive to be free. All of us have an ideological perspective, whether it is articulated clearly or mostly hidden. The important thing for us is to become aware of our ideological presuppositions and to test whether they further or hinder the liberating activity of God.

In this realm, there is no neutral, non-ideological ground. Capitalist ideology permeates our institutions and media as thoroughly as does oxygen the air we breathe. Usually those who deny they are ideological, or proclaim to be neutral to ideology, have so internalized their acquiescence to the status quo and the capitalist ruling class that they lend it their support without even being aware of it.

The task, then, is seriously to address the question, "Which side are we on? To which ideology do we subscribe?" For us Christians, the enterprise is "exploration into God." Christianity is more than a collection of stories and ideas recorded in the Bible. To live as a Christian demands continued biblical *interpretation* and the acting out of that interpretation in our daily lives. When God's gift of faith is separated from the whole meaning of the covenantal relationship between God and the people — especially at the point of concrete physical human need — this faith is declared to be dead. ("So faith by itself, if it has no works, is dead." James 2:15)

Central to biblical revelation is the announcement of God's active purpose to destroy such perversion and to call the people back to a faith for which "doing justice and loving kindness" is the essence. Liberation theologian Jose Miguez Bonino points out in *Christians and Marxists:*

> God has to break in again and again into the life of God's own people and destroy, transgress, contradict, relativize these very signs of the divine presence in order to restore God's intention and to save humankind from self-deception, alienation and destruction.

As we reflect upon whether we are straying from God's intent, it is important to realize that our very reading of the Bible is focused by our ideological lens. We will probe the meaning of this in the readings and exercise of this session.

From the start, we should also acknowledge that we, as editors of this study guide, have consciously chosen to embrace the worldview and the political and religious ideas that have developed from the life experience of the working class and the poor. To decide otherwise — to accept the ideology of the capitalist ruling class — we believe, is religious idolatry and contrary to the unfolding of God's plan. Therefore, this session gives special attention to the tacit alliance between Christianity and capitalism so that Christian faith may be liberated from alien ideology and freed to proclaim the Word of God.

The first article by George McClain of the Methodist Federation for Social Action discusses how certain ideas take hold in the institutions of a class society and how Christianity, as we know it in North America, is, for the most part, held captive by both indirect and direct pressures within capitalism.

The second reading, a "Declaration" by several bishops of Chile, is followed by Pablo Richard's trenchant critique of the bishops' ideological presuppositions. These documents appeared during the time of the Allende government in Chile and lay bare widely-held Christian notions which strip the Gospel of its power and hope for the exploited.

Dave Kalke's analysis of two corporate executives' speeches unveils the strategies employed by global capitalism in the ideological struggle to insure that its ideas remain the dominant ideas of the time. Particularly instructive are the attacks on church groups who are challenging the morality of transnational corporate activity in the Third World.

The next reading, "Apostles of Reaction," also by George McClain, is an analysis of a so-called "evangelical" organization within the United Methodist Church which has an underlying new-right political bias. Its value, for readers of various backgrounds, lies not so much in the details regarding this particular group as in the example it provides for unmasking the capitalist ideological biases of self-styled "evangelical" and alleged "biblically-based" movements that have arisen in virtually every mainline Christian communion in North America. ■

Rachel Burger

The Idolatry and Promise of the Church

by George D. McClain

The Spirit of the Lord is upon me,
because God has anointed me to preach
good news to the poor.
God has sent me to proclaim
release to the captives,
and recovering of sight to the blind,
to set at liberty those who are oppressed,
to proclaim the acceptable year of the Lord.

(Luke 4: 18-19)

The above passage is the key to understanding the social mandate of the Christian Gospel, for with these words Jesus announced his ministry, and therefore shaped the nature of the ministry we carry on in his name.

The meaning seems quite straightforward and, in fact, radical in its implications, placing the Christian message implacably in opposition to economic poverty and political oppression. Yet, we repeatedly encounter interpretations, both among liberals and conservatives, which would divest the Gospel of all radicality.

For instance, the author of the *Moffatt Bible Commentary* writes:

> On Jesus' lips the ''good news'' has a purely religious import. . . . The term *the poor* is to be taken in its inward spiritual sense . . . and similarly the expressions *captive, blind, oppressed* indicate not primarily the downtrodden victims of material force, such as Rome's, but the victims of inward repressions, neuroses, and other spiritual ills due to misdirection and failure of life's energies and purposes.

The Rev. George D. McClain is Executive Secretary of the Methodist Federation for Social Action and editor of the MFSA bi-monthly publication, *Social Questions Bulletin*.

This sort of ''spiritualizing'' of the Bible and Christian message permeates all North American church life. How is it to be explained?

Christians today who work among those who are victims of economic poverty and political oppression immediately challenge the Moffatt commentary as a serious distortion. In seeking to uncover the reasons for this type of interpretation, these Christians are discovering the usefulness of Karl Marx's understanding of how ideas are rooted in economic reality.

Marx's analysis is predicated upon the importance of ''material'' life, that is, the basic and essential day-to-day tasks of meeting human needs. This philosophical outlook of *materialism* (not to be confused with the notion of consumerism and a desire for more and more ''things'') recognizes that our consciousness and our ideas are decisively shaped by the experiences we have in the course of living and working in order to survive as human beings. Materialism differs from the philosophical outlook of *idealism* (not to be confused with commitment to high principles) which contends that people's consciousness and ideas are primarily shaped by exposure to ideas themselves and by mysterious forces beyond our control. Gracie Lyons, in *Constructive Criticism*, gives the following explanation of the difference:

Suppose we're trying to explain the fact that many of the older white women in our community organization don't speak out at neighborhood meetings. An idealist approach might yield explanations such as "Women are just naturally more passive," or "It's just women's instinct to be receptive rather than aggressive." A materialist approach, on the other hand, would focus its attention on the concrete work experiences of women, experiences determined by the way labor in our society has been divided along sex lines. If a woman's daily life experiences consist mostly of doing unpaid housework, and raising children in the isolation of the home, we can easily see the material basis for her quiet behavior.

In our society, ideas are usually accounted for by idealist explanations. These tend to obscure the down-to-earth struggles by certain groups and assure that idealism, not materialism, dominates the cultural and religious scene.

While Christians would not go all the way with some versions of Marxism which account for mental or spiritual phenomena solely on the basis of philosophical materialism, our long-standing idealistic bent desperately needs to be corrected by the materialist perspective.

Marxism asserts that the trends in intellectual history depend upon who controls the economic base by which a society meets its material needs; that is, by who controls the means of production. The capitalist ruling class controls the economic base which generates the essential elements for human survival — food, shelter, clothing, etc. It also dominates the political, cultural, legal, and governmental institutions (called the superstructure), which tend to perpetuate the economic system and the interests of the ruling class who are its chief beneficiaries. For instance, the legal system in a capitalist society always protects the supposed "right" to accumulate wealth and to own unlimited amounts of "private" property. Were this not the case, capitalism could not exist.

Thus, through control of the economic base, the capitalist class is able to influence political and cultural institutions and the ideas and images which they continually generate. The current spate of narcissistic and self-centered pop psychology books, such as *Looking Out for #1* and *How To Be Your Own Best Friend*, embody, in a remarkably crass way, the individualism and selfishness which capitalist institutions foster. This perspective on the source of dominant ideas provides us with a powerful tool for understanding why the church as an institution has tended to give support, first to feudalism and then later to capitalism and now even to monopoly capitalism and the transnational corporations.

Given the constant pressure on religious, cultural and educational institutions to provide ideological support for capitalism, it is not surprising that religious thought tends to take place within certain limits which appear to be self-imposed but are in fact imposed by the exigencies of the system. This means that the institutional church is constantly under pressure to interpret the Scriptures, celebrate the Sacraments, and preach the Word of God in a manner acceptable to the capitalist view of life — often called the "American way." Clergy who have spoken out against racism, sexism, capitalism and imperialism often bear significant scars — such as losing their pastorates — as a result.

Most of the time these limits are imposed, not through overt coercion, but rather through the internalization of the prevailing cultural ideology, which includes a stress on individualism, self-sufficiency, personal responsibility for one's lot in society, the supremacy of "free enterprise," and a visceral and unquestioned anti-communism.

While normally the limits on the church's social thought are indirect and self-imposed, if necessary these limits could become overt and direct. Imagine for a moment what would happen if the church in North America suddenly were to put its whole institutional weight behind a movement to reject capitalism. Corporations would begin to threaten the financial livelihood of churches and their vast array of institutions by cutting off direct and indirect corporate and foundation contributions as well as the large personal gifts that enable the churches to command such vast resources. Significant membership losses would follow not only among the capitalist class, but also among those in the middle and working classes who rightly or wrongly identify their personal well-being with the existence of capitalism. In recent years, even the few and generally mild questions raised about aspects of capitalism by the National Council of Churches and the World Council of Churches have been met with threats by the wealthy to withhold contributions or leave member denominations. Further down the line, we could expect governmental authorities to use their powers to curb the privileges the churches enjoy, such as tax-free status, and to find other "legal" ways to harass the church.

Sometimes the assumption is made that while right-wing fundamentalist Christianity clearly plays the role of defending prejudice and free enterprise while countering alleged communism, middle of the road or "liberal" denominations do not participate in this defense of the status quo. This is not true. Although explicitly right-wing religious lobbies and churches may act as the "shock troops" against any deviation from the tacit Christian-capitalist alliance, so-called moderate and liberal churches and their leaders are perhaps more effective in providing religious support for capitalism. In fact, as the North

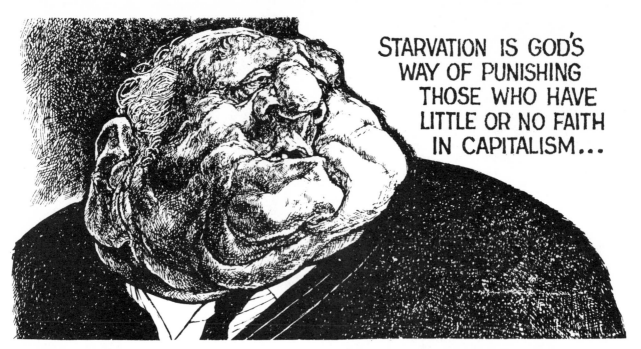

STARVATION IS GOD'S
WAY OF PUNISHING
THOSE WHO HAVE
LITTLE OR NO FAITH
IN CAPITALISM...

American peoples have become educated and secularized, the unsophisticated forms of other-worldly religion (biblical literalism with emphasis on the fear of hell and escape to heaven) have been increasingly less useful in providing the individualistic and spiritualized interpretations of Christianity required by capitalism. Thus, liberal churches have developed theologies which do not conflict with natural science and literary criticism of the Bible. They have also specialized in providing for every age level a sense of community (something very lacking in a competitive society). Finally, they have developed various forms of community outreach, mostly of a charitable nature, that meet gaps in the delivery of social services rather than address their underlying causes. For example, they provide meals for senior citizens, host child care facilities and sponsor government funded non-profit housing. The Advertising Council of America even encourages this religion-in-life approach.

Several mechanisms are employed to proscribe church life in such a way as to render it safe for capitalism. One is to stress individual concerns, basically in isolation from social realities. Here the emphasis is on a "pastoral" orientation which provides personal and religious support for the inevitable crises of life. Generally speaking, these crises are not interpreted in the counseling situation as possible openings through which God may be calling a person to move toward a new, broader, more biblical and political understanding of life. How many times, for instance, have women counseled with pastors about a basic dissatisfaction with their lot in life, only to have their socialization as subservient housewives and full-time mothers be reinforced rather than challenged? How

seldom has any pastor ever told a dissatisfied worker, "Well, you know, to work for someone else's personal gain is by definition to be ripped off — no matter how well they pay you!"

Another technique is that of interpreting every biblical passage so that only psychological and "spiritual" realities are taken seriously. The principalities and powers which oppress are here limited to spiritual, interior ones — personal sin, the temptation to dishonesty, low self-esteem, etc. As in the earlier example regarding Jesus' announcement of his ministry, to free the oppressed applies only to the *spiritually* oppressed; to liberate the captives means to free only the *spiritually* bound.

Finally, to the extent that social issues are confronted, the technique is to treat the victims as objects of charity (as do most hunger projects) rather than as persons to be empowered to change the system which created hunger and oppression. Where specific divisive issues do emerge and the church cannot avoid a choice, a frequent tactic is to treat the issue as one to be debated or studied, so that "both sides may be heard." If a side is taken, then care is taken to limit the matter to a harmless resolution and avoid, if possible, actually engaging in any action that confronts an evil and demands a change. "Politics is really for the politician." "We don't know enough about the issue to get involved." "The church's job is to be involved not in the conflict but in reconciliation." These are frequently used rationalizations for passivity. If some action is taken, it may well be offering the church's "good offices" to both sides in the dispute, a thoroughly non-controversial role which in most cases serves to maintain the status quo.

When Marx stated that religion was the opiate of the people, he was commenting on the role of organized Christianity in his day. In the Prussian state, Christianity was expected to play precisely that role and to constitute a justification for the feudal order. Here were the instructions given by the preacher at the court of Potsdam, as cited by Jose Miguez Bonino in *Christians and Marxists:*

> What matters is to stimulate the attachment to the old constitution, to alert the people against a freedom and an equality applied to themselves, to show the need for differences between social conditions and to lend influence and authority to our works by means of intelligent allusions to the consequences of the furious passion for freedom of the French Revolution.

Whether one looks at Christianity past or present, the churches, with some notable exceptions, do play this role of opiate, justifying the existing order and keeping people unclear about the cause of so much human suffering . . . suffering which could be radically diminished if the profit motive were not the final arbiter of life in our society.

Given this pessimistic analysis of the alliance between the churches and capitalism, we may wonder if there are any possibilities for a church to cross the boundaries informally set for it and respond to the Gospel.

Marxist criticism of religion, as generally interpreted, would assert that religion ultimately is based on an illusion and can make no lasting contribution to the building of a new, non-capitalist society.

Before rushing to reject this possibility, we should acknowledge how helpful Marxist criticism of religion is in unmasking how religion becomes permeated with a capitalist ideology and how religious institutions, even "liberal" ones, tend to play a reactionary role. Religion under capitalism has served as an opiate of the people, a mystifier of the actual realities of society and for this we in the churches must repent in the full biblical sense of turning away from serious wrongdoing toward a radically new life.

Marx serves the function of a modern day prophet to the church in our era, indicting it for its idolatry and enabling Christians again to take seriously Jesus' teaching, "No servant can serve two masters. . . . You cannot serve God and mammon (money)."

As Christians seeking to be faithful, we know the basic stance of capitalism is anti-Christian, for it is built upon the maximizing of personal profit, the nurturing of an impulse to be grasping, the promotion of individualism instead of community, the exaltation of the strong over the weak, and the subordination of human life to economic gain. As biblical people, we know the judgment of God in calling the church away from idolatry and back to faithful obedience. We also know of significant instances of the church throwing its support behind revolutionary efforts, as in the role of the black church in the United States in the struggle against racism and in the current involvement of countless Latin American laity, religious, and priests in the struggle against capitalism on their continent. In some smaller or larger way, most of us know of circles of Christians who have broken through the acceptable limits imposed upon the church to be active and uncompromising agents of radical change.

We, therefore, may proclaim the hope that the church — or at least a saving remnant thereof — can be the courageous and effective bearer of the Gospel message that the will of God is opposed to capitalism and to the church's alliance with capitalism; further, that the way of obedience in our time is to call for a new social and economic order built not on exploitation, but on the sharing of God's gifts among all the people. Early in this century Karl Barth wrote, "Real socialism is real Christianity in our time." Perhaps now is the time when such words will fall onto fertile soil and, in the grace of God, bring forth a hundredfold yield. ■

Declaration
by Several Bishops of Chile

It is the policy of the editors of this guide to change sexist terms such as "He" with reference to God, whose being embraces male and female, and "man" as a generic term for people or humanity, which encompasses men and women. Since the documents by the Chilean bishops were issued at a certain time and place in history and editing them would have changed the ideological thrust, we left them in their original form.

When we reflect on the situation in our country, we, the bishops of the Central area of Chile, feel compelled to address the Catholics of our dioceses.

We start with a fundamental fact: Chile is a country involved in a dynamic process of change. Our reflection and our words flow from the perspective of our Christian faith and are not based on human science.

There will always be change. It is our human condition to seek that ultimate goal already promised by Christ: The final resurrection when He will come again. Mankind will always be looking for a model of a more just and truer society, because men carry in their heart the restlessness of our Creator who said: "Possess the earth." And whether people are believers or not, they will feel the command of Christ to make this earth more fraternal; because "this is my commandment: That you love one another as I have loved you."

This is the positive plan of God. Every step in the process of change should lead effectively to a more just life and to one filled with more fraternal love, if that love is oriented by the Gospel of Christ. For change is misdirected when it is inspired by materialistic concerns or when it does not take into account the complex nature of man, which encompasses both strength and weakness, good and evil, a mixture of grace and sin.

The above declaration was issued by several Chilean Catholic bishops on June 1, 1973, from Santiago, while the Popular Unity government was still in power. Salvador Allende, a Socialist physician, had been democratically elected President by the Chilean people, but was killed in a coup when the present military Junta overthrew his government in September, 1973. English translation by the Ecumenical Program for Inter-American Communication and Action (EPICA), Washington, D.C.

Within this framework, we wish to say a word about our situation in Chile.

We are troubled by the chain of events in our country, by the way things are moving. It pains us to see long queues of Chileans — millions of hours lost every week — suffering the humiliation of living under these conditions. We resemble a country devastated by war.

We are also concerned about the black market, unleashed by the immorality of those who traffic unjustly with foodstuffs and other essential products.

In principle, we do not approve the exodus of professionals. The country should find realistic and effective ways to avoid this drain on our human resources. It is the moral duty of every Chilean to remain in the country where he was born and which gave him an opportunity to become a professional.

We are also concerned because the communications media do not tell the truth and even more because they incite the people to hatred. When they destroy truth and love they fall short of their fundamental duties; they are immoral.

We watch with anguish the rising inflation that is overwhelming us and its attendant crisis for our economy.

These days we are witnessing the problem of the copper miners at El Teniente with all the implications that it has for the life of the labor unions and the progress of our economy. We condemn the violence that arises from this labor conflict for we believe that this suffering could have been avoided.

We realize that mere words do not touch the problem and that wise counsel is not enough. We know that the role of the church is not to offer technical solutions, but we want to add some reflections that may clarify the situation in which we live, without pretending to have all the answers.

THE DIVISION BETWEEN SOCIALISTS AND CAPITALISTS IN THE COUNTRY IS FALSE

Socialism and capitalism are two ideological expressions that have been converted into symbols. To attempt to reduce the whole Chilean problem to these two words is an over-simplification which does not accord with reality. Reality is much more complex than symbols and systems, because we human beings are much more than words.

Our reality includes myths and utopian models and obviously these will not solve everything.

Until now, the word socialism represents a system as yet quite undefined in Chile, nor is it possible to affix the label of capitalism to all that exists today.

We cannot build a society on the principle that we are a collection of mutual enemies. Peace will not come with the domination of one group over another. The good of society requires the contribution and collaboration of everyone and the plain recognition of the rights of all. Justice demands this and only on the basis of justice can peace be maintained.

We ask that Chileans concentrate on what unites us rather than on what divides us. It seems to us more important to deal with concrete individuals, with names and faces, than to judge others according to definitions or words. Men are more important than systems and human beings more than ideologies. Ideologies are divisive while our history, our blood, our common language, human love and the common task that we Chileans face today should help us create a single family. Our words here have no other purpose nor any other hope than that of helping us look at ourselves as equals, as brothers and sisters. We Chileans don't deserve to live in a climate of anguish, uncertainty, hatred or vengeance.

THE IDOLATRY OF POWER

The struggle for power, the strategy for obtaining it, strengthening it or resolving it appear to be a goal of human life, especially in politics.

The price that must be paid for such power is no longer considered important. This power constitutes an idol and an illusion for many people. We forget that our faith teaches us that each person's life is sacred. Every person is my brother or sister.

Power can easily corrupt the heart of him who possesses it. History has shown this. He who loves power falls prey to his own trap.

We are concerned about the tendency towards absolute statism, without adequate popular participation.

Power should only serve as a means to achieve the common good. More than needing persons in power, we need servants. Christ never sought power. He insisted that he came to serve: "Whoever would be great among you, let him be as a servant" (Mark 10:48).

The idolatry of power necessarily leads to the breakdown of moral values, to ambiguity between what is moral and what is immoral. The principle of Machiavelli, "the end justifies the means" is always there, latent in the human heart.

The church has always denounced totalitarianism. This name hides every absolute or "total" system, generally based on ideologies which have little in common except the fact that they never tolerate any counter-position, any criticism, or any force that serves to balance extremes.

Let us recall the words of Christ: "One cannot serve two masters." It is impossible to serve God and money. Sincerely, one cannot serve God and idolize power.

We have all sinned and we are all guilty. We sin through action and even more through omission. We act cowardly. Not speaking out can be evil. We must take steps to be more sincere and truthful.

ORIGINAL CONTRIBUTION OF CHRISTIANS

Our goal is to build up the Kingdom of God; to build up the church at the service of mankind and of the society in which we live. That can only be accomplished by following the Gospel, becoming truly converted and being ever more faithful to the spirit of Christ. This is challenging and justifies our commitment, but it is also an arduous, difficult and conflictive task, given the nature of the human heart.

We say "no" to falsehood, "no" to excessive power, and "no" to hatred. Like the apostles, we have believed in love and love always inspires sincerity, justice, mercy and brotherhood.

The Christian path is the only viable one: We believe it is the best, because it touches the human heart in attempting to transform structures.

We are making an effort to understand the impatience of those who seek apparently more efficacious ways to improve the country, but in the end the only truly liberating path is that which follows the criteria and mind of Jesus Christ. That is why the church has denounced the errors and the evils of capitalism as well as of Marxism.

What really counts is the integrity of a person's life, being true to what one believes and in what one does.

The greatest contribution that the church can make to the country is to provide loving Christians who struggle to build peace. That is our problem: We are not Christian enough and perhaps we talk too much and do too little.

The feast of Pentecost is approaching. For those of us who believe in the activity of the Holy Spirit, this will be an opportunity to ask God to repeat that miracle. People who spoke different languages came to understand each other and to close the gap between them. Love brought them closer together. A country can only be built on love.

The Virgin was present at Pentecost. She is the Mother of the church. She has been the Mother of our country since its beginnings. She will help us overcome the difficult situation of Chile today. This is our message, our fervent wish and our prayer.

Raul Silva Henriques	Raul Silva Silva
Emilio Tagle	Carlos Gonzalez
Augusto Salinas	Fernando Ariztia
Alejandro Duran	Ismael Errazuriz
Enrique Alvear	∎

Response
by Pablo Richard

Pablo Richard, a Roman Catholic layman, was national director of the Christians for Socialism movement in Chile from 1970-1973. Since his exile from Chile after the coup, he has served as a research associate at the Centre Lebret in Paris, and at this printing was doing research in Costa Rica. English translation by the Ecumenical Program for Inter-American Communication and Action (EPICA), Washington, D.C.

On June 6, 1973, El Mercurio published a document by the bishops of the Central Region of Chile. El Mercurio summarized this document fairly well under the following heading: "Bishops State: Chile Resembles a Country Devastated by War." Oddly enough, the newspaper, La Prensa, used a similar heading. The document provoked indignation among the Left and a feeling of shame and scandal among those Christians committed to the building of socialism.

The bishops' statement is not an isolated action, but falls within the process of change that Chile is undergoing. This statement is an historical fact with irreversible consequences. It contains the position of the institutional church at this moment in the class struggle. In analyzing this document, we do not judge the bishops' intentions. We presume they had the best of intentions. However, history is determined by facts, not intentions. As Christians and as revolutionaries, we have the right and the duty to publicly and fearlessly analyze the position of the bishops.

The revolutionary process in Chile causes anguish among the rich while it gives hope to the poor. The rich man views the downfall of the capitalist system as the ruin of his own house. His farms and factories are lost. His laws are broken. His temples of justice are desecrated. The forces of order are thwarted. His schools, colleges and universities are threatened. His newspapers and radio stations are unmasked. For the wealthy, it is chaos and destruction. On the contrary, the poor view the collapse of the capitalist system as the collapse of their jail and the opening of prison doors. The takeover of farms and factories, the crumbling of the bourgeois "order," and the possibility of having their own schools and universities, etc., are signs of liberation and hope. Thus, the same realities that cause anguish within the bourgeoisie, bring hope to the poor and exploited.

The bishops' document breathes anguish and pessimism. It expresses the feelings of the rich, not the feelings of the poor and exploited. The bishops see the situation in Chile as one of long queues, as a country devastated by war, by the black market, by the exodus of professionals, and as one where the communications media foster hatred and destroy truth and love. There is inflation, violence, the idolatry of power, statism, etc. . . . "We don't deserve to live" — say the bishops — "in a climate of anguish, uncertainty, hatred or vengeance. We say 'no' to falsehood, 'no' to excessive power, 'no' to hatred."

The bishops' document does not reflect the hope of the poor and the exploited. It communicates nothing of the joy and hope which grows among the exploited when an industry is socialized or when farms and distributing companies are expropriated. The bishops do not reflect the growing hope of the poor who are glad to see the legal judicial system of the bourgeoisie broken; nor the growing hope of the poor when popular power is strengthened, when their vanguards are multiplied or when officers of the Armed Forces begin to understand their problems and soldiers regard themselves as brothers of the workers. Nor

again do the bishops reflect the growing joy of the poor when the forces of order begin to realize that the workers are not bandits nor thieves; nor the growing hope of the poor when they see the possibility of having their own newspapers, magazines, schools and universities; nor the increased hope of the exploited when they gain strength, when their consciousness grows and their class organizations are strengthened. This hope of the poor is not reflected in the bishops' statement.

Certainly there are queues, inflation and a black market. But why do the bishops see only these problems? Why don't they denounce the causes of these realities? Why don't they rejoice at the positive events? Why do the bishops share the anguish and concern of the rich and not the pain, struggle and hope of the poor?

In a revolutionary process, anguish characterizes the bourgeoisie while hope is the distinguishing mark of the exploited, but there is still another distinction between them. The exploited feel, live and think of history as the history of class struggle. On the contrary, the bourgeoisie is unable to understand this profound reality of history. If the bourgeoisie, as a social class, could understand history, they would disappear as a class. When they refer to social classes, they refer to income, prestige, to their cultural or educational level. They do not comprehend the profound laws of the march of history. For the bourgeoisie, a confrontation between social classes does not exist.

The bourgeoisie disguise the class struggle by blaming false or superficial contradictions. They speak, for example, of a confrontation between "democrats" and "Marxists." Those with more fascist attitudes reduce class struggle to a confrontation between civilization and barbarism, between order and chaos, light and darkness, truth and falsehood, etc. The revolution of the exploited for them is barbarism, chaos, totalitarianism, falsehood and darkness.

Another tactic of the bourgeoisie used to hide or deny the class struggle is to resort to the complexity of society. They say that to talk about the exploited and the exploiters is an oversimplification. To them, reality is "extremely complex." Of course reality is complex. Theoretically, one can discover five, eight or 20 social classes, but in practice there is a fact that is not complex, but a very simple reality: Some people are on one side and some are on the other. One can observe reality in two ways: From books or on the street. In books, one finds many social classes. This is correct. But in a street confrontation, there are always two groups. This is also a fact.

The bourgeoisie thinks it is an oversimplification to divide the country into capitalists and socialists.

There are so many degrees and forms of capitalism and there are so many models of socialism. This is all true. But, when we get down to cases, we have one group that wants to maintain capitalism and another that is trying to build socialism. The Christian Democratic Party (DC) plays with many theories in order to determine the kind of socialism they uphold. But the fact is that the DC is fighting against the building of socialism in Chile.

Still another maneuver that the bourgeoisie uses to hide and deny the class struggle is to preach pacifism, moralism, individualism, fundamentalism and spiritualism. They talk about peace, unity and love, opposing these values to class struggle which is presented as war, violence, hatred and divisiveness. In these ways, they hide the fact that the class struggle is correctly aimed at going beyond social classes, for it is properly trying to build up love, solidarity and peace.

The bourgeoisie reduces the class struggle to moralistic preaching. The esteemed virtues are honesty, hard work, and responsibility. Wealth is the fruit of hard work and honesty. Poverty is the result of vice and laziness. There are no exploited or exploiters, but only honest people (the bosses and the "decent people") and a tremendous number of lazy people, thieves, vicious and ignorant types (the exploited and "the poor"). It does not matter to what group one belongs, as long as one is honest and consistent in one's beliefs. They try to bring into disrepute leaders of the political Left because of their conduct and way of life. I do not deny the importance of honesty and persistency, but I unmask the bourgeoisie's use of labels to hide the class struggle by employing moralistic discourse.

The same can be said about preaching integration, fundamentalism or individualism. The class struggle is denied by resorting in an exclusive way to that which unites us and not to that which divides us, and also by calling people in an exclusive way to a "conversion of heart" as the only way to transform reality. They also speak about "fundamental truths," about "eternal and immutable principles" in order to deny the dialectic reality of a concrete historical process. I don't deny the importance of "personal conversion," nor of certain values which unite all Chileans, nor of certain universal truths, etc., but we must unmask the recourse through their ideology to this kind of preaching.

The bishops' document, apart from its intentions, specifically uses all the ideological arguments we are describing. They speak of the "complex" situation of mankind and society in order to hide simple facts. They resort to personal and moralistic preaching: "What really convinces people is the integrity of life, and persistency . . ." The document denounces the "idolatry of power" and opposes to it a personal attitude of "service." We agree with the document when it denounces low politics and unprincipled political struggle, but can we reduce class struggle to the idolatry of power? Are healthy politics opposed to a personal attitude of service? The exploited, who have offered their lives in the service of politics — have they done so because of vanity or ambition?

The document asks us to look for "what unites us and not what divides us." Why then do they not denounce the abuses of the bourgeoisie against the exploited, if they are also part of that humanity which is common to all Chileans?

We could quote the whole document and show how it directly employs the ideological preaching of the Chilean bourgeoisie. Christians cannot accept this ideological simplification of the Gospel. Because of faithfulness to the church and to Christ's message, and because of solidarity with the poor and exploited, we respond to the bishops' document with respect, but with Christian firmness. The Gospel is a liberating historical fact, not a moralistic, pacifistic, fundamental message. The message of the Gospel is unambiguous. No one expects the church to pronounce itself in favor of the Popular Unity coalition or of any other political party. But we demand that it should pronounce itself clearly — about whether it is on the side of exploitation or on the side of liberation. The Chilean process does not admit spectators or arbitrators. It does not admit ambiguous situations. Christ very clearly divided his audience: One group followed him, the other group murdered him. And it was not the poor, nor the sick, nor the oppressed who crucified Christ. It was the powerful, the Pharisees, the ones who administered the temple, those who loved wealth more than the Kingdom of justice and brotherhood.

We are concerned about the bishops' statement. It points in a very dangerous direction: To a path against history, against revolutionary changes, against the poor and exploited. I do not judge intentions, only facts. We, as Christians, have an inheritance which can become a dead weight. To remain static in history means to be crushed by it. The church suffered the French Revolution because it was feudal. Will it suffer the socialist revolution because it is a church compromised with the bourgeoisie and with capitalism? ■

Unmasking the Corporate Missionary

by David Kalke

The remarks below are excerpts from a speech delivered by D.J. Kirchhoff, the president of Castle & Cooke, Inc., to the Merchants and Manufacturers Assn. The entire speech was printed in *Barron's Business and Financial Weekly* on Feb. 19, 1979. While the speech has been reprinted in other publications (*The Christian Challenge*, October 1979, and *The Witness*, January 1980, with rebuttal), the editors of this volume were unable to obtain reprint permission from either *Barron's* or Castle & Cooke. In a letter to us, Rafael Pagan, vice president of Castle & Cooke Foods, indicated that he believes our book is biased because we didn't use the work of several "respected professors" he suggested. His letter, sent before he saw our materials, concludes, ". . . we cannot agree nor authorize the publication of Mr. Kirchhoff's speech, any other of our statements nor portions of those statements on this issue in the above book." We have subsequently consulted with copyright lawyers and have excerpted within legal limits.

D.J. Kirchhoff's remarks and the refusal of reprint permission by Vice President Rafael Pagan suggest that the transnational corporations are on the defensive. They, along with other transnational executives, are beginning to feel the pressures being placed on them by individuals, groups and organized movements which are challenging a system based on profits for a few at the expense of social development and the meeting of basic human needs for the many. A careful analysis of the strategies for this defensive posture is in order as we examine the tools used to prop up the capitalist system:

> I want to speak with you today about a campaign being waged against Castle & Cooke by some so-called "public interest" groups, many of them church-related. This campaign has challenging implications for everyone in this room — and for everyone who believes in the opportunity for people to grow in a climate of personal and economic liberty.
>
> I strongly believe that those values — especially as represented by the U.S. corporate community, because of our spectacular economic success — are under siege, and in greater danger today than at any time since the industrial revolution. . . .
>
> What concerns me today is a direct assault on our economic system. This siege is spearheaded by what can only be called a "movement" — an amorphous group of people who believe, as an act of faith, that capitalism is inefficient, wasteful, unjust, inhumane, exploitative, monopolistic and profit-oriented at the expense of the worker.
>
> These may sound like 19th Century Marxist cliches, and indeed they are. But cliches aside, this movement is totally committed to these distorted perspectives. It seeks, by whatever means, to bring about what is euphemistically called "social change," and it poses a very real threat to corporate survival. . . .
>
> It is ironic that our principal antagonists, or at least our principal visible antagonists, come from the church community. Eliot Janeway puts it best: "The Kremlin has found a new outlet for its well-known technique of harnessing the religious cadres it detests to the political conspiracies it hatches." Spokesmen from prestigious church organizations have confronted Castle & Cooke at annual stockholders' meetings with charges so outlandish that they would not normally warrant any comment. We have been accused of depressing the social conditions of our host countries, holding down wages and contributing to Third World malnutrition by exporting goods for profit. . . .
>
> Because of our policy of public accountability, we brought those church critics to our overseas facilities and allowed them to inspect conditions for themselves. It was to no avail. They returned to our most recent annual meeting last April and repeated the same general and groundless charges in support of a radical resolution. They were determined not to be confused by the facts.

The Rev. David J. Kalke is a worker-pastor of the Metropolitan New York Synod, Lutheran Church of America. He is a national staff member of Theology in the Americas, and has lived in Chile and traveled extensively in Central America.

Labels on the file cabinet drawers: OUR FACTS, ABSOLUTE FACTS, THEIR FACTS, BARE FACTS, NEUTRAL FACTS, UNSUBSTANTIATED FACTS, DEMO FA, DISPUTABLE FACTS, INDISPUTABLE FACTS, UNDEMONSTR. FACTS

While most churches provide greatly needed missionary services among the poor and needy, some church groups, dedicated to a non-specific "theology of liberation," respond to ideologies alien to the church and confuse "social change" and "political ministry" with sound religious commitment.

They truly believe that profits are synonymous with greed, and that greed is the principal motivator of the corporate mind. Eliminate us, they say, put production into the hands of the workers, redistribute corporate wealth, and you have eliminated a major sin of Western civilization.

Even terrorist campaigns waged by international guerrillas find aid and comfort in the secular church.

The intentions of these particular groups may appear to be overtly Christian, but their work pays blind homage to the purveyors of revolutionary violence. . . .

However, churches beg for criticism when they forsake the ethics of civilized — and Christian — conduct.

When a church group contributes $85,000 to terrorist revolutionaries in Rhodesia, who oppose the concept of free elections in a multi-racial society, it forfeits any immunity from criticism. . . .

Another major Protestant church has been credited with funding Puerto Rican terrorists who are suspects in a wave of bombings which killed and maimed dozens of innocent victims in New York City. This church group can be clearly identified and should receive maximum publicity for this culpable act.

The principals involved in the decision to fund this "ministry" should be held fully accountable before their membership and the American public.

Through these church groups, millions of tax-exempt dollars are being laundered into the coffers

of this movement to decimate the free market and end personal liberty and economic opportunity in the Third World. At the same time, these organizations are using tax-exempt privileges to attack our traditional political, social and economic institutions here in the United States. . . .

We must overcome Western civilization's growing sense of guilt. *There is nothing evil about profit*, in spite of the semantic games played by the agitators. If it were not for profit and incentive, the Western world would not be providing food, hard and soft goods, technology, services, and loans to the rest of the world. . . .

The survival of truth and common decency are never certain, and must be fought for constantly. We are at war, but it is a guerilla war. It is being fought in the courtroom, the boardroom and the media. The enemy is organized, discernible and has ample resources.

Castle & Cooke does not intend, after 127 years, to forfeit its principles to guerrillas of any political stripe.

I am convinced that our path, rather than theirs, is the one that offers more hope for the future, but it cannot be accomplished in a vacuum or by one corporation. Let's revitalize our corporate leadership and take the offensive, in the best tradition of American capitalism.[1]

Kirchhoff's words do not represent the isolated remarks of one president attempting to defend his corporation from a few public critics. His speech is one of a series of cleverly-articulated rebuttals as transnationals attempt to clean up their image and isolate their enemies. By his own admission, Kirchhoff is concerned about more than Castle & Cooke. He is speaking for and to the capitalist class. Behind his words we can see the ideological arguments used to justify and rationalize the international flow of dollars through the transnationals' accounts. He projects his concerns for "everyone who believes in the opportunity for people to grow in a climate of personal and economic liberty." In order to appreciate the significance of Kirchhoff's remarks, we must view them in the larger context of transnational strategies.

In September 1975, over 250 persons involved in public relations and advertising divisions of the world's largest transnational firms came from 20 countries to Geneva, Switzerland. These capitalists came to develop — as the invitation to the meeting put it — "a strategy to meet future attacks on the multinationals." While no master plan was devised and passed which would suggest a conspiracy theory, their discussions did concretize several approaches for dealing with critics. The strategies they developed can be seen in subsequent public relations efforts during the last few years. Indeed, as we will see below, some of these suggested approaches are evident in Kirchhoff's remarks.

The three-day symposium involved a series of presentations and small working groups designed to improve the image of the transnationals. The problem which needed most attention, as stated by Charles J. Hedlund, president of Esso Middle East (based in New York), was one of information. "During the oil crisis we did a good job in profits, but a bad job in information."

While no final document was produced nor official minutes provided of the meeting, one Swiss journalist, Urs P. Gasche, did note the following elements as common ingredients for a counter-strategy of the transnationals for dealing with their critics:

1. The critic is to be identified as an opponent of the system and thus discredited as a discussion partner.

2. Dubious motives need be attributed to the critic: Ideological or national prejudices, envy, stupidity, ignorance and lack of experience. Hence, s/he is again discredited as a discussion partner.

3. When criticism is global or circumstantial, the contrary is "proved" by means of isolated instances (e.g. description of an individual project).

4. When criticism is indisputable around a specific case (e.g. in the case of ITT in Chile), emphasis is put on the fact that it is an individual case, moreover still under investigation.

5. In any case, it should be said in public that defending free enterprise is in everybody's interest. Therefore, it should be shown, especially in the mass media, that criticism of multinationals is basically criticism of free enterprise, and that behind it are the enemies of the free world, whose view of life is based on Marxism. One Swiss executive reportedly began a discussion by saying, "There is only one enemy, and he is in Moscow."

If we reflect a few moments on the media image of the transnationals over the last four years, we can note a change in the way they project themselves. Oil companies are presented as friends of the environment. Other large corporations are seen as the promoters of cultural events. Still others present themselves as the family businesses that got a little too large; they now take credit for providing jobs. Others are portrayed as the means by which problems such as hunger and illness can be overcome.

In the case of Castle & Cooke, we are reminded that it was founded in 1851 (by two lay missionaries of the United Church of Christ) and that it is primarily involved in the production of food (Dole bananas, pineapples and mushrooms, Bumble Bee tuna and vegetables). In another speech delivered Sept. 12, 1979, to the Financial Writers' Assn. in New York, Kirchhoff goes on to say the following about his company: "We have 31,000 stockholders; 42 per cent are women. Our shares are typically held by small

investors. Half of our stockholders own fewer than 200 shares each. Only 10 per cent own 1,000 shares or more each." This small company attempting to live out the "missionary objectives of its founders" is now one of the world's largest agribusiness corporations.

Public relations and advertisements are being designed to present the transnational within the traditional understanding of the family or small business, as illustrated in these remarks by Castle & Cooke Vice-President Pagan:

> I'm honored to be here today in such distinguished company to discuss religious principles and multi-national capitalism within the framework of Third World aspirations for a better life for a majority of the world's people.
>
> I speak to you in two capacities. First, as an officer of a U.S.-based multinational corporation — or MNC — founded in Hawaii 128 years ago by two Protestant missionaries from the Mainland — Messrs. Castle and Cooke — who believed that a successful business enterprise and personal and social decency are compatible with, and indeed mutually reinforce, each other. Today, Castle & Cooke is a worldwide agribusiness with facilities in more than 20 countries. Two of its most important subsidiaries were founded by American immigrants of Italian Catholic and Russian Jewish origin. As I will describe later, Castle & Cooke works with local landowners, businessmen and workers — Filipino Moslems, Thai Buddhists, Latin American Catholics and African Animists — to create wealth and to help build communities that can support economic and social growth, and political and personal liberty.
>
> And second, I am here as the son of a retired

23

Puerto Rican businessman who became an Episcopal priest and who until recently — he is now past 80 — worked with farm laborers to assert their basic human rights, and persuaded landlords to respect the dignity of all who depend on them. I was raised in a multiracial society and spent a great part of my life in or in relation to the developing world and have witnessed poverty at very close range.[2]

They present themselves as moral institutions which still have the human touch. They present themselves as being concerned about local and neighborhood issues, while they may be involved in red lining or in removing capital from certain areas to other parts of the world where labor is cheaper and profits higher. Chemical Bank, with investments in Pinochet's Chile, employs a Corporate Social Policy Advisor whose task is to listen to the concerns of neighborhood or special interest groups. Channels are being developed to hear complaints, to neutralize the voices of the poor and the oppressed without effecting the necessary structural changes being called for which would enable workers and nonshareholders to participate in an economic democracy.

Recently, I was part of a religious delegation given an audience with a team of Chemical Bank officials, including the head of the International Bank, the Corporate Social Policy Advisor, the head of the Bank's Latin American desk and other high ranking executives. They appeared to be a rather well-versed team for "hearing the concerns of church persons." An atmosphere of openness and dialogue enabled us to discuss Steve Bikko and Chemical Bank's commitment to change within the apartheid system of South Africa. But when it came to discussing the Chemical Bank's investments in Chile, the head of the International Bank stated: "Economic conditions have improved dramatically since Pinochet has been in power . . . with the economic well-being of people at large in the process of improvement . . . indeed there has been some social dislocation (his words for torture and systematic repression), but one dare not conclude that there is a correlation between repression and the economic system . . . human rights is a question of degree . . ." And then the conversation broke into a discussion of the Soviet Union. The liberal facade soon gave way to the hard line typified in the strategies outlined above: 1) linking critics to the Moscow line, 2) discrediting the members of our delegation "who hadn't been in Chile recently," and 3) a defense of the capitalist system.

I don't mean to single out Chemical Bank, but merely to illustrate that these public hearings and efforts to listen to concerned groups are not designed to effect change; they are designed to prevent it. As a result of such meetings, no corporation commits

itself to restraining its profit motive, nor does it change its relations to the Third World, its basic employment policies, practices or pay scales. Rather, these are efforts, as seen in the Geneva symposium, on the part of the transnationals to improve their image and to neutralize opposition.

It is within this context that we must place Kirchhoff's comments. He comes before the Merchants and Manufacturers' Assn. to defend not only Castle & Cooke, but the entire profit making system and most especially the transnational corporation. His remarks do not deal with the specific activities of his corporation in the internal politics of Honduras (the Central American country where Castle & Cooke has been accused of cooperating with a military regime in the repression of workers' movements). Rather, his speech is a call to enlist his colleagues in a McCarthy-like campaign against critics.

Kirchhoff's remarks come at a time when the political, economic and social relations of the transnationals are being questioned by an increasing number of Third World governments, organized labor, church leaders and concerned American citizens. They come at a time when a growing number of U.S. politicians are becoming concerned about the role of U.S. corporations in Third World politics. The role of ITT in its efforts to block the election of Salvador Allende in Chile; of United Brands in bribing the president of Honduras; of General Motors in cooperating with the apartheid government in South Africa; of Coca Cola in union busting in Guatemala; of the increased profits of companies operating under right-wing military dictatorships in Latin America: These have created a growing awareness among some Congresspersons of the contradiction between capitalism as an economic system and democracy as a political system. These scandals have created a new awareness among the general public as well. A recent Harris poll indicates that only 18 per cent of Americans express significant confidence in business leaders, compared to 55 per cent in the early 1970s. Kirchhoff and the other defenders of the transnational corporations have correctly perceived the difficult times they face.

ANALYSIS OF TACTICS

Within this context we can begin a more careful analysis of Kirchhoff's position. Four dimensions have been singled out for special consideration: 1) the use of a McCarthy-like approach, 2) the projection of the transnational as the protector of democratic capitalism, 3) the avoidance of issues and 4) the self-concept of the corporation as missionary.

> . . . we thought we were dealing with well-meaning — albeit not too well-informed — Christian clergymen who in their idealism wanted to be certain that

we were fair with our employees and business associates. Our record for fair play and the development of economic opportunity for people would be easy to demonstrate to any fair-minded person — and certainly Christian clergymen would be that.

Despite their harsh initial attack at the annual meeting and believing we were dealing with fair-minded, if uninformed, people, we invited their chief spokesman to visit some of our facilities — to see for himself. His criticism soon showed political and ideological biases. Our work with Communist-dominated unions in one country was commended while most of the criticism regarding our labor relations was directed against an area where we work with unions affiliated with the AFL-CIO.

The clergyman's trip was followed by a reintroduction of the same resolution, supported, interestingly enough, by quotes from a midwestern Socialist newspaper and from NACLA — the North American Congress on Latin America — a pro-Castro organization based in Oakland, CA, and New York City. It was also followed by a flurry of anti-corporate and anti-government articles in the local press of one of the countries visited. . . .

I am still concerned, however, with the persistency and activity of a highly vocal and political minority within those groups. With the support of various pro-Marxists, this activist minority has created tax-exempt institutions to develop strategy, to select target companies, and to coordinate the overall effort of church radicals. One of these institutions, the Interfaith Center for Corporate Responsibility (ICCR), a project of the National Council of Churches, is based in New York City. It is well-financed and staffed, and counts on extensive research support from NACLA as well as other organizations in the New Left camp, such as the In-

stitute for Policy Studies (IPS) which has been so prominent on the Op-Ed page of the *New York Times* in recent months, defending Vietnam and Afghanistan, while attacking U.S. motives in the world. . . .[3]

A RETURN TO McCARTHYISM

Perhaps the most repugnant aspect of Kirchhoff's remarks is his attack-by-innuendo approach. Rather than dealing directly with the questions of his critics, those posed by the North American Congress on Latin America (NACLA) and the Interfaith Center on Corporate Responsibility, he first attempts to discredit these organizations. In the spirit of McCarthy and the Geneva symposium, he tries to link them to the "Kremlin," to accuse them of using "19th Century Marxist cliches" and to imply connections with international terrorist organizations. His tactic is one of "red baiting," a tactic of the McCarthy era which defenders of democracy had struggled to lay to rest. Kirchhoff attempts to avoid the criticism of several internationally respected secular and religious research centers by merely labeling them "Marxist." He assigns to them an ideology heretofore invoked to strike fear and disbelief in the minds of his listeners, but a tactic which loses credibility today as more and more respected people, including Christians, become socialists.

He attempts to create an image of assault, the good guys vs. the bad guys. The good guys are the trans-nationals, the defenders of "personal and economic liberty;" the bad guys are the Marxists, the intellectuals and now members of the various churches. In this climate of emotionalism, he concludes his remarks by declaring war on the enemy. "We are at war, but it is a guerrilla war. It is being fought in the courtroom, the boardroom and media. The enemy is organized, discernible and has ample resources." (The total budget of NACLA, whose attack is so upsetting to Kirchhoff, is less than one half of his annual salary.)

While Kirchhoff's remarks against his critics may strike us as insubstantial, the return to the tactics of McCarthy is serious. By attempting to discredit his critics, he clearly hopes to divide the popular forces united in their efforts to change the role of the transnational.

DEFENSE OF "DEMOCRATIC CAPITALISM"

A second tactic is to portray the transnational as a friend of the people, as the defender of democracy and capitalism. The defense of the so-called "free enterprise system" is portrayed to be in everybody's self interest. "Like all publicly-owned, U.S. based corporations, we are accountable to our shareholders, to our employees and their unions, to regulatory agencies, to the U.S. Congress and to the people and governments of the 20 host nations outside the United States where we have facilities." Kirchhoff implies throughout his remarks that capitalism and democracy are one and the same. Yet how do we, much less people under military dictatorships as in Honduras, exercise control over transnationals? How are they accountable to us? Those who make decisions must own stock — not exactly "free" elections. Those critics who have purchased stock are now being written off as "Marxists." Unions organized to represent workers are busted; their leaders are jailed. Yet Kirchhoff tries to convince his audience that Castle & Cooke is accountable to the people.

How does a transnational remain accountable "to the people" when "the people," be they we or peasants in Honduras, have no access to the decision-making body governing the transnational? In the speech referred to above, Kirchhoff uses the term "democratic capitalism" to describe his understanding of our political and economic system. How Kirchhoff defines the democratic participation of "host governments," "people" and the U.S. taxpayers in the transnational corporation remains unclear. In fact there is no participation.

Quality control and product integrity are paramount to our corporate objectives, but they do not transcend in importance our employee relations, or the contribution we make to the welfare of the communities in which we participate. This has been an integral part of Castle & Cooke's success, and we are proud of it. . . .

The following internal document from Castle & Cooke's subsidiary, the Standard Fruit Company, reveals that the company authorized "special" payments to the commander of the 4th batallion (Lt. Col. Gustavo Alvarez), who directed the military raid on the Las Isletas plantation in Honduras. The document also shows that the company makes "special" payments to police officers, customs officials and newspaper reporters.

Standard Fruit Company, Honduras Oct. 16, 1976
Financial Authority Policy Manual   Section: 1-1-5

APPENDIX 1
PROCEDURE FOR "SPECIAL" PAYMENTS

The Treasurer will dispense the funds in accordance with Section I of the Financial Authority Policy and in accordance with the Special Payments Budget approved by the Home Office. All payments will be approved by either the Controller or the Assistant Manager and the Treasurer.

Special payments will be collected in sub-account 568 entitled "Special Expenses" and charged to appropriate cost centers in accordance with the department making the request. Payment Documents and maximum amounts are shown below:

Recipient	Document	Record Retention	Maximum Amt. Per Payment
1. Commander 4th Battalion-La Ceiba	Voucher	Accounting	$2,700
2. Commander 4th Battalion-La Ceiba	Voucher	Accounting	$150
3. Administrator of Aduana Other Officials to dispatch ships	Voucher	Accounting	$500 / $60/Ship
4. Various Police Officials in La Ceiba	Voucher	Treasurer	$100/Payment
5. Various Police Officials in Olanchito	Voucher	Treasurer	$100/Payment
6. Two Newspaper Reporters	Check	Accounting	$100/Person/Mo
7. Christmas Gifts	Materials Requisition	Accounting	$10,000
8. Various	Will normally be made by voucher	Treasurer	$100/Payment

We practice good business and good citizenship in every country in which we do business. As a result, we are welcome by the people and governments wherever we are involved. . . .[4]

AVOIDING THE ISSUES

"I like to think we are bearing constant witness to the missionary objectives of our founders." Kirchhoff's homily avoids the accusations of his critics and is rather an expose of a value system used to defend and justify the role of the transnational corporation. By attempting to discredit his critics and spouting the pious platitudes for "democratic capitalism," Kirchhoff hopes to bypass the serious accusations being made against Castle & Cooke. In 1977 it was alleged that Castle & Cooke was involved in union busting activities in Honduras. It was alleged that company vehicles were used by the military on a raid against a workers' cooperative. An internal document from Castle & Cooke's subsidiary, the Standard Fruit Company, indicates that Honduran military and police personnel have been on their payroll. Unfair salaries and poor medical plans for workers have been concerns. Other sources have alleged close cooperation between Castle & Cooke executives and the Honduras police that led to the arrest of over 200 trade unionists.

These accusations against Castle & Cooke go unanswered in Kirchhoff's remarks.

The World Council of Churches (WCC) is another source of support for the anti-business movement. Its increased interest in the Third World has been marked by a radical theology and has led to its involvement in direct support of the South African Marxist guerrillas with funds and other resources obtained from various religious congregations. They, for example, have repeatedly protested violations of human rights directed against western democracies and allies, while grievous infractions in Marxist states, such as North Vietnam's treatment of the boat people, are ignored.

Although a non-church related group, NACLA's personalities and material seem to be ever present in the system. NACLA collects, evaluates and disseminates data which is primarily hostile to the interests of the United States. NACLA profiles the assets and personnel of American multinationals, and these profiles become targets of opportunity for anti-business militants.

NACLA is tax-exempt and has received financial support from the World Council of Churches, the National Council of Churches, and the Institute for Policy Studies, among others.

NACLA has spawned a network of subsidiaries. One of these related activities is the Corporate Data Exchange (CDE), whose purpose is to identify stockholders of giant companies that allegedly control the U.S. economy. The Corporate Data Exchange recently released an agribusiness directory which profiles 222 major food producers. Very recently, the publication was used by Congress-man Fred Richmond from New York — who refers to it as a "Congressional Textbook" — in his attack on the food industry. This publication was made possible through grants by a group of well-meaning organizations, such as: The United Presbyterian Church, The United Methodist Church, The Seed Fund, The Presbyterian Church in the United States, The United Church of Christ, and The Marianist Provincial House. This, in my opinion, is an incredible example of the Marxist utilization of church money to influence our government and public opinion. . . .

But what of the moral and ethical base of the activists within the churches who use this material as though it were Christian Gospel? What of the use of the contributions of the members, your donations and mine, to further the radical movement, to sway government and public opinion? Do these people represent the opinion of either the average clergyman in the pulpit or the churchgoer in the pew? I think not, and I have hundreds of letters from clergy and laity to demonstrate this. . . .

I started out today by talking about the disenchantment of businessmen to the anti-business feeling of the general public. Could that feeling be any other way if avowed enemies of the free enterprise system can impose a tyranny of ideas and push their positions and attitudes into the halls of Congress, the newspapers and broadcast media of America, and the pulpits of our churches?[5]

THE ROLE OF THE CORPORATE MISSIONARY

Kirchhoff's missionary zeal, attributed to the company's founders, is determined to set the agenda for the church's mission. A fourth corporate tactic is the bringing together of a rationale for the capitalist system and a system of religious beliefs which can support it. It is an effort to enslave the Gospel to the needs of an economic system on the defensive.

By appealing to the company's missionary founders and the large donations of transnationals to churches, Kirchhoff gives the message to the progressive Christian sector that the corporations and their economic power will attempt to regain control over the church's missionary agenda. "Confronting any church organization is neither an easy nor a comfortable task. It is somewhat akin to kicking your dog or tripping your grandmother. However, churches beg for criticism when they forsake the ethics of civilized — and Christian — conduct. . . . We must determine whether the churches' funding, your contributions and mine, are being used for the exempt status of groups who are blatantly political in their organized attack to undermine the basic economic structure of our society." His McCarthy tactics are directed against those sectors of the church which have helped those persons with whom he disagrees. By labeling these persons "terrorists," Kirchhoff would dehumanize them, camouflage their legitimate struggle

"Of course I'm a Christian! But I'm not an extremist Christian."

for liberation and would forbid the church from being involved with them. In this way he also tries to discredit the World Council of Churches' contribution of food and medical supplies to the Patriotic Front in Zimbabwe.

Kirchhoff appeals to the old dichotomy between the sacred and secular by creating the category of "secular church" to describe those Christians involved in social change. This is a "church" he would like to see destroyed as it threatens the interests not of the Gospel, but of the "basic economic structure of our society." He attacks the theology of liberation as another secular tool divorced from "religious commitment."

It is on this level of developing ideological supports for the transnationals that progressive Christians are challenged to be alert. Who determines the agenda for the progressive Christian? The Gospel? An economic system? Can the church, as an institution, withstand the inevitable pressures from the capitalist class?

Kirchhoff has indicated a more aggressive role in the future for the transnationals. We can expect to see more efforts from their representatives to make the missionary enterprise serve their corporations. The unity of those Christians standing with the poor and exploited will be challenged. We need to remain strong as the corporate missionaries begin to develop

tactics designed to divide and conquer us. The missionary agenda of the church dare not fall prisoner to the objectives of the transnational corporation. By using religious symbols and values, the dominant class hopes to develop yet another weapon which can help them maintain and justify their power.

TIP OF THE ICEBERG

The remarks by Kirchhoff are but the tip of the iceberg. There is a much larger effort on the part of monopoly capitalism to build public support for transnational enterprises. We Christians will need to be as innocent as doves and as wise as serpents as we move forward in our analysis of their work. We may see further attempts to divide the Christian community through continued efforts to discredit certain sectors. The ideological struggle is being advanced on new levels.

One thing is clear: The capitalists and their transnationals are on the defensive. They have felt our strength. ■

1. D. J. Kirchhoff, "The Corporate Missionary", excerpted from *Barron's Business and Financial Weekly*, Feb. 19, 1979.
2. R. D. Pagan, Jr., excerpt from talk entitled, "Religion, Politics and U.S. Business Abroad".
3. D. J. Kirchhoff, excerpt from talk given to Financial Writer's Assn., Sept. 12, 1979.
4. Kirchhoff, *Barron's Business and Financial Weekly*, *op. cit.*
5. Kirchhoff, from talk to Financial Writer's Assn., *op. cit.*

Apostles of Reaction
by George D. McClain

"Highly visible, well-organized and institutionally successful," was how one seminary president recently described the Good News Movement. Formally known as "A Forum for Scriptural Christianity Within the United Methodist Church," the organization's nature goes well-beyond that of a forum. The leaders of Good News, in fact, have as their goal nothing less than to negate the church's commitment to social justice and to align the denomination with reactionary tendencies, both theologically and politically. Their vehicle is the well-financed Good News organization, which, in 1977, had an income of $363,000.

Much of their success lies in providing a focus for the legitimate concern of many in the church for more serious attention to evangelism and church growth.

We are convinced, however, that many who consider themselves part of Good News out of their authentic concern for evangelism, would want to question their affiliation if they were acquainted with the theology, social views, tactics, and affiliations of the Good News leadership.

Good News leaders are now giving their major attention to the United Methodist General Conference of April, 1980, where they hope to move the denomination from its moderate stance toward a reactionary one. A major struggle is underway, one with enormous significance for the future.

Convinced that such a reactionary shift would subvert the capacity of the United Methodist Church to proclaim a holistic Gospel of "good news to the poor," the Methodist Federation for Social Action (MFSA), offers this critical evaluation of the leadership's theology, social views, tactics, General Conference strategy, and political and religious links, as well as the organization's structure and funding.

The Rev. George D. McClain is Executive Secretary of the Methodist Federation for Social Action and editor of the MFSA bi-monthly publication, Social Questions Bulletin. This article first appeared in two parts, in consecutive issues of the SQB, November-December 1978 and January-February 1979.

While the MFSA does not pretend to be neutral in the continuing debate over the future direction of the church, care has been taken to be fair in this evaluation. It is based on recent and current publications and statements; facts have been carefully documented, and unfounded accusations avoided.

THEOLOGY

According to its brochure, Good News gives a voice to a "silent minority" of United Methodists who "share five basic tenets of Biblical faith: Inspiration of the Bible, the Virgin Birth of Jesus Christ, Christ's death as atonement for sin, the physical resurrection of Christ, Christ's literal return." Although Good News prefers to describe its stance as "evangelical" or "orthodox," its theology is actually that of a rigid, traditional fundamentalism.

Biblical literalism. Good News leadership describes Scripture as the product of literal, verbal inspiration: "These 'God-breathed' Scriptures are reliable in every particular, having as their substance truth without admixture of error." They reject the possibility that the Pentateuch contains "tradition" which is not historically factual, and they criticize denominational seminaries for teaching the standard view that the book of Isaiah has more than one author. They insist biblical miracles must be interpreted in a very literal way, attacking United Methodist curriculum for lacking sufficient "supernaturalism." Their view virtually rejects a hundred years of scholarship regarding the literary and cultural background of the Bible.

Doctrine of God. The central theological doctrine for Good News leaders is that of Christ's substitutionary atonement. Despite a variety of Christological formulations in the New Testament, Good News leaders insist that Christ must be understood along the analogy of Old Testament temple sacrifice, in which "the sinless Son propitiated the holy wrath of the Father." The consequences are ultimate: "Those who die without him as Savior will spend eternity in a state of damnation, a self-chosen separation from the Heavenly Father."

The doctrine of God here is harsh and condemning

and not at all balanced by the pervasive New Testament theme that God in Christ is above all a God of love. To us, the New Testament understanding of God is incompatible with literal eternal damnation. Furthermore, the Good News doctrine of God allows no recognition of divine redemptive activity which is not articulated in Christian terms.

Scholasticism. In doing theology, Good News leaders appear much more concerned with the correctness of the words and doctrines used to describe faith than with the adequacy with which faith is expressed in life. Their concern for the correct repetition of doctrinal formulae out of the past constitutes an uncreative scholasticism inhibiting the creative movement of the Holy Spirit. It also prevents Good News leaders from acknowledging the legitimacy of the varieties of Christian experience expressed by ethnic and racial groups and women, often in a non-traditional form and language. This scholasticism also hinders any genuine advances in our understanding of God's revelation.

Intolerance. Good News leaders have little sympathy with those who stand on theological ground different from their own. What does not square with their theology is usually called "humanism," "liberalism," or even "radical secularism" — terms which appear to be interchangeable in the Good News' lexicon. Theological pluralism within the denomination is rejected — unless this "pluralism" is one "that has as its base Scriptural inerrancy." In other words, the only acceptable "pluralism" is one which includes all biblical literalists, while excluding everyone else. Good News' intolerance provides the driving force behind their crusade to turn the denomination from its alleged "humanism."

Unbiblical Approach. Despite all the contentions of Good News leaders, their theology is *not* biblical in our view. Their literalistic interpretations and scholasticism stultify the living Word; their doctrine of God takes insufficient account of God's loving, compassionate and forgiving nature, and their intolerance of diversity within the denomination repudiates the Apostle Paul's metaphor of the church having many parts but one Body.

POLITICAL VIEWS

Although the Good News brochure claims the movement "has avoided reactionary fundamentalism which ignored society's ills," Good News leaders reflect an extremely negative attitude toward the denomination's social witness. For instance, rather than defending the church's role as advocate of peace in Vietnam, women's rights, and economic and racial justice, they condemn such activism for creating hostility between denominational leadership and local churches.

Death Penalty.

Who says the execution of a murderer is wrong? You cannot find it in the Bible. If you say it is wrong, you are telling God that he is wrong. God commands that sin shall be punished — not just as a deterrant and not just to rehabilitate — but because *divine justice must be done.*[1]

It is as though the New Testament had never been written and grace, redemption, and forgiveness had never been heard of. Here we see the practical outgrowth of the stress on divine wrath rather than God's love and compassion. Furthermore, their position ignores the built-in injustice that the death penalty always falls heaviest upon poor and minority persons.

Big Business. Their pro-big business stance is apparent from the unquestioning defense of multinationals' role in less developed countries and the castigation of church-sponsored corporate responsibility efforts as "abrasive advocacy of causes alien to people" in local churches. This includes a rejection of church shareholder resolutions which have been directed against such targets as corporate support for apartheid in South Africa, neo-fascism in Chile, runaway shops and infant formula abuse.

Apartheid in South Africa. Good News leaders are lending support to apartheid in South Africa. In September, 1978, Good News chairman Paul Mickey of Duke Divinity School and Executive Secretary/Editor Charles Keysor both served as local organizers for appearances by a team of five white South African defenders of apartheid, all leaders of the Christian League of Southern Africa. The group's visit to Duke Divinity School was reportedly cancelled because of student protest against this visit by these Christian apologists for apartheid.

World Hunger. Official United Methodist positions regarding world hunger were sharply attacked in 1978 in two major articles in *Good News* magazine. In a stunning display of selfishness, these articles opposed an international system of food reserves, a simple lifestyle, and a national policy which would assure every human being access to food as a matter of right. The possibility that "we in the U.S., who constitute 6 per cent of the world's population, [are] somehow guilty because we consume 35 per cent of the world's goods and services," is emphatically rejected.

Their answer to the world food problem, as well as to U.S. farmer's woes, is near absolute free enterprise, for it is government controls and regulation which, in their view, cause hunger. Rather than a new international economic order, they call for "more widespread adoption of the only economic system that is a demonstrated success — free competitive market capitalism." This remarkable analysis completely ignores how, under a profit-oriented market economy, foreign companies and local ruling elites have taken the best land in Third World countries, only to grow products like tea, sugar and coffee for export while the native populations are subjected to ever-increasing malnutrition and repression.

Women's Rights. Good News leaders are opposed to the Equal Rights Amendment. They show no recognition of the burdens borne by the numerous women who must work to support their families, yet are denied equal pay for equal work.

Good News leaders are opposed to the organized women's movement and attempt to caricature it in extremist terms. They contend the denomination supports what they call "the extremist leadership of the radical feminist movement" or "hard core feminism." Even basic assertiveness by women is misrepresented as denial of dependence upon God or of interdependence between men and women.

Sexuality. Good News leaders focus perhaps more energy on issues related to sexuality than on any other cluster of issues. They oppose the United Methodist position on abortion which affirms "the legal option of abortion under proper medical procedures."

The church has carefully stated that "a decision concerning abortion should be made after thorough and thoughtful consideration by the parties involved, with medical and pastoral counsel." Nevertheless the Good News leaders claim that the church supports a "pagan" view of "supreme selfishness."

Three crucial considerations are missing from the Good News analysis: 1. The abortion question is a moral dilemma which eludes a uniform Christian solution for the legitimate, competing claims of fetus and mother. Therefore to foreclose, ahead of time, the option of a safe, medically-supervised abortion to those facing this dilemma is to be insensitive and extreme. 2. There has been a dramatic reduction in deaths, especially among poor women, since the time when illegal abortion was the only option. 3. A human fetus in the early stages is *not* a child but a *potential* human being.

The issue of homosexuality continually evokes the longest and strongest editorial blasts in *Good News* magazine. The Good News leaders contend that Scripture, Christian teaching, and the millions of United Methodists in the pew all support the position that homosexuality is an unequivocal evil that must be uprooted from the church and, in fact, excluded from the entire society. Good News leaders successfully urged passage at the 1976 General Conference of a resolution stipulating that no national church funds may be used "to promote the acceptance of homosexuality." This has had a particularly repressive effect upon the open discussion the church sorely needs. Denominational officials are now very fearful of being attacked for sponsoring any sharing of views about homosexuality, for no rational discussion could take place without hearing voices advocating a greater acceptance. One seminary has even denied admission to a homosexual theology student from the predominantly gay denomination, the Metropolitan Community Church, for fear of losing church funds.

The fact is that the denomination is undecided and confused and contradictory on the issue of homosexuality. Good News leaders find this situation not only frustrating but unbearable. They desperately

want to settle the issue, not by allowing free and open discussion over whatever time is necessary for a consensus to emerge in the church, but by forcing their extreme stand upon the church.

TACTICS

Misrepresentation. Though they claim they are only concerned about "spiritual" matters rather than any social and political agenda, a close reading of their literature reveals that they have their own social-political agenda. They do not in fact oppose the church involvement in social-political matters; they only oppose it when it does not further their own positions.

Good News leaders sometimes grossly misrepresent organizations or positions which they oppose. Liberation theology is equated with violence, even though numerous theologians and practitioners of liberation theology like Dom Helder Camara are pacifists and all caution that violence is to be resorted to only, if at all, as a very last option when all other avenues for resisting the violence of oppression have been exhausted.

Witch Hunts. The tactics of Good News leadership regarding homosexual persons in the ministry are so lacking in human compassion and sensitivity that the description "witch hunts," given by the editor of the denominational clergy magazine, *The Circuit Rider*, is quite correct. Good News leadership cannot let rest, even temporarily, the carefully considered and overwhelming decision of the New York Conference to affirm Rev. Paul Abels' ministry at Washington Square Church, where Abels was unanimously asked back; nor can it allow the reluctant act of Bishop Ward in reappointing him when the bishop had been given no other choice by the conference. Nowhere have they more clearly demonstrated their lack of tolerance for the ambiguities and confusion of a church which has not made up its mind about homosexuality.

Good News leaders, in the fashion of witch hunts, want to identify transgressors, drive them out into the open, and punish them in public. Even bishops can be targets. Bishop Ward is accused of "following the path of least resistance, capitulating to local pressures" and creating a "vacuum in episcopal leadership (which) allows the church to drift . . . onto dangerous reefs."

The *Good News* editor charged Bishop Ward and the other bishops (Wheatley, Carroll, Armstrong) who shared messages with a local church-sponsored conference on homosexuality with setting aside church law, being divisive, subverting the church, and "hastening the already-alarming hemorrhage of membership loss." The editor insisted the Council of Bishops "deal decisively" with these bishops if they were to protect their credibility, prevent further erosion of their power, and stave off adoption of a term episcopacy.

McCarthyism. The Good News leaders' witch hunt tactics in their recent attack against the Women's Division of the Board of Global Ministries are reminiscent of McCarthyism. On the basis of rumor-mongering to the effect that "the Marxist views of staff-persons in the Women's Division have long been a topic of conversation in United Methodist circles," the Good News Evangelical Missions Council called for the mass resignation of the entire Women's Division staff. These charges can only be seen as an attempt to discredit the Women's division by the revival of the appeals to fear and hate employed by the late Senator Joseph McCarthy.

Division and Suspicion. The endless confrontations which Good News leaders create with boards and agencies of the denomination serve continually to foment division and suspicion. The Board of Discipleship is attacked because church school literature is not fundamentalist enough. The Board of Global Ministries is criticized for seeing evangelism in holistic terms and mission as a two-way street not limited to sending missionaries. Church and Society is blasted for its involvement in coalitions and advocacy. United Methodist Women is attacked for championing women's rights and called a "totalitarian ecclesiastical empire." United Methodist seminaries are attacked for not teaching a narrow fundamentalism and accused of leaving "the historic Christian Gospel unstated and undefended." Good News leaders urge ministerial students to desert our denominational seminaries for certain unaffiliated, supposedly more "evangelical" seminaries, namely Asbury, Fuller, Gordon-Conwell, and Trinity Evangelical.

Good News leaders also promote division and suspicion by their strong push for "selective giving," which involves withholding apportionments from World Service or the Interdenominational Cooperation Fund or refusing pledges to United Methodist Women. This constitutes a rejection of the UM connectional system itself and the introduction of a potentially fatal sectarian intolerance into our denominational life.

The United Methodist Women are a special target of Good News efforts to create divisions within the church. The Good News Task Force on Women sends its newsletter *Candle* without any charge to any UM woman, bombarding her with continued attacks upon UMW study material.

PLANS FOR 1980

Good News leaders felt they achieved some important successes at the 1976 General Conference and now they are expending great energy to formulate and enact an "evangelical agenda" at the 1980 General Conference in Indianapolis. This time around they expect to spend even more than the $10,000 they expended in 1976.

The process began at a January 1978 "political strategy think tank," where 30 persons worked for three days on their General Conference agenda. This is outlined in the first of what will be eight or nine pre-General Conference issues of the Good News Political Strategy Committee's newsletter, *Words to the Wise*.

Issues for 1980 which have been targeted thus far include:

• Making United Methodist Women's units optional in local churches. This would legitimize the dissension fostered by the Good News Task Force on Women and the Esther Action Council.

• Remove mandatory requirements for ethnic and sexual representation on church agencies.

• Allow use of other than denominational curriculum in UM churches. This would legitimize Good News' current promotion of its own and other fundamentalist materials.

• Change the style of the Board of Church and Society from monitoring legislation, advocating the needs of the dispossessed, cooperating in action coalitions, and taking stands, to being a politically irrelevant private chaplaincy to government workers and legislators.

• Make specific a "core of doctrine," which could enforce Good News sectarianism on the entire church.

• Eliminate subsidies to seminaries and replace them with tuition vouchers which seminarians could use in any seminary, including independent "evangelical" ones.

• Prohibit absolutely the appointment of any homosexual minister.

• Repeal the UM position supporting the legal option of abortion.

• Allow groups other than the Board of Global Ministers to send missionaries. This would legitimize Good News' threats to send out their own fundamentalist missionaries.

• Allow "selective giving" to World Service, thus making each denominational program vulnerable to attack by pressure groups such as Good News.

• Either administer "euthanasia" (their word) to the Consultation on Church Union (COCU) or give it a different basis, presumably a fundamentalist one.

To accomplish these goals and others which inevitably will be added, the Good News strategy is to develop position papers; to elect "evangelical" delegates to General Conference; to encourage petitions, especially with local church and annual conference endorsement; to influence elected delegates; and to organize an "evangelical" caucus of 40 or more volunteers to lobby with delegates at the site of General Conference.

STRUCTURE/FUNDING

Good News leaders have fashioned a powerful organization to effect their purposes. The decision-making body is the board of directors, consisting of 25 clergymen, 10 laymen, and 5 laywomen, and chaired by Dr. Paul Mickey, associate professor of pastoral theology at Duke Divinity School. The board appears to be self-perpetuating and not structurally accountable to the general membership.

As of August, 1977, the Good News paid staff consisted of nine persons, six of them full-time.

A wide variety of activity is made possible by enormous and rapidly growing financial resources. Good News income was over $363,000 in 1977, almost 40 per cent over 1976. The overall increase was due mostly to large gains from sales of confirmation material and profits on summer convocations. The most remarkable figure is the $116,583 received for 1977 in a category simply called "contributions," indicating that Good News may well be heavily subsidized by large gifts from rich supporters.

ALLIANCES

South African Connection. As mentioned previously, the top Good News leaders are lending support to the pro-apartheid Christian League of Southern Africa. Listed with Chairman Paul Mickey and Executive Secretary/Editor Charles Keysor as local contacts for the apartheid supporters' U.S. tour in late 1978 is Edgar C. Bundy, long-time head of the Church League of America and widely recognized as a leader of the Far Right in the United States. Mickey, Keysor, Bundy and the other tour contacts were asked by the Justice Department to register as "agents of a foreign principal" because they considered the Christian League representatives to be involved in political activities.

Thus, there is a major link between Good News and an international right-wing agency which is also supported by at least two leading figures of the Far Right, Edgar C. Bundy of the Church League of America and Senator Jesse Helms of North Carolina, who went to the Senate floor to protest the Justice Department request that Mickey, Keysor, Bundy and other tour organizers register as foreign agents.

Eagle Forum Connection. The Eagle Forum is a national organization headed and founded by Phyllis Schlafly, who also heads the powerful Stop-ERA lobby and has affiliations with a variety of Far Right organizations, including the John Birch Society,

American Conservative Union, and Young Americans for Freedom.

The Eagle Forum opposes the Equal Rights Amendment, abortion rights, and government-funded day care programs and supports neighborhood schools (anti-busing), law and order against aggression by other nations (pro-military spending), prayer in schools, and the right of religious bodies to designate different roles for men and women.

While continually attacking the ecumenical bodies of which United Methodism is a part — the Consultation on Church Union, the National Council of Churches, and the World Council of Churches, Good News leaders have been seeking out their own interdenominational ties. Since 1977 they have been planning common strategy with reactionary caucuses in other denominations. Other groups involved are the southern Presbyterian "Covenant Fellowship," the northern Presbyterian "Presbyterians United for Biblical Concerns," and the Episcopalian "Fellowship of Witness."

NEW FAR RIGHT?

The emergence of the New Far Right is currently the cause of increasing concern. Last year, for instance, a wide range of liberal and moderate organizations established an information clearing-house on New Far Right activities. Supporting groups included the National Education Assn., American Library Assn., AFL-CIO, and various church organizations.

While there are always exceptions, New Far Right groups tend with a high degree of correlation to be

pro: Death penalty, nuclear power, local police, FBI, CIA, greater defense spending, prayer in the schools, property rights, free market economics, "right to work" laws, and a constitutional convention to prohibit abortion. Usually they are *anti*: Busing to desegregate schools, gun control, ERA, abortion rights, government regulation of business, women's rights, unions, religious ecumenism, homosexual rights, sex education and the Panama Canal treaties.

Far Right groups, like all extremists, have an apocalyptic, conspiratorial world view which intensifies their sense of alienation.

> The ideological extremists . . . because of their isolation from the world, feel menaced by unknown dangers. The paranoic tendencies which are closely associated with their apocalyptic and aggressive outlook make them think that the ordinary world, from which their devotion to the ideal cuts them off, is not normal at all; they think it is a realm of secret machinations. What goes on in the world of pluralistic politics, in civil society, is a secret to them. It is a secret which they must unmask by vigorous publicity.[2]

As sociologist Edward Shils concludes, extremists see "the world" as the realm of evil, against which they must defend themselves and which they must ultimately conquer.

The other characteristic of the New Far Right is its tendency to concentrate on single issues, or on a very few issues; but in doing so to involve adherents of these single issue campaigns in a large network of extremist politics.

Now, what about the Good News leadership?

Does it represent the presence of the New Far Right within our denomination?

The known ties of Good News leaders to the Christian League of Southern Africa (in company with Edgar Bundy of the Church League of America) and to Phyllis Schlafly's Eagle Forum certainly point in this direction.

Furthermore, there is a very high correspondence between the New Far Right consensus on issues and the positions of Good News leadership. Good News leaders' positions correspond to the standard Far Right positions on the death penalty, free market economics, government regulation of business, ERA, abortion, religious ecumenism, women's rights, homosexual rights, the Panama Canal treaties, and racial and ethnic quotas.

Furthermore, Good News leadership reflects the paranoic tendencies, the apocalyptic and aggressive worldview, the suspicion of conspiracy, and the felt need to unmask secret evil which characterize extremism.

Taken together, these factors force upon us the conclusion that the leadership of the Good News movement constitutes the presence and influence of the New Far Right in United Methodism today.

THE CHALLENGE

The social situation in the United States today provides fertile ground for the growth of ultraconservative attitudes. As Americans we have seen the end of our post-World War II boom and prosperity and are now plagued with "stagflation," a new condition of high inflation combined with economic stagnation. The average American, accustomed to rising economic expectations, is now fortunate if wages keep up with living costs. Women and minorities find themselves increasingly pitted against each other and white males for a limited supply of jobs and promotions. Meanwhile corporations, intent on increasing their profits, have managed to shift a large portion of the tax burden from their shoulders to those of the middle class. Together with widespread family breakdown, these factors have created an unsettling climate conducive to the growth of right-wing activists who pinpoint scapegoats and offer simplistic solutions, as with California's Proposition 13 on tax reduction.

Religious fundamentalism, with its moral absoluteness, its otherworldliness, and its holy war mentality, also thrives in a climate of fear and uncertainty. The wedding between militant fundamentalism and reactionary politics is a natural and recurring one.

The New Far Right presents a special challenge. What is "new" is its sophistication in political tactics, fund-raising, mass organization, and coalition building. It is these characteristics which also make the New Far Right presence in the UMC a special challenge, for Good News leaders have been demonstrating considerable sophistication in these areas. Thus they constitute a greater long-term threat to the church's mission and life than earlier far rightist groups in the church such as the Circuit Riders of the 1950s.

Good News leaders would prefer to conceal their reactionary politics under a camouflage of "evangelical" concerns. However, in pretending that their program is spiritual and not political, they are at their most hypocritical, for Good News leaders have a political agenda — and a very reactionary one, as we have shown. Good News leaders not only wish to neutralize the church's commitment to social justice and its threat to entrenched principalities and powers of privilege. In addition, their political ties and social views suggest an ultimate goal of aligning the church with the reactionary politics of the privileged sectors and giving religious sanction to their policies of oppression.

It is apparent that Good News leaders have taken advantage of many United Methodists of evangelical persuasion who support a more vigorous evangelism but who by no means wish to be used to support apartheid in South Africa or witch-hunts in the United States, nor to promote the social agenda of the Far Right or to purge the United Methodist Church of all non-evangelicals.

The emergence of fundamentalist extremism in the church calls for a two-fold response. The church must make clear that a divisive sectarianism which sets out militantly to "save" us all, which condemns non-fundamentalists as humanists, which employs distortions, confrontations, McCarthyism and witch hunts to get its way, and which would align the church with those who "rob the poor and crush the afflicted," simply is out of step with the spirit of Christ as United Methodists have come to understand it.

Furthermore, in a time when many are weary and tempted to withdrawal and resignation, our church must discover a new vision of human community which addresses the real fears upon which the Far Right is capitalizing. To the articulation of such a just and loving vision — grounded in Scripture and based on economic justice, racial and sexual inclusiveness, and respect for human dignity — we call upon all United Methodists and offer our hand in partnership in this task. ∎

1. G. Russell Evans, "What About Capital Punishment?" *Good News*, March/April 1978 pp. 98-108. See also July/Aug. 1978, pp. 3-4.
2. Edward A. Shils, *The Torment of Society*, 1956, pp. 231-234; quoted in Shriver, *A Briefing on the Right Wing*, pp. 2-3.

Group Exercise

For the first hour, have group members participate in a discussion around each of the readings for this session. The following questions can serve as a guide:

The Idolatry and Promise of the Church

1 How, in your experience, have you seen certain social implications of the Gospel discouraged or rejected by the institutional church?

2 Do you agree that the prevailing ideas of a society are those of its dominant class? To whatever extent you accept this, what new light does it shed on religious life in the United States?

Chilean Bishops Declaration and Response by Pablo Richard
"Corporate Missionaries" and Response by David Kalke

3 Build a contrasting description of the idealist and materialist worldviews from your reading of these documents.

4 How are the responses of the dominant class in the face of revolutionary ferment and change (e.g., defensiveness, blaming superficial contradictions, emphasis on pacifism, moralism, individualism and class collaboration) being used in the current capitalist crisis to resist the efforts of those who champion the poor and working people?

Apostles of Reaction

5 What religious groups do you know which bear similarity to the Good News Movement? How is their support of dominant capitalist interests expressed — or masked?

For the second hour, invite members to participate in a liberation theology method of reading a biblical passage as follows:

Session 1 has pointed out that we do not approach the Scriptures in an antiseptic way, but we are already conditioned by our philosophical, ethical, political and class backgrounds. We must begin our interpretation, then, with a certain "suspicion" about the preconceived ideas with which we approach the Bible, and about our methods. For a better understanding of this, spend 10 minutes reading the following excerpt from theologian Juan Luis Segundo's **The Liberation of Theology**, and then the passage from Mark 12: 28-34.

Suspicion and Bible Reading
A LIBERATION METHOD

Christianity is a biblical religion. It is the religion of a book, of various books if you will, for that is precisely what the word "Bible" means. This means that theology, for its part, cannot swerve from its path in this respect. It must keep going back to its book and reinterpreting.

Attached as it is to a book, traditional theology does not, however, assert its independence from the past or from the sciences which help it to understand the past, such as general history, the study of ancient languages and cultures, the history of biblical forms, and the history of biblical redaction. On the other hand, traditional theology does, implicitly or explicitly, assert its independence from the sciences that deal with the present. . . . This seems to be based on the naive belief that the word of God is applied to human realities inside some antiseptic laboratory that is totally immune to the ideological tendencies and struggles of the present day.

Now liberation theology starts from the opposite end. The suspicion of such a theology is that anything and everything involving ideas, including theology, is intimately bound up with the existing social situation in at least an unconscious way.

Thus, the fundamental difference between traditional academic theology and liberation theology is that the latter feels compelled at every step to combine the disciplines that open up the past with the disciplines that help to explain the present. And the theologian feels this necessity precisely in the task of working out and elaborating theology; that is to say, in the task of interpreting the word of God as it is addressed to us here and now . . .

Each new reality obliges us to interpret the word of God afresh, to change reality accordingly, and then go back and reinterpret the word of God again, and so on.

Two preconditions must be met if we are to use such a methodology. The first is that the questions rising out of the present be rich enough, general enough, and basic enough to force us to change our customary conceptions of life, death, knowledge, society, politics and the world in general. Only a change of this sort, or at the very least a pervasive suspicion about our ideas and value judgments concerning those things, will enable us to reach the theological level and force theology to come back down to reality and ask itself new and decisive questions.

The second precondition is intimately bound up with the first. Theology cannot somehow assume that it can respond to the new questions without changing its customary interpretation of the Scriptures. Moreover, if our interpretation of Scriptures does not change along with the problems, then the latter will go unanswered; or worse, they will receive old, conservative, unserviceable answers. . . .

The method these two preconditions suggest has four decisive factors. First, there is our way of experiencing reality, which leads us to ideological suspicion. Secondly, there is the application of our ideological suspicion to the whole ideological superstructure in general and to theology in particular. Thirdly, there comes a new way of experiencing theological reality that leads us to exegetical suspicion, that is, to the suspicion that the prevailing interpretation of the Bible has not taken important pieces of data into account. Fourthly, we have our new way of interpreting the fountainhead of our faith (i.e., Scripture) with the new elements at our disposal.

—Excerpted from **The Liberation of Theology** by Juan Luis Segundo, S.J. pp. 7-9.
Copyright © 1976 by ORBIS Books, Maryknoll, N.Y., 10545. Reprinted by permission.

One of the scribes who had listened to them debating and had observed how well Jesus had answered them, now came up and put a question to him, "Which is the first of all the commandments?" Jesus replied, "This is the first: **Listen, Israel, the Lord our God is the one Lord, and you must love the Lord your God with all your heart, with all your soul, with all your mind and with all your strength**. The second is this: **You must love your neighbor as yourself.** There is no commandment greater than these." The scribe said to him, "Well spoken, Master; what you have said is true: That God is one and there is no other. To love God with all your heart, with all your understanding and strength, and to love your neighbor as yourself, this is far more important than any burnt offering or sacrifice." Jesus, seeing how wisely he had spoken, said, "You are not far from the kingdom of God." And after that, no one dared to question him any more.

—Mark 12:28-34

Now answer the following questions:

6 What crises are arising in our country today that provide cause for "a pervasive suspicion about our ideas and value judgments?"

7 How does "ideological suspicion" regarding the Christian-capitalist alliance raise questions regarding the conservative and liberal religious notions of Christian salvation?

8 How would the passage from Mark be interpreted by business executives who see transnational corporations as "missionary efforts"? (For example, in their answer to the question, "Who is my neighbor?")

9 In what directions would new interpretations move us?

Note: At the end of this session, please preview the Group Exercise for Session 2, which involves preparation before the meeting around mutually agreed upon assignments.

Capitalism in Crisis

Inflation. Unemployment. Recession. Preparations for war. Everyone agrees that these are signs of a serious and prolonged economic crisis, anticipated to grow worse during the 1980s.

Now we can be certain of some other things besides the proverbial "death and taxes." One is that whenever economic crises explode — whether as gas or heating oil shortages or rising health and food costs or the like — it is always the working class and the poor who suffer most. "You can depend on it." And the capitalist system is able to manipulate for its own ends the unemployed, the aged, the sick — those who are able only with great difficulty to fight back.

Superb ironies characterize the system: While millions seek adequate housing, 30 per cent of the housing work force seeks work; and the way capitalism works its way out of industrial depressions (27 of them in 122 years) is to fire workers, then counter consequent high unemployment by inaugurating programs to get them back to work. Facts like these have led economist Harold Freeman to say: "The days when people can be persuaded to accept nonsense of this order and magnitude are by no means over but they may be slowly ending and we may someday look back on these days with disbelief. . . . If masses of people begin to reflect on these conventional features of an economy which provides fortunes for a few and misfortunes for many and for which grown men and women can give no sensible justification, it may be the moment of dangerous truth for U.S. capitalism."

But before that moment arrives, many hurdles must be overcome. One is the ideological hurdle addressed in the first session. We have been served up a lifetime of analysis from the perspective of capitalist ideology. The same capitalist class which owns the means of producing social wealth and directs our labor also finances prestigious universities that train the "experts" who lobby Congress and advise our political leaders. These same capitalists own and control the radio and TV stations, newspapers and publishing houses. They tell us that the news they produce is "objective," nonideological — "the truth" — "and that's the way it is."

The idea that truth is non-ideological, that it stands above and beyond material circumstance and human need goes back at least as far as Plato, who first developed and synthesized idealist philosophy. From the time of the ancient Greeks, ruling classes have found it convenient to define truth in this fashion. It enables them to characterize their ideology as timeless and "truthful" while contending ideologies can be dismissed as "false" or "unrealistic" when applied to timeless and absolute categories.

But there is another view, based on a materialist world outlook, as described in Session 1. It is a perspective developed from an ideological commitment to the interests of the working class and the poor. Its purpose for understanding the world is to change it — not to justify the status quo. It uses Marxist tools of analysis. The view from the bottom looks quite different than the view from the top. Those on the bottom are forced to do all they can to try to change the system to make it work more in their favor. The people bearing the brunt of capitalism's destructiveness have little choice in the long run but to struggle for revolutionary change.

The people on the top find it exceedingly difficult to see beyond the beauty of the world they have the power to create materially and ideologically for themselves. Those in the middle must make an ideological choice. *Which Side Are We On?*

The two readings selected for this session attempt to analyze problems from the ideological perspective of the working class and the poor. Together they provide an overview of the economic and political realities we face at the beginning of the 1980s.

The first article, "What Makes It a Crisis?" focuses on the domestic economy. It indicates the depth of our economic problems while examining the origin of the present crisis and how it affects us on and off the job. It provides evidence that we are not experiencing merely another of the regular and recurring "downturns" in the "business cycle," or simply a drop in "leading economic indicators."

The second reading offers a view of the present crisis in its international dimensions, showing how it emerged historically on the basis of the contradictions inherent in the world capitalist system. It examines inflation, monetary policy, the role of gold, special drawing rights, the dollar crisis — concepts which all of us find difficult to comprehend. A short glossary is provided to aid our understanding.

Many of us instinctively draw back when we encounter such difficult subjects. We will need each other's encouragement and support to gain comprehension of the economic forces that shape our lives. We can no longer abandon this task to the "experts." If we are to take charge of our own future, we must unlearn much of what we have been taught, and begin again. This is a difficult and time-consuming chore, for which the few readings and glossary here are insufficient. A suggested bibliography for additional study can be found at the back of this book.

In the Group Exercise following the readings, we evaluate which class interests and ideological perspectives are most often served by the daily press. As Christians, we find that once we cast off the idolatry of the past and begin to use a new set of tools with which to analyze the world around us, the old information takes on new meaning, and becomes useful in our efforts to construct a more just and equitable world. ∎

What Makes It a Crisis?

by The Union for Radical Political Economics

Most people living in the United States need little reminder that we're in the middle of a serious economic crisis. Corporate and government economists have tried to minimize these problems for years, of course — exhorting us to be patient and to excuse the inconvenience. Their recommendations have hardly solved the problems. More and more people are facing economic dislocation and hardship. The prospects for immediate relief seem dim. The crisis persists. . . .

The media usually talk about the economy by referring to "leading economic indicators." This suggests that our problems can easily be summarized with arrows on graphs: This leading indicator points down and that one points up. But if we look just at "leading indicators," we're likely to develop abstract and artificial analyses of our problems. We need to begin with the facts of our own lives. Those facts leave little doubt that the crisis has not been laid to rest.

Many of us have experienced the crisis *on the job*. Bad times always assault workers' wages and this crisis has been no exception. Workers' average real spendable weekly earnings, measured in constant 1967 dollars, reached a peak of $95.73 in 1973, fell to $90.53 by 1975, and was $89.62 in 1979.

People have also felt the crisis in their flesh and bones. Employers are often pressured during crises to speed up the pace of work. This has clearly happened as the crisis has evolved. The rate of industrial accidents had begun to increase in the mid-1960s, climbing by 27.7 per cent from 1963 to 1970.[1] By 1976, according to a government survey, a quarter of all U.S. workers were exposed to risk of death or injury on the job because of unsafe working conditions.[2] And, partly reflecting these deteriorating conditions, a recent opinion survey found that "the number of Americans dissatisfied with their

work or their employers" had reached a 25-year high.[3]

The crisis has also pushed many of us *off the job*. The current crisis is partly a crisis of unemployment, and the problems of joblessness have not abated.

Unemployment itself has assumed sweeping proportions. In 1967, according to official government measures of unemployment, there were fewer than 3 million unemployed workers. By 1975, those numbers had jumped to almost 8 million unemployed workers, or 8.5 per cent of the civilian labor force. (This was the highest annual rate of unemployment in the U.S. since the Great Depression.) Unemployment reached a peak of 9.1 per cent in May, 1975. By October 1977, there were still almost 7 million unemployed workers, or 7 per cent of the labor force. Most observers agree that real rates of unemployment are nearly double these "official" figures.[4] The average unemployed worker remains jobless for approximately 10 weeks. This means as many as 15 per cent of all Americans are unemployed at some point during an average year. And the burdens of joblessness are barely mitigated by the varieties of unemployment insurance available to some workers; it appears that no more than one-half of unemployed workers in the United States are currently receiving unemployment compensation.[5]

Finally, some groups of people experience these problems with special intensity. Women and minority workers are especially hard hit. Unemployment rates are also particularly high in certain regions — older central city ghettos most specifically and the Northeastern region of the country more generally. The crisis is placing mounting pressure on many families to abandon their communities and neighborhoods in order to move — somewhere, anywhere — where they might stand a better chance of finding work.[6]

Almost all of us also feel the crisis as *consumers*. Inflation keeps emptying our wallets and purses. Back in the 1960s, an annual price increase of three per cent seemed high. But prices have increased at least three per cent per year since 1968 — the longest sustained period of inflation since price statistics were first systematically recorded around 1800. By 1972, consumers' prices were increasing an average of almost nine per cent a year. The rate of inflation for the period from August 1978-August 1979 was 11.5 per cent and climbing.

Most families in the United States, moreover, have felt inflation even more sharply than these figures indicate. Households in the bottom 80 per cent of the U.S. income distribution spend an average of 70 per cent of their incomes on four basic necessities: Food, shelter, medical care, and energy. Between 1970 and 1976, the cost of these four basic necessities increased more than 44 per cent more rapidly than the cost of other goods and services.[7]

Finally, many of us feel the crisis *in our communities*. The crisis has seriously affected the quantity and quality of social services. Schools have been hit hard. Hospitals have been closed and medical services curtailed. Housing has grown more and more expensive to maintain and the housing stock has aged considerably. Fiscal crises have meant that public transportation has not been maintained either; buses and subways have deteriorated rapidly in many cities.

All of these dimensions of the crisis have had a profoundly insidious effect on the social and political

atmosphere. On the one hand, people feel fatalistic because the crisis seems so deep. In 1975, for instance, 81 per cent of a representative sample of U.S. residents reported that they felt "none," "little," or, at best "some" control over their own economic condition.[8]

On the other hand, the crisis has also created profound divisions among working people. We're encouraged to blame each other for the crisis — to blame it on labor unions demanding higher wages, or on illegal immigrants "stealing" our jobs, or on environmentalists "costing" us our jobs. The blame is placed everywhere but where it belongs — on a corporate-controlled system of production for profit. And one of the main reasons for this divisiveness is that different groups bear the impact of the crisis to different degrees. Increasing inequalities of income reflect these tendencies: Over the past six years, the income of a family at the top of the income distribution has increased, on average, almost 25 per cent more rapidly than that of a family around the 20th percentile in the income distribution.[9] Gaps among us have been widening along almost every dimension.

The crisis has hit us all in different ways, in short, and it has been serving to keep us fatalistic and divided. That must change if we are to protect our own interests. If it is to change, we need a new understanding of what the crisis represents.

WHAT MAKES IT A CRISIS?

There are three important characteristics of the current situation which make clear that it must be considered as a "crisis" — potentially as severe as the Great Depression — and much more than some kind of serious "recession" in the economy.

The first reason is that the economy itself is behaving differently than an economy usually behaves after a serious recession. No economic "recovery" can go on very long in capitalist economies unless there is a lot of new investment in plants and machines — in the capital goods which give a sharp boost to recovery and provide the basis for future profitable production. "But the distressing fact," as *Business Week* reports it, "is that the level of capital investing is the United States is still lower than it was in 1974, with the increase in investing coming more slowly than in any previous postwar recovery."[10] This sluggishness in investment is not unique to the United States; the pattern persists in every advanced capitalist country. "Moreover," as *Business Week* concludes, "there are signs that the flatness in investment outlays that has haunted the recovery overseas from the start may remain with the global economy for the rest of the decade."[11]

Can investment be easily sparked? The Organization for Economic Cooperation and Development (OECD) concludes that "business confidence about the sustainability of growth is much weaker than prior to the recession."[12] This low confidence has held down investment, in their view, "despite widespread measures to encourage investment."[13] So, from the point of view of investors, the economy is in a vicious circle. Policy stimulus doesn't work because confidence is low. Confidence is low because investment is low. Investment is low because policy stimulus isn't working. Such is their analysis, *Fortune* concludes in a recent editorial, that the prospects for more investment "are far from encouraging."[14]

The second reason this is a "crisis" is that it is affecting the whole world capitalist economy. It is "universal" rather than geographically specific and contained. All of the advanced capitalist countries are suffering similar problems in similar ways. The OECD reports semi-annually on the "economic outlook" in its 24 member countries — the major advanced capitalist countries of the world. Its most recent report (July 1977) had nothing but somber facts:

> In the majority of Member countries the expansion has remained hesitant and unemployment has continued to rise. The rise in industrial production has recently slowed down again and capacity utilization rates remain generally low . . .
>
> The overall prospects for any significant reduction in inflation next year are not particularly good. . . . In many countries, inflation has stopped decelerating and has even accelerated.[15]

The common problems are leading to similar solutions. Each country is tempted, as its own problems persist, to raise tariffs in order to protect its industry from the competition of foreign imports. When some countries do it, others are forced to follow suit. In any period of continuing economic crisis, the threat of protectionist wars looms constantly. The shadow is currently growing longer every day. *Fortune* recently expressed its concern in clear and ominous language:

> In the early 1930s, an epidemic of trade restrictions nearly strangled international trade, and thereby helped sink the world into the Great Depression. But at least lessons were learned, and the 1950s and 1960s brought sustained progress toward free trade among the nations of the world. In most of the developed nations, at least, protectionism became a waning cause, lacking any broad base of support. And yet in 1977, rather suddenly, protectionism has once again become a dangerous presence in the world economy.[16]

The international monetary system is in serious disarray. Tariff wars will only complicate matters. "It is a livable situation" for now, as an international banker put it recently, but "it can't continue much longer."[17]

There is a third reason why the current period must be viewed as fundamentally different from ordinary recessions. After normal recessions, basic economic and social relationships are similar to those which existed before. There is a slow-down, then a resurgence in economic activity. But structural changes in the economy are minor.

During economic crisis, in complete contrast, nearly everything changes. The world looked completely different after the Great Depression than before it. And institutions are changing their shape very rapidly during the present period. Corporations are shifting the location of their activities to such an extent that entire cities and regions are affected. Labor unions are being forced to adjust their collective bargaining policies. Municipal governments are changing their basic policies and social services. The national government is contending with the failure of old policies and the necessity of entirely new ones. The list goes on. What it means is that the basic institutions of our economic system are changing the way they work. The structure of the economy is at stake. The crisis is a stage on which the script for a new structure is being written while the play is being acted almost simultaneously. Ten years from now, the economy will look very different as a result. . . .

WHEN DID THE CRISIS BEGIN?

If the crisis is so serious, some of us may ask, how could conditions have deteriorated so suddenly? Hadn't we already solved the problems of prosperity? Wasn't the business cycle "obsolescent"? Didn't the crisis start in 1973 or 1974?

Many of us have had the impression that the crisis started just a few years ago because corporations, the government, and the media had not begun to talk about serious problems before then. We had begun to experience assaults on our working and living conditions, of course, but we were usually told that these were isolated wounds, easily cured by band-aids. Those of us not directly affected were told to ignore them.

In fact, however, the crisis did not appear suddenly. It is now possible to recognize, with the help of a little hindsight, that the conditions leading to the crisis had begun to emerge during the middle of the 1960s. A brief historical review of the emergence of the crisis can help underscore how deeply it has taken root.

Some signs of trouble had first appeared in the late 1950s. Profits were lagging and corporations did not have enough money to maintain investment. During the 1960s, they began to borrow heavily and the government reduced corporate tax burdens through investment tax credits and accelerated depreciation allowances. These devices helped inflate the economy, generating resurgent prosperity. Government expenditures on the Vietnam War, ballooning from year to year, further heated an economy which was already beginning to show signs of too rapid growth.

By the late 1960s, all of the early seeds of stagflation had been planted. The economy was apparently growing too fast. Prices were beginning to rise. Wages were beginning to rise. Competition from foreign businesses was beginning to reduce profit mar-

gins of U.S. corporations. In response, corporations were beginning to speed up the pace of production. Angered by rising prices and increasingly intensive work, many U.S. workers began to protest — both through slow-down on the job and wildcat strikes over working conditions. The spreading protests were making it more and more difficult for corporations to keep their lines running smoothly. "Many manufacturing executives . . . (had) openly complained in recent years," the *Wall Street Journal* observed in 1972, "that too much control had passed from management to labor."[18]

Some of these conditions had also been spreading abroad. The surging U.S. economy was over-heating other advanced capitalist countries. Prices were beginning to rise, working conditions were deteriorating, and workers were also beginning to protest — sometimes much more militantly than in the United States. By the late 1960s and early 1970s, the intensifications of worker protest had become an epidemic throughout the advanced capitalist world. Between 1969 and 1974 in the member countries of the OECD (excluding the United States), the annual average number of strikes was three times the level in 1946-50 and double the level of 1951-67.[19]

Instability in production spread quickly to instability in the market. As inflation began to accelerate and international competition among large corporations also intensified, the international economy began to experience tremors. Exchange rates fluctuated more and more rapidly. The dollar was losing its power as a standard world currency. Interest rates began to rise and fall among countries. The United States tried to stabilize the situation with dollar devaluations both in 1971 and 1973, to no avail.

By the early 1970s, in short, the world economy was becoming increasingly fragile. The international economy was extraordinarily vulnerable to any kind of sudden shock when food and energy prices began to spiral in 1973-1974. Given those extra jolts, conditions deteriorated more and more rapidly. And the timing of those events made it appear to many that bad weather and higher prices had somehow "caused" our exploding problems. The media fed us these myths.

We are suggesting, in complete contrast, that the inflation of food and energy prices did not "cause" the current economic crisis at all. They were, in fact, partly caused by the crisis. The crisis had begun to develop in the 1960s. By 1973, the world economy was strained and staggering. If the food and energy crises provided the knock-out punch, the boxer was already bloodied and wobbling on his feet.

WHY DIDN'T THEY TELL US?

This kind of account seems novel, in large part, because we were being fed a very different kind of story during the late 1960s and early 1970s. The character of the emergent crisis was disguised over the years for two reasons. One involved errors of omission while the other involved clear acts of commission.

The omissions can be attributed to mainstream economists. Orthodox economists largely believe that capitalism is capable of stable equilibrium. Under the influence of John Maynard Keynes, this had led, during the 25 years after World War II, to a spreading belief that governments could keep capitalist economies growing smoothly with stable prices. The primary postulate of the "new economics" popu-

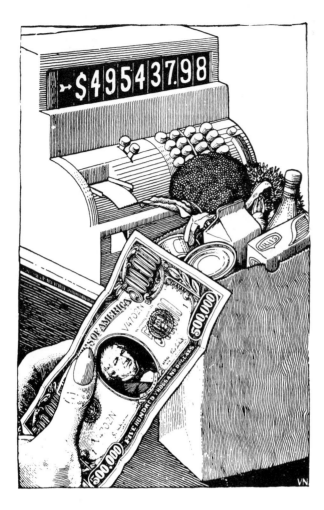

able of curing instability and/or that governments can help them restore stability. They believe that capitalist economies build fundamentally upon *harmonies* of interest, rather than *conflicts* of interests. That analytic orientation leads them to believe that the economy can and will right itself soon *even when the facts do not support that belief.*

Many corporate and government officials know better, having recognized that the world capitalist economy was in trouble since the late 1960s and early 1970s. They have kept silent because they have been pursuing policies clearly designed to protect their interests and reduce peoples' power as the crisis has developed.

It had become clear to corporations and many government officials, as early as 1970, that the developing crisis would require harsh consequences for people if corporate interests were to be protected. Economic growth could no longer jointly satisfy both corporations and working people. Economic contradiction and crisis was going to mean, more and more, that corporate interests would have to be served *at the expense of others.* There was no longer enough margin in the economy to permit mutually beneficial policies.

Corporate and government policies soon reflected this. *Business Week* had clearly issued the warning in October 1974:

> It is inevitable that the U.S. economy will grow more slowly . . . Some people will obviously have to do with less . . . The basic health of the U.S. is based on the basic health of its corporations and banks. . . . Yet it will be a hard pill for many Americans to swallow — the idea of doing with less so that big business can have more.[21]

Government had begun to take the warning seriously. During the recession of 1969-1970, during the wage-price controls of 1971-1973, and during the downturn of 1973-1975, U.S. government policy partly reflected a clear and self-conscious decision to try to restore economic stability by forcing workers to pay the price. As one business observer remarked about the Ford Administration's policy in 1975, it was a policy of "benign neglect; there is no program and it has been done on purpose. (They) want to let the economy take a deep bath . . ."[22]

This orientation still dominates corporate and government policy. Corporate leaders are still complaining that people have too much power and that they are not yet free enough to pursue the kinds of investments which (they say) they might otherwise consider. *Fortune* expressed this continuing complaint as recently as October 1977:

> But the best antidote . . . would be resumption of vigorous economic growth in the industrial world. Unfortunately, the prospects are far from encour-

larized in the 1960s, as James Tobin put it, was "that government policy could and should keep the economy close to a path of steady real growth."[20]

The prosperity of the 1960s convinced most economists that their theories were correct. The economy seemed to be growing stably. That impression led them to treat the problems of the early 1970s as temporary aberrations. This was like the annual reports on the Vietnam War during the previous decade. Anticipating opposition to the war, the government had repeatedly told us that there was "light at the end of the tunnel" and that "victory lay just ahead." By the early 1970s, the economists were feeding us the same kind of message about the economy: The "recovery is in sight," they told us. Our problems have been caused by "accidents," there's no need to "panic," and the economy will "smooth itself out soon."

These palliatives seem comical in retrospect, of course, because their predictions have proved to be wildly inaccurate at every turn. It does not appear that most mainstream economists misled us deliberately. Rather, economists have omitted any mention of the emergent economic crisis because their theories don't know a crisis when they see it. Mainstream economists believe that capitalist economies are cap-

aging, for the economies of many nations are laboring under . . . heavy depressants not easily shaken off . . .

(One) great depressant might be called "social drag." It can be defined as the combined effects of the excessive costs, inefficiencies, and disincentives that government imposes on economic activity in the private sector. . . . Social drag includes such things as:

- Welfare payments and unemployment benefits so generous that they erode incentive to look for work and to accept work that is offered.
- Busybody regulation not disciplined by rational cost-benefit calculation. . . .
- Statutory minimum wages, which reduce employment opportunities for unskilled workers, especially young people.
- Government-granted privileges that enable labor unions to establish unreasonable work rules and to force wage increases far in excess of productivity gains . . .

Social drag is both inflationary and depressive. Extra costs translate sooner or later into higher prices. What's more, the growing scope of welfare-state entitlements unrelated to work help create an excess of claims upon the output of the economy. . . .

On the supply side, social drag diverts resources from investment to consumption, dulls incentives to work and to invest, and channels enormous numbers of working hours into such unproductive activities as administering unsound regulations and trying to comply with the same.[23]

No wonder corporations and the government don't talk very much about how fundamental they think the problems in our economy have become. Many people depend on welfare benefits or unemployment compensation or labor unions or minimum wages or government social services. The more that people begin to hear corporate suggestions that these programs are in the way, the more those people will begin to

question the "needs" of corporations which seem to require higher priority.

Since the late 1960s, in short, corporations (and their friends in the government) have begun to regard *our* interests as conflicting with *theirs*. It's time that we begin to view *their* interests as in conflict with *ours*. ∎

...Trabajar...
...Ahorrar...
...Prosperar...

The Republican Party

GOP ad reads "to work, to save, to prosper."

---

1. *President's Report on Occupational Safety and Health* (Washington, DC: U.S. Government Printing Office, 1972) Appendix B, pp. 71ff.
2. *New York Times*, Oct. 3, 1977, pp. 1, 22.
3. *New York Post*, Aug. 10, 1977, p. 59.
4. See "Counting the Underemployed" in David M. Gordon, ed., *Problems in Political Economy: An Urban Perspective* (Lexington, Mass.: D.C. Heath, 1977), 2nd ed., pp. 70-75; and Richard Du Boff, "Unemployment in the United States," *Monthly Review*, November 1977.
5. See *Economic Indicators*, July 1977, p. 13.
6. Recent data show that those who are most likely to move are those who can — particularly young people between the ages of 20 and 24 — while older people find it much more difficult to move.
7. See Leslie Ellen Nulty, *Understanding the New Inflation: The Importance of the Basic Necessities* (Washington, D.C.: Exploratory Project for Economic Alternatives, 1977), pp. 6,8.
8. Cited in Jeremy Rifkin, *Own Your Own Job* (N.Y.: Bantam Books, 1977), p. 130.
9. Nulty, *op. cit.*, p. 16.
10. *Business Week*, Oct. 17, 1977, p. 61.
11. *Ibid.*, p. 20.
12. Organization for Economic Cooperation and Development, *Economic Outlook*, July 1977, p. 20.
13. *Ibid.*, p. 20
14. *Fortune*, November 1977, p. 103.
15. *Economic Outlook, op. cit.*, pp. 6,5,11.
16. *Fortune*, November 1977, p. 103.
17. Quoted in *New York Times*, Sept. 28, 1977, p.D16.
18. Quoted in David M. Gordon, "Capital vs. Labor: The Current Crisis in the Sphere of Production" in URPE, *Radical Perspectives on the Economic Crisis*, 1975, p. 33.
19. Richard Hyman, "Strikes in the 'First World': Institutionalization and its Limits," University of Warwick, mimeo, September 1977, p.10.
20. James Tobin, *The New Economics—A Decade Later* (Princeton: Princeton University Press, 1975).
21. *Business Week*, Oct. 12, 1974.
22. Quote from Pierre Rinfret, business consultant, in *Newsweek*, Feb. 24, 1975, p. 65.
23. *Fortune*, November 1977, p. 103.

The Present Crisis and the Danger of War

by *People's Tribune*

Terms appearing in bold face type are defined in the glossary following this article.

A most pressing issue today is the growing danger of world war — a result of the economic crisis within the world capitalist system. The International Monetary Fund has asserted that widespread inflation has imposed both **monetary** and **fiscal** restraints that leave "little room for maneuver" to improve the economy. The *New York Times* commented: "The portrayal by the (IMF) of a world that has bound itself into an economic strait jacket is the gloomiest of a series of analyses put forward by economic watchdog institutions in recent months." (*New York Times*, Sept. 12, 1977, p. 1)

It has been two years since the above assessment. At his writing (September 1979), forecasts of the leading economic institutions have become gloomier. Now there is even less room to maneuver. If we are to understand the present crisis and the growing

This article was adapted and edited by Peggy Case from three articles which first appeared in the *People's Tribune*, the newspaper of the Communist Labor Party: Oct. 1977, Sept. 1978 and Feb. 1979. Reprinted with permission.

danger of war, we must examine certain fundamental principles of the political economy of the capitalist system. This article will discuss gold and currency relations, the causes and significance of inflation, credit, some measures adopted by leading powers to get out of the crisis, and war dangers growing from the capitalist crisis.

GOLD AND CURRENCY

In order for **commodities** to be exchanged, **value** must confront value in the market. In other words, people will exchange commodities with each other which are equivalent in terms of the amount of average human labor embodied in them. The widespread exchange of a vast spectrum of commodities demanded the development of money as a means of measuring their value and exchanging them. Karl Marx examined in detail how the value of any commodity is determined, and how money historically evolved with the development of commodity circulation. (See *Capital*, Vol. 1)

Historically, the role of "universal equivalent" fell to gold. Gold was suitable not only because of its physical characteristics, but also because of its own high value — the large amounts of human labor expended in the production of a relatively small quantity of the precious metal over the history of commodity circulation.

As capitalism developed, gold was replaced in circulation by printed paper notes representing a certain quantity of gold. Paper money functioned as a medium of exchange within countries, and was stamped with a national identity. However, in international trade, printed notes were superseded by the transfer of the precious metal itself.

Speaking of gold money, Marx noted: "When (it) leaves the home sphere of circulation, it strips off the local garbs which it there assumes, as a standard of prices, of coin, of token and of a symbol of value, and returns to its original form of gold bullion." This gold bullion, as "money of the world serves as the universal medium of payment, as the universal means of purchasing, and as the universally recognized embodiment of all wealth. Gold's function as a means of payment in the settling of international balances is its chief one." (Karl Marx, *Capital, Vol. 1*, International Publishers, 1975, pp. 142-143.)

As **imperialism** emerged, and until the aftermath of World War I, international debts were traditionally settled in gold bullion. In the period between the two world wars, as a result of the growing productivity of labor and the greater amounts of commodities available for circulation, gold was supplemented as world money with the U.S. dollar and the British pound. These currencies could function as world money because they were "convertible"; that is, each monetary unit could be converted into a fixed quantity of gold.

INFLATION

The main disruption in the circulation of paper money arises from inflation, when additional paper currency is printed that is not accompanied by a corresponding increase in gold reserves. As a result of inflation, the amount of paper money in circulation has increased, while the gold content of each unit, i.e., the value content, has therefore decreased. Hence, the money is worth less. In other words, inflation is not the same thing as a simple raising of prices. Inflation is a cause of rising prices. If each unit of paper, or symbolic money has less real value behind it, it can be used as exchange in the marketplace for fewer goods. More of these paper units are needed for each purchase because each is worth less than before. Thus, the price is higher. We are concerned here with inflation and not monopoly price-fixing policies which also raise prices.

Inflation increases in response to the developing **economic contradictions of capitalism**. It is a means by which the government finances the expansion of capitalist control all over the world, and pays for the military interventions necessary to secure areas which resist or revolt. It is also a means by which the government attempts to overcome market stagnation resulting from the overproduction of commodities by printing more money to allow commodities to circulate.

It is not possible for modern capitalism to function without inflation. As much as politicians may claim that they can eliminate inflation, or balance the budget, the internal laws of the capitalist system are bound to assert themselves.

Business Week commented recently that "the 14 years of high and volatile inflation since the Vietnam war turned hot in the summer of 1965 have put an end to a century of relative price stability in the United States. In the years since, inflation has become institutionalized — deeply embedded in the soul of the U.S. economy." (*Business Week*, Jan. 29, 1979, p. 78)

Inflation is "deeply embedded" in the capitalist system itself. Capitalism must expand or die. If a capitalist enterprise stands still, it cannot survive competition. It must constantly expand production, expand its share of the market, improve its technique. And given the social relations under capitalism, it is not possible to expand without producing inflation.

In every reproduction cycle — the journey a given **capital** takes from its initial advance in the form of **means of production** and labor power, through the process of production and circulation as commodities, back into the capitalist's pocket as money enriched with **surplus value** — the capitalist cannot consider the cycle complete until a portion of the surplus value has been put once more into the form of capital so that the scale of production can be expanded.

The extraction of surplus value is the foundation of capitalism. What the capitalist calls profit, comes about as a result of the transformation of human labor power into a commodity. The workers sell their labor power to the owners of capital, to use as they please for a given period of time. The workers are paid for their labor power at its value, the cost of maintaining them and their families at a level conforming to a given cultural standard. The capitalists are always trying to push the cost of labor to the minimum needed for survival; the workers are always struggling to raise it to a level of greater comfort. But in the time that they labor for the capitalist, workers create far more value than they are paid for. Ever increasing quantities of commodities are thrown into circulation beyond the power of the workers to buy back. Additional currency can then be thrown into circulation. Prices rise (because the currency glut has made each unit worth less) while real wages fall, since the workers are able to buy less with their wages.

CREDIT

The various forms of credit are major means of expanding the money supply. It is not necessary actually to "print dollars;" the government need only increase the amount of money available through the banks as credit.

Commercial credit represents shares of the total capital of the economy. Stocks, securities, commercial paper, etc. are promises of payment against the future production of surplus value. When economic stagnation occurs, demands for payment must be met. The government, through its Federal Reserve System, creates money and credit to meet these demands. Inflation thus acts as a subsidy for the capitalist class.

Expansion of productive capacity and actual capi-

tal is the basis upon which the entire structure of credit is built. While the expansion of credit and other forms of money take on a life of their own, they must always expand with the scale of reproduction necessary for the economy to grow.

Credit has another inflationary dimension. Consumer credit, as distinguished from the commercial credit discussed above, is extended primarily to the working class. It accounts for 17.8 per cent of disposable income. Most people are familiar with the fact that were it not for credit cards, charge accounts and other forms of consumer credit (mortgages, loans, etc.) they would be unable to buy basic necessities. Consumer credit, a major factor in inflation, allows producers to consume at usurious rates of interest what they could not otherwise afford. More "fictitious" money is poured into circulation, increasing overall inflation.

Inflation has become essential to the functioning of the system, whether it comes in the form of government increasing the actual supply of paper money to pay for military adventures and avoid stagnation in the circulation of commodities, or in the form of credit.

As long as international balances between countries were settled in gold, the problem of inflation was confined within national boundaries. However, when currency is being exchanged across national boundaries, it is another matter.

Despite all the efforts of capitalist governments to overcome the difficulties created by the inability of the workers to buy all the commodities they produce, the glut of commodities clogs the market. The economy stagnates. Production must be curtailed; workers are laid off. In an effort to get rid of this glut in foreign markets, there is an official devaluation of the currency. Its foreign exchange rate is adjusted to correspond to its decreased gold content, thus lowering the prices of commodities in foreign markets. Devaluation becomes a means of gaining a competitive advantage in terms of international trade, but it is at the expense of the working class. The commodities rise in price in the domestic market, thus lowering workers' standard of living. And inroads are made into the foreign market which results in a loss of production when the domestic commodities can no longer compete with imported goods.

Other countries will inevitably try to respond to a devaluation with trade barriers, erecting tariff walls around themselves to protect their domestic markets. This was the situation during the 1930s. But the present crisis has its own specific character. To understand how it differs from those which preceded it, it is necessary to review some history.

WORLD WAR II

On the eve of World War II, the capitalist world was in the grips of a massive crisis of overproduction. Unemployment reached unprecedented levels. Inflation and devaluation failed to relieve market stagnation significantly. Unified by common currencies (the "sterling area," the "dollar area" the "franc area," etc.) trade blocs corresponding to colonial spheres of influence, solidified.

The war that developed from the crisis was triggered by the attempted German expansion into, and economic enslavement of, eastern Europe and European Russia. The British, French and U.S. imperialists hoped that the Nazis would destroy the Soviet Union. However, when Germany attacked the West as well, the imperialists were forced to enter the war as allies of the Soviet Union.

The Second World War was primarily a military extension of the political battle over the fate of the colonial world. The division of the world into trade blocs, united by common currencies and protected by tariffs, resulted from insulated colonial systems that would not allow the free penetration of international capital. Although the war failed to destroy the first socialist country and thus release that market to the imperialists, it spelled the doom of direct colonialism. The British and French economies, shattered by the war effort, ultimately yielded their colonial empires to **neocolonialism**.

By remaining out of the war until 1941, the United States managed to accumulate 70 per cent of the world's monetary gold reserves, which flowed to the United States for haven from the war and in exchange for arms and industrial goods. The war, fought across Europe and Asia, devastated the major industrial centers of two continents. After the defeat of the Japanese and German fascists, the industrial plant of the world, with the exception of the United States, lay in ruins.

The economies of the advanced capitalist countries again, with the exception of the United States, were crippled. Pre-war currency relationships had been destroyed by the outflow of gold and capital, and the massive inflation required to finance the war. With the major portion of the world's monetary gold concentrated in the United States, the dollar remained the sole sound currency in the capitalist world, and was, though briefly, "as good as gold."

In 1944, a conference of representatives from the leading capitalist countries was held at Bretton Woods, NH, to prepare for the rebuilding of the capitalist economies devastated by the war. The main achievement of the Bretton Woods Conference was the establishment of an international monetary system on whose basis international trade could be re-established. To this end, the conference set up two international institutions, the International Monetary Fund (IMF) and the International Bank for Reconstruction and Development (World Bank).

Based on the objective position of the United States as the center of world imperialism, the U.S. dollar was placed at the center of the monetary system erected at Bretton Woods. A system of fixed exchange rates between currencies was established, based on the convertibility of the dollar into gold on demand at the rate of $35 to an ounce of gold. These exchange rates were only allowed to fluctuate with 1 per cent of their established parities. Devaluations were allowed only in exceptional instances and by common agreement within the Fund.

At the conclusion of the conference the dollar was the sole convertible currency. Its fixed rate to gold did not allow it to be devalued; its role in international trade was that of world money, a substitute for gold. The outpouring of dollars from the United States in aid, trade, and investment provided the reserves upon which the value of other currencies was based.

The organizational structure of the International Monetary Fund, whose purpose was the monitoring of exchange rates and granting of temporary assistance in financing balance of payments deficits, ensured absolute control by the United States. For example, in order to be a member of the IMF, countries were required to put up quotas in gold and currency, which provided the assets that would allow the Fund to function. Representation in the Fund and voting rights were allocated in proportion to a country's quota. The United States, which provided nearly 30 per cent of the initial capital, exercised veto power, by virtue of its enormous block of votes over all decisions of the Fund.

NEOCOLONIZATION AND THE MARSHALL PLAN

In the immediate post-war period, the functions of the IMF and World Bank were temporarily superceded by the Marshall Plan. The Marshall Plan re-vived the West European economies under U.S. hegemony, at the expense of the European industrialists and the old European direct colonial empires. The colonies were opened to the penetration of **international finance capital**, under the leadership of Wall Street. The neocolonial exploitation of these areas by finance capital was the engine that drove the reconstruction of the West European economies under the Marshall Plan. (See "Contradiction of Finance Capital" in Session 3 for an explanation of the distinction between industrial capital and finance capital.) The vast superprofits from neocolonial exploitation yielded a raise in the living standard of the working class in the imperialist centers and aided co-optation of key sectors of the labor movement. This advanced a change in political conditions. The Cold War and an increasing anti-communism replaced the relative unity achieved to defeat the fascists during the World War.

The revival of Europe's capitalist economies began the collapse of the Bretton Woods system. To rebuild the economies of Britain, Western Europe and Japan it was necessary to protect their domestic markets because of the loss of their direct colonies. Tariffs and other restrictive barriers were raised around Europe.

While the continual trade deficit of the United States created a flood of dollars onto the continent in the form of aid, investment and the purchase of commodities, the protective barriers around Europe were particularly restrictive to U.S. manufactured goods. Nor could the United States, under the Bretton Woods system, devalue the dollar to gain a competitive advantage in European markets. A devaluation of the system's central currency would have created monetary chaos.

By 1958, the European currencies had become convertible, that is, they could be freely exchanged for other currencies and gold on the basis of the rates of exchange established at Bretton Woods. As the European economies revived, their productive capacity increased. The need for dollars as the lubricant of world trade declined, leaving massive dollar reserves in Europe's central banks. It became clear that the U.S. gold reserve, in relation to outstanding dollar liabilities, was no longer sufficient to maintain the Bretton Woods fixed rate of convertibility. European central banks, taking advantage of the dollar's convertibility, began exchanging dollars for gold to build up their own gold reserves. The flood of dollars from the United States was accompanied by an outpouring of gold. The post-war scarcity of dollars, the new world money, had, in a decade, turned into a "dollar glut," as the central position of the dollar was used by the financiers to buy up the key sectors of the world capitalist economy.

STANDARD DRAWING RIGHTS

By 1960, the legs of the Bretton Woods system began to buckle. Between 1961 and 1967, under the auspices of the IMF, discussions were held on how to supplement world reserve assets (dollars and gold) to overcome the paucity of gold and the glut of dollars.

As a result of phenomenal post-war rise in productivity, and the emergence of the neocolonies as commodity producers, the mass of the world's commodities outstripped the supply of gold necessary to circulate them. Dollars could only continue to perform this function if ever increasing amounts were printed out of all proportion to U.S. gold reserves.

At the Rio de Janeiro Conference of the IMF in 1967, in order to relieve the pressure on the dollar, and supplement the dollar and gold as international reserve assets, the IMF established an artificial reserve asset known as "Special Drawing Rights" (SDRs).

SDRs are allocated to participating member countries in proportion to their IMF quotas. Participating members are obligated to accept SDRs from one another in settlement of payments deficits and in exchange for convertible currencies. Exchanged through the IMF, SDRs have no value outside of the common agreement among nations, enforced by the economic and political might of the United States, that these reserves will be accepted as payment on debt.

Special Drawing Rights created an inflationary solution to inflation. Dollars and gold were supplemented by the new "paper gold" with no value behind it. But the alternative to the creation of SDRs was a continued inflationary glut of dollars grossly overvalued in relation to gold and concentrated in Europe's central banks; the massive default by debtor nations, particularly the neocolonies virtually devoid of reserve assets; and the collapse of the capitalist economy. Thus capitalism maneuvers out of one crisis, but only by creating the conditions for an even larger crisis in the future. The rules of the game within the capitalist system guarantee that such a dilemma will occur over and over again.

The creation of SDRs proved the fundamental weakness of the dollar. Currency speculation intensified, leading to a series of monetary crises and devaluations throughout the '60s. Yearly it became more apparent that the capitalists were unable to maintain the rates of exchange established at Bretton Woods.

Further fundamental changes were necessary in the system to avoid monetary crises and the destructive migrations of short term capital as a result of currency speculation.

By the late '60s and early '70s most of the neocolonies had completed the transition from being pre-dominantly commodity consumers to being commodity producers. **Transnational capital** had gone all over the globe in search of the highest rate of profit, financing production where the labor costs were cheaper and raw materials closer. As they began throwing increasing quantities of commodities on the world market, the international financiers gained at the expense of European and U.S. industrialists whose domestically-produced commodities could not compete, and, of course, at the expense of the laboring colonial peoples, whose products were beyond their means to buy.

The mounting glut in the world market, and the inability of the dollar to respond with a devaluation that would give U.S. commodities a competitive advantage, aggravated the contradiction between the industrialists and the financiers. The industrialists proposed monetary reforms that would advance protectionist trade policies, while the financiers advocated reforms which would continue to allow their capital to roam the globe freely in search of maximum profit, independent of national boundaries.

But one thing was clear to all. While at the conclusion of World War II the massive concentration of gold in the United States provided a gold cover for dollar liabilities of almost 60 per cent that figure plunged by the late '60s. Gold reserves failed to cover the dollar to the extent legally fixed by the Federal Reserve System. Any sizeable movement of European central banks to convert their dollars could have left the cupboard bare.

Thus it is not surprising that on Aug. 15, 1971, following a meeting at Camp David with a handful of economic advisors, President Nixon suspended the convertibility of the dollar. The action had become absolutely essential. The fabric of the Bretton Woods system was tearing at the seams.

THE NIXON SHOCKS

The package of economic measures known among economists as the "Nixon Shocks" were unacceptable to the Wall Street financiers. It was, however, *not* because of the suspension of convertibility of the dollar and ensuing dollar devaluation. On the contrary, it was common knowledge in economic circles that these measures were unavoidable. However, the rest of the package turned toward protectionism in favor of U.S. industrialists, and included the 90-day wage and price freeze, a 10 per cent investment credit to businesses investing in American-made equipment, and a 10 per cent surcharge on imports. The United States was being led onto the road of protectionism. Europe responded in kind.

Wall Street was losing control over the President, who was putting forth the policies of the economic nationalists with this package. Had Nixon not been abandoned by the most powerful sector of the U.S. capitalist class, the Wall Street financiers, it is doubtful that the Watergate scandal would have materialized. With Nixon out of the picture, the international financiers, under the leadership of Wall Street, intensified efforts to reform the international monetary system. The main issues in the debate were the role of gold, the dollar, and SDRs, and whether fixed exchange rates were possible any longer.

Wall Street pressed for increasing the role of SDRs and phasing out the role of gold. They opted for a system in which the IMF, firmly in their control, became the clearing house of international trade. The opposition, most articulately expressed by France, demanded some form of return to a gold standard, claiming that the U.S. proposals would only enhance U.S. domination of the international monetary and economic system.

A debate that began almost as soon as the European currencies became convertible in 1958, reached a head in the monetary chaos following the "Nixon Shocks."

The removal of Nixon was accompanied by the construction of the Trilateral Commission, a body of financial and political leaders from the United States, Western Europe and Japan. This commission, formed at the initiative of David Rockefeller, was both a recognition of the contradictions between West Germany, Japan and the United States, and a forum for finding solutions mutually acceptable to the world's leading financiers.

With SDRs functioning, the Trilateral Commission constructed, and the IMF and Trilateral Commission functioning as organizational centers of transnational capital, the financiers moved decisively.

The oil crisis of 1973, with its quadrupling of the price of oil, produced a flow of dollars to the OPEC countries, particularly Saudi Arabia, which lacked the population and productive capacity to absorb vast quantities of manufactured goods and thus acted as a sponge to absorb excess dollars. This allowed Europe temporary relief from a glut of dollars. With convertibilty suspended, these dollars were open to wild market speculation that would drive their value down. Instead, these dollars flowed to Saudi Arabia and were recycled back into U.S. and European banks and through IMF loan facilities into the non-oil producing neocolonies. Wall Street used this flow of wealth to set up reactionary neocolonial centers to exercise their dictatorship through the dispensing of dollars and arms.

With recession already on the horizon, amid monetary chaos and stalemated monetary reform negotiations that had dragged on for years, the international financiers had taken a calculated risk. In unleashing the oil crisis, they achieved their ends at great cost — world depression. But the depression (labeled only a recession in the United States due to its milder impact here) allowed the IMF to consolidate its hold on the capitalist world. The oil crisis completed the economic strangulation of the neocolonies, and forced European, Japanese and U.S. industrialists to accept the domination of the international financiers and their monetary policies, at least for the near future.

Behind the maneuvering for absolute economic and political control over the neocolonies, lies the necessity for the imperialists to stem the tide of socialist revolution in Africa and Latin America. IMF lending facilities continue to plunge the neocolonies deeper into debt, while the "conditions" placed on these loans are dictated by transnational capital through the IMF and the World Bank.

It is convenient to continually blame the "Arabs" or OPEC for the oil crisis and the inflation which has grown more problematic each year. However, the price of oil is quoted in terms of U.S. dollars, which have become less than half of what they could be exchanged for in 1967. The oil producers have little real freedom to go against the interests of the leading Wall Street capitalists. Basic control of the oil industry and all the subsidiary aspects of it which allow for delivery of finished products, are in the hands of the leading financiers.

The period from the Bretton Woods Conference to the oil crisis marks the rise to hegemony of transnational capital led by Wall Street. Struggling against the industrialists within their own class, against the

53

growing economic prestige of socialism and against socialist revolution throughout the neocolonial world, the international financiers have consolidated their strength while producing crises of unprecedented proportion. Mounting debts are being mediated by artificial currencies. The entire non-industrial world is caught in a spiraling debt. Markets are glutted while commodity circulation stagnates. The outcry for tariff barriers and other forms of "moderating free trade" grows daily. With their entire income absorbed in refinancing debts, the neocolonies have no recourse but to borrow further when a glutted market cannot absorb the products of their labor. The industrial nations lose maneuvering room as their currencies fluctuate wildly in an attempt to gain momentary economic advantage.

THE DOLLAR CRISIS

For over a year, headlines in the daily papers have detailed the continued decline of the dollar. From President Carter to the leading spokesmen for Western Europe and Japan, public officials have all expressed alarm. But the fall of the dollar is nothing new, as we have seen. Since 1971, when the United States suspended the convertibility of the dollar into gold in foreign trade — and hence the fixed ratio of the dollar to gold — a constantly deepening monetary crisis has engulfed the capitalist world.

Dramatically spiraling inflation and the plunge of the dollar are blamed on many things, but most especially on the U.S. balance of trade deficit, which in turn is blamed on increased oil imports. However, the fall of the dollar does not merely result from the persistent trade deficit and resulting loss of faith in the dollar's strength.

A trade deficit is not necessarily a bad thing. A trade deficit reflects more imports than exports. This is often the result of an expanding economy, which absorbs raw materials and other imports for expanded production of manufactured goods. Trade deficits also reflect a situation in which U.S. multinational corporations or U.S.-owned foreign corporations produce or assemble products abroad which are then "imported" into the U.S. market, i.e., the Dodge Colt (Japan) or the Ford Fiesta (Germany). As far as oil is concerned, the oil bill accounts for less than 20 per cent of the trade deficit.

The dollar's fall really represents its changing relationship to other currencies — its *exchange rate.* While public confidence and international trade balances are factors which influence the money speculators' buying and selling, the exchange rate is based on real, concrete factors. Although the gold standard is no longer officially in effect, gold, whose quantity and quality can be accurately measured and assessed, remains the standard of measure of the value of currency.

The fall of the dollar continues to be reflected in all the money markets by the rise in the price of gold from $35 per ounce a decade ago, to over $800 per ounce in January, 1980. Gold has not mysteriously become more valuable, scarce or expensive to produce; the dollar has become cheaper, devalued in relation to gold. The official denial of gold as a standard has had no effect on its function as such.

The glut of paper currency rolling off the printing presses, and the extension of massive doses of credit, have produced the inflation of the U.S. dollar and its fall in relation to other currencies. As devaluation makes commodities cost more in the domestic market, it also allows imports to rise in price and still remain competitive — thus fueling more inflation.

The greatest benefactor of currency creation is the Pentagon. The U.S. military budget is the largest in history. The tremendous expansion of the military apparatus is absorbing massive quantities of social wealth. Health, education and job programs are being slashed and sacrificed. Public hospitals are forced to close in many cities. School districts all over the country have cut back on educational programs, and in some cases simply shut down for lack of funds (e.g. Toledo, OH). Arms production, military payrolls, and nuclear weapons arsenals are expanding.

A case in point: The House of Representatives voted to slash $1 billion from government jobs programs. Cutting 125,000 CETA jobs, they almost simultaneously appropriated $2.4 billion for a nuclear aircraft carrier as part of the largest money appropriation ever to the Pentagon.

Public revenues are created by increasing the amounts of money in circulation. Through taxation and direct expenditure, this money is then absorbed into the military apparatus.

If the capitalists really want to improve the exchange rate of the dollar, to stop its "fall," their solution is simple: Reduce the quantities of dollars in circulation, to bring them into better relationship with other currencies and make less credit available. It sounds simple, but of course there are consequences either way. A consumer debt of $1.3 trillion was the basis of recovery from the 1973-75 recession. How will the glut of commodities keep circulating? How will the military expand?

The periodic sale of a portion of the U.S. gold reserve is an attempt to "call back" some of the "surplus" dollars glutting the world market. However, by selling gold reserves, the dollar is forced to rely solely on U.S. military and political strength for backing. By separating paper currency from its backing in precious metal, the capitalists have entered dangerous water. In commodity exchange, value must confront value. Deprived of the value that precious metal embodies, paper currency could fall to the value of the paper on which it is printed.

The reluctance of U.S. officials to halt the fall of the dollar is understandable. The cheaper dollar is an effective barrier against imports into the United States, which become more expensive. At the same time, U.S. manufactured goods become cheaper in markets abroad.

It is the workers who carry the brunt of the consequences of this situation, however. Spiralling taxes, rising prices — these are the fringe benefits for the working class which accompany the capitalists' profits from expanding military production.

The falling dollar is only a symptom of a society that is increasingly sacrificing the standard of living of its working class for the creation of a monstrous war machine. The benefactors of this war machine are the capitalists who profit from arms production. The growth of the military budget is inseparable from the overall crisis which is leading us to war and even further attacks on the economic and political conditions of the workers.

There can be little doubt that the standard of living for most U.S. workers, particularly minorities, is under increasing attack. The fall of **real wages** in recent years can only signal further stagnation in distribution, and an intensified glut of commodities on the world market.

This spreading crisis expresses the incompatibility of modern social production with capitalist private appropriation. Commodities cannot circulate. But driven by the **anarchy of production**, capital continues expanding. Production of industrial raw materials, food, cotton, wheat, trucks and oil have all doubled in the United States since 1967 and continue to expand. This expansion is taking place within a contracting market. At the same time, the gobbling up of smaller producers and the mergers of other medium and large producers has accelerated. Under increasingly monopolized ownership, further revolutionization of the means of production results in increased productivity, more and cheaper commodities, produced by fewer and fewer workers.

POLICY STRUGGLES

The convergence and intensification of overproduction, credit and monetary crises are bound to produce an industrial crisis. The economy is threatened with collapse. The present struggles within the capitalist class concern how to forestall further crisis or eventual collapse of the economy. Although inevitable, collapse is not imminent. Owing to the international interconnections of the decisive section of the capitalist class — the Wall Street grouping — there is still room in which to maneuver.

However, that maneuvering is constrained by the increasing struggle of the medium and small, relatively independent industrialists, who, under the banner of "fiscal restraint" and the "tax revolt," are demanding a contraction of credit. Apparently, they fail to recognize that any contraction of credit, or a "balanced budget," especially as it affects the consuming capacity of the growing masses of the unemployed and otherwise impoverished workers, would further aggravate the present glut of commodities, triggering a more rapid economic decline.

Although the ultimate interest of all capitalists are the same — maximum profit and preservation of the system — there are differences in the short term interests of different sectors (Ed. note: See Session 3 for more on this subject). The Wall Street grouping continues to press for expansion, especially of the military budget and its complex network of industries. Increased military spending is a point of agreement between the leading financiers and the most vocal advocates of "fiscal restraint" and a balanced budget. The military build-up is intimately related to the sweep of economic and monetary realignments discussed above. Politically, these realignments are expressed in the growing consolidation of the world anti-Soviet front. For example, in September 1979, a Defense Department study was released which discussed the merits of sending U.S. arms to China.

Parallel to the development of the now deteriorating U.S.-Soviet detente was the amassing by the East European and Soviet Bloc of a considerable debt to the West. Why is the socialist bloc willing to amass this debt?

The debt allows them to purchase advanced technology to further expand their industrial base. It would be foolish not to avail themselves of the vast resources of the West. Balance of trade deficits with the West allow them to develop their means of production and simultaneously sustain a constantly rising standard of living for the people.

While the socialist bloc countries import technology and machinery, they have refused to open their doors to a flood of consumer goods. While a market for Western goods certainly exists, it is clear that to import consumer goods would remove the stimulus to further expand their own industrial base.

It must also be noted that the socialist bloc has solid reserves of gold and "hard" uninflated currency. It is not necessary under present conditions to transfer these reserves. They merely finance and refinance interest payments against their debt. For the capitalists, lending to the socialist camp allows them limited access to an external market. But it is precisely the nature of especially the Soviet market that clarifies the nature of the war danger.

Soviet socialism represents a highly developed economic system. It has both a large industrial base and growing consumer demand. It represents, to the capitalists, precisely the kind of market they need to relieve their glut of manufactured goods. On the other hand, the Chinese market, is considerably less developed. A flow of industrial and consumer goods would soon exceed the economic and monetary limits of the Chinese economy to absorb and exchange for them. In contrast, because of its highly developed economy, the Soviet market could absorb vast quantities of industrial commodities and exchange "hard currency" reserve assets for them.

As much as the capitalists may attempt to replace gold and "hard currency" assets in international trade, they cannot really succeed. There is, of course,

still room for maneuver within the capitalist system. The drive to exploit the market and non-union labor of the U.S. South by transnational capital is presently a key part of these maneuvers. But with the increasing resistance of Latin American and African countries, and the growing awareness of the necessity to organize the U.S. South, the possibility of a military solution for the capitalists is drawing nearer. Sooner or later they will be tempted to use the massive military machine to gain by violence what they so desperately need — the highly developed Soviet market with its gold and hard currency reserves.

CONCLUSION

The developing contradictions of the capitalist system leave the capitalists with little choice but to try turning back the tide of socialist revolution and gain access to the socialist world's markets and assets. The neocolonies in Latin America, Africa, Asia and the Middle East are increasingly rebelling against the stranglehold of international capital, and the repressive political regimes it necessitates. More and more the various national liberation struggles are turning to socialist ideas for guidance, and socialist countries for support in freeing themselves.

There has been a growth in the tactics of the Cold War in the past year, an increasing consolidation of anti-Soviet propaganda in the United States. Confrontation politics are heightening in areas where U.S. interests are most directly threatened — the Caribbean, the Middle East, Africa. The tactic of blaming the Soviet Union for every revolutionary movement in the neocolonies is an important aspect of this propaganda. It is used to justify U.S. support for the counter-revolution ("protecting" the smaller nations from the "Soviet menace"). It also justifies an expansion of the U.S. military budget and armament production which is so necessary to the economic health of many leading industrialists. By creating the illusion that the Soviet Union is the cause of unrest everywhere, the leaders of the capitalist world attempt to divert people from examining the real source of their misery and underdevelopment — the ever-expanding exploitation of people and resources needed to keep the capitalist system going.

As the crisis develops, the danger of war increases on many fronts. There is fear of a nuclear holocaust on all sides. It is not in anyone's interest to initiate a nuclear war. But small wars can easily escalate, and rational people are not always the ones in positions of power.

Revolutionary wars of liberation continue. Whatever one may think of the motives of the Soviet Union in giving material support to these movements, the fact remains that the Soviet Union and its East European allies have aided movements which

weaken capitalism by their success. Since capitalism provides no more than the illusion of development, liberation movements increasingly look to socialism as the viable option.

The need to expand in a shrinking world means capitalists in the leading countries — Germany, Japan, the United States — are faced with few options. Different sectors vie for implementation of different tactics to rescue the system. No one tactic has yet predominated. Some would like to stop short of military confrontation with the Soviet Union and attempt to peacefully penetrate the socialist markets, while trying to hold the line against any further revolt in the neocolonies or further erosion of the domestic market. Carter and Kennedy exemplify this tendency on the political level. This policy cannot prevail given the degree of crisis outlined above. Each U.S. attempt to stop a revolt aided by the socialist countries heightens the level of confrontation with the Soviet Union.

Others — primarily representing the industrial wing of finance capital — are increasingly advocating policies of direct military confrontation with the Soviet Union, protectionist trade policies against European and Japanese commodities, gun-boat diplomacy in relation to the neocolonies, and strengthening of anti-labor policies in the United States. As this sector increases its political power, the danger grows that war will develop among the leading capitalist countries also, as each group of industrialists struggle to survive the crisis at the expense of its competitors.

Nationalist tendencies are clearly on the rise in every major capitalist country, and in a few of the major socialist countries. Wars can arise between socialist neighbors when one country sees its security threatened by possible alliances of a socialist neighbor with capitalist enemies, or other socialist countries expressing nationalist tendencies. But nationalism has no place in a socialist world. Nations were historically a product of capitalist development — arising with the need to protect domestic markets. Once competition is eliminated as the driving force of economic life on a world-wide basis, there will be no markets to secure for blocs of competing capitalists. The basis for production is entirely different under socialism. (See Session 4)

We are entering a time of mounting economic crisis and rapid change. There will be significant realignments at the political level. Socialist countries are also affected by the maneuvering and policy changes going on in the capitalist world. Their response is not always in tune with the socialist principles of internationalism and peaceful resolution of conflicts among socialist countries. The socialist system is based on planned production to meet human needs,

so military production for defense drains valuable resources that could be used to strengthen the economy. War is, therefore, very unhealthy for socialism.

On the other hand, a capitalist economy has needs (which must be distinguished from the human needs of the people living in it) for new markets to relieve the glut of commodities, new sources of cheap labor and raw materials, and a way to get rid of surplus goods without losing the profit generated in their production. War has historically provided at least temporary relief from crises inherent in capitalist production. World War II did bring an end to the Depression. However, the nuclear balance of terror which defines our reality now, has placed some restraints on even the most notorious hawks.

It is not at all clear how long this restraint will be maintained as the capitalist crisis deepens. It is therefore crucial that progressive people in the United States do all they can *now* to counteract an escalation of Cold War policies, anti-communist propaganda, gun-boat diplomacy and nationalistic chauvinism. The struggle between capitalism and socialism will intensify in more and more countries. We cannot have peaceful times until this historic struggle is completed. Capitalists do not give way without a battle, and people will continue to battle for socialism because it has more promise for them. The present crisis can become a catalyst for uniting the oppressed and speeding the socialist transformation, or it can be the catalyst for another world war — one which no one is likely to win.

We in the United States have the capacity to build a strong movement for peace — a movement to eliminate the options of war against the Soviet Union or between capitalist powers. Such a movement will have to be part of our efforts to resolve the present crisis in a way that is most beneficial to the majority of people in the United States *and* around the world.

■

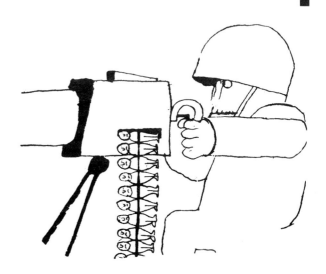

A Glossary for Political Economics

by Peggy Case

Terms defined are listed in the order in which they appear in the preceding article.

Monetary policy adjusts the size of the national money supply. In the United States, the Federal Reserve system determines monetary policy by expanding or contracting the supply of currency and the availability of credit.

Fiscal policy determines the amount of taxation, level of government spending, and the amount of public debt which will be accumulated.

Commodities are products of labor which satisfy some human want and are produced for sale. The term is used to distinguish those objects which are made for sale to another from things made for one's own use. The capitalist mode of production is characterized by the predominance of commodity production. Under capitalism even labor power has become a commodity to be bought and sold.

Value determines how a certain portion of one commodity is exchanged for a commodity of a different kind. This term has been used by economists as shorthand for *exchange value*. It should be distinguished from *use value*, which refers to the utility of an object. The (exchange) value of any commodity is determined by the labor time required to produce it under normal conditions of production and with the average degree of skill and intensity of labor prevalent at the time. If it takes an average of one hour to produce a pair of shoes, and one hour to produce a dozen loaves of bread, then one pair of shoes and 12 loaves of bread are equal in value. They could be exchanged and no one would be cheated. Value should not be confused with *price*. The price of a commodity is determined by market conditions, and tends to fluctuate around the value — sometimes going above, sometimes below it.

Peggy Case is an activist who lives and works in Pontiac, MI. She prepared this glossary to accompany "The Present Crisis and the Danger of War."

Imperialism refers here to the current stage of capitalist development, which began around the end of the 19th Century. In the sense that imperialism refers to a policy of conquest and plunder in other lands, it existed long before capitalism. Marxists, however, use the term to define the dominant features of present-day capitalism. The term is sometimes used interchangeably with "monopoly capitalism." Modern imperialism has the following characteristics:

- the territorial division of the whole world among the greatest capitalist powers;
- a concentration of capital and production developed to a stage in which international capitalist monopolies have been formed and now play a decisive role in economic life;
- a merging of bank capital with industrial capital into an oligarchy of "finance capital";
- the export of capital, as distinguished from the export of commodities.

Economic contradictions of capitalism refer to the opposing forces inherent in the capitalist mode of production. For example, the main contradiction of capitalism is between the *social character of production* (many people work together to produce something) and the *private character of appropriation* (only a few own the products of the labor of many because they also own and control the means of production). As a result of this contradiction others arise: The owners of capital and the owners of labor power have opposing interests; the imperialist countries are in contradiction with the dependent developing nations; there is a contradiction between the constant expansion of production as demanded by competition and the actual contraction of the market for the commodities produced. In each case, the economic contradiction calls attention to the struggle between two opposing forces.

Capital refers to the materials that are necessary for production, trade and commerce. It consists of all tools, equipment, factories, raw materials, commodities in process, means of transport and money used for the purpose of generating a profit. For example, money capital is used to buy tools, raw materials and human labor power. However, not all money is capital. Money becomes capital only when it is used in a way that expands its value. Value is expanded by establishing a particular social relationship with the producers of value — the workers — and thus extracting *surplus value* (see below).

Means of production are those things people need to produce the necessities of life — land, raw materials, tools, factories. The means of production should be defined in relationship to the *mode of production* as one of its subdivisions. The means of production plus the workers who use them comprise the *forces of production*, one of two components of the mode of production. The other component is the *relations of production*, which refers to the class division in a society between those who own its means of production and those who do not, and are obliged to work for those who do. Viewed the other way around, from the general to the specific, there is a basic Marxist category, mode of production, comprised of the forces of production (the means of production plus labor) and the social relations of production (owners and workers).

Surplus value is the value produced by the worker which is not paid for in wages. It is the source of profit that goes to the employer. For example, the wage laborer sells labor power (ability to work) to the owner of money, land, factories and instruments of labor (capitalist). The capitalist buys labor power at its value, which is determined, like the value of every other commodity, by the labor time needed for its production (i.e., what it costs to maintain the worker and sustain his or her family at a particular, culturally-determined standard of living). Having bought labor power, the employer is entitled to use it, that is, to set it to work for the whole day — say eight hours. Meanwhile, in the course of four hours (*necessary* labor time), the worker produces sufficient value to pay back the cost of his or her own family's maintenance; and in the course of the next four hours (*surplus* labor time) he or she produces a "surplus" product or *surplus value*, for which the capitalist does not pay. This unpaid portion of labor is the source of all profit. Surplus value is the source of wealth of the capitalist class.

Neocolonialism is a term that has come into current use to describe present day imperialism. Under *colonialism*, imperialist powers directly control the government, economic relations of the colony and the military which maintains colonial rule. Examples include British and French rule in Africa prior to the 1950s. Neocolonialism refers to the economic, political and military relations imposed by the United States, Britain and other imperialist powers to retain domination over nominally independent nations. Examples include South Korea, Kenya and much of Latin America.

International finance capital is the money capital of the foremost financiers of the leading capitalist nations. It is controlled by an international cartel dominated by the U.S. Wall Street (Rockefeller) grouping. International finance capital flows freely around the world in search of maximum profit and shows no allegiance to national boundaries or political authority. Therefore, it is sometimes referred to as **transnational capital**. (See Session 3, "Contradictions Within Finance Capital.")

Real wages are a measure of purchasing power in relation to a standard, once inflation is taken into account. The general standard now in use is computed for the year 1967. Real wages are distinguished from *nominal wages* — the actual numerical value of the wages received. For example, if a worker is paid $100 a week, her or his nominal wages are $100. But, the cost of living has gone up 216 per cent since 1967 (as of June 1979). This means that the worker with nominal wages of $100 per week has real wages of less than $50 a week. So, $100 today purchases less than half of the food, rent, medical care and other items that it could in 1967. Although nominal wages have increased in recent years, workers' real wages have fallen.

Anarchy of production is a term used to characterize an economic system in which there is little, if any, central economic planning. For example, under capitalism decisions about what to produce, how much to produce, etc., are made by a few individuals — not on the basis of need, but rather on the basis of maximizing profit. Consequently, many frivolous commodities will be made; many necessities will be in short supply if they are unprofitable; and overproduction in some sectors will be a recurrent problem. Therefore, production will be *anarchic* — without order or regularity. ∎

Group Exercise

The readings for this session contain many economic concepts which take awhile to assimilate. Spend some time discussing these concepts (inflation, credit, surplus value, real wages, etc.). It is important to review any parts of these articles which, at first, may be unclear. A group discussion generally produces much greater insight than individual reading. Everyone can make a contribution by providing examples that clarify meaning. After you have re-examined the difficult passages, have your group evaluate whether or not the analysis developed in these readings offers a credible explanation of the current economic crisis.

Choose one of the following activities: "**A**" or "**B**."
A. Before meeting, have everyone in your group agree to watch a particular network news show on a given evening. For example, perhaps everyone will watch the CBS evening news on Wednesday. Take some notes as you watch, keeping the following questions in mind:

1 How many separate items were covered in a half hour broadcast? What depth of coverage was given to each?

2 What fears were stimulated? What hopes were encouraged? How much weight was given to the positive accomplishments of people? How much to the negative?

3 What explanations were offered for the problems and crises of the day? What solutions were suggested?

4 Who did the newscasters define as the prime movers of the day's events? What contribution did working people appear to make? Political leaders? Businessmen? Women? Minorities?

5 Whose class interests were represented in the choice of items covered and the content of that coverage?

Using the above questions as a guide, have your group discuss the broadcast they watched. Try to develop a composite picture of the kind of world portrayed by the evening news. Examine those images and compare them to the worldview developed by members of your group.

B. Ask each group participant to prepare for this exercise by clipping one article from your local newspaper. Bring a clipping to your meeting which analyzes some major aspect of the global or national economy, corresponding as much as possible to the subjects covered in the two readings for this session. Summarize the content of your article for other group participants: What is the major problem or crisis being defined? What causes are given for the problem? What solutions are suggested? After each person has completed her or his summary, have your group compare and contrast the analysis these articles develop with the two readings selected for this session. Use the following questions as guidelines:

1 Which articles offer a more comprehensive view of the problems we face, the causes of those problems, and the solutions possible?

2 Can you identify specific class interests represented by the newspaper analyses and the readings selected?

3 How do the newspaper articles mis-identify the causes of economic crisis? How do they reinforce divisions within the international working class?

Class Struggle in Our Times

Class analysis does not lend itself to a simplistic formula which can be reduced to a mere "we," the workers, and "they," the capitalists. This division overlooks the complexities of class relations as well as the various forces at work within them which we must understand to build a movement for substantive social change.

Class struggle takes on different forms and dynamics at any given moment in history. By using a class analysis to clarify the forces and powers at work within a concrete situation, terms like oppression, exploitation, manipulation, domination, repression and subjugation become vivid expressions of a struggle between workers and capitalists.

For example: Workers in an oil refinery in central Minnesota went on strike in the early '70s. Striking workers were not arrested by the boss, or physically harassed. Instead, the owner summoned a private security force, surrounded the factory, and had workers flown in from a branch plant in Oklahoma to break the strike.

And we ask: How do we interpret class struggle when worker is turned against worker? How can we deal with the fact that workers from Minnesota were betrayed by workers from Oklahoma who were protected by hired security guards? Finally, how do we combat the capitalist class when their assets enable them to mobilize in this way?

A class analysis would have helped the Oklahoma oil workers understand their struggle as united with that of their co-workers in Minnesota, and vice versa. Minnesota workers could have anticipated the options of the capitalists for breaking the strike, as well as their own options for success, had they better knowledge of the various political, economic and social forces at work.

This is another way of saying that the primary source of change is within the things that change. As Frank Cunningham explains in *Understanding Marxism*, "Everything is composed of elements that work together or require one another and at the same time work against one another. As Marx and Engels put it, things are 'unities of opposites,' or they contain 'dialectical contradictions.' In order to survive, a living organism must acquire energy (i.e., eat food), and it must also expend energy (get food). Since living creatures expend energy to gain nutrition, the two work together. But these elements also work against one another since the two activities never perfectly balance. Rather, the creature is either assimilating more than it expends (it grows) or it expends more than it assimilates (it dies)."

We see this in the contradiction between the forces and the relations of production within the United States. Capitalism requires that the forces of production include a smooth functioning, low paid work force, and even a "reserve army" of unemployed workers to reap profits and grow. At the same time, this work force has the capacity to organize and overthrow the capitalist class. Therefore, capitalism requires something that finally becomes incompatible with its continued existence.

From the perspective of the workers, then, class struggle is the attempt to channel organizing efforts around their interests into unified action. At certain moments in history, unified action is more possible than at others. While the first and foremost factor is the organization and consciousness of the workers, other factors, both national and international, determine the intensity of the struggle and the possibilities for structural change at any given moment. At stake here is more than the efforts of a few workers in one factory; e.g., one oil refinery in central Minnesota. The fact that the working class exists across the globe means that class struggle in one place carries with it an international dimension which should be evaluated in relationship to political and economic factors elsewhere.

For the capitalists, class struggle is an at-

tempt to maintain a production process which will support their interests — increased profits and expansion. This means that they must prevent, or keep to a minimum, working class mobilization. Capitalists also use a regional, national or even global analysis to estimate the strength and weakness of the working class. The flight of capital from the Northeast of the United States is related to their awareness that labor is less organized and therefore cheaper elsewhere, be it the J. P. Stevens mills of the South or the textile mills as far away as South Korea. Many times the ruling class is divided over its understanding of the working class and what is needed to contain it while keeping profits high.

The state, or the government, is not outside of class struggle; historically it has sided with the ruling class. Ownership of capital tends to confer political power. "Money speaks" has become the phrase to describe the extent to which capital has penetrated the decision-making aspects of our society. This ranges from controlling election campaign funds, to decisions effecting the opening of new factories and jobs, to questions of energy.

The state, then, is used by the capitalist class to exercise control over, and protection for, the production process. While the working class has gained some concessions from the state, such gains have been minimal and over a long period of time have failed to loosen significantly the grip of the capitalist class over the everyday-lives of most of the population.

As government, so all institutions in our society must be looked at from the class perspective. Whose interest do they serve? What is their social function? Who is involved in making decisions? Who shares the profits?

Class struggle is complex. It is fought on many fronts (political, economic, ideological, religious, social, cultural, etc.) Interests are sometimes hidden. Actors shift sides. Leadership changes. It is important to understand, that though we are either on one side or the other, class struggle is not simply side "A" versus side "B." It cannot be visualized or participated in simply by identifying who's who and what Board of Directors interlocks with what conglomerate. If we look at the ruling class, for example, we would not see a unified elite operating in coordinated fashion and making clean decisions for routine implementation in world affairs.

Class struggle is better understood by asking questions about political power and its function in capitalist society, its relationship to economic power and the production process. Political reality is more complex than the usual issues surfacing during election years. Forms of political power in the capitalist system include economic constraints (initiated by government or business or both), administrative authority, political repression, ideological coercion, etc. Developing political consciousness requires an all-encompassing new perspective on the forces that make up our capitalist system; it will also require new forms of organizing.

The first two articles in this session, "Contradictions Within Finance Capital" and "The National Association of Manufacturers" will introduce the structure of the capitalist class as it exists in the current phase of monopoly capitalism. They will help us to see the divisions within the ruling class itself and how these divisions have grown from the forces within capitalism.

Monopoly capitalism is that phase in capitalist development where money is controlled by the banks and employed by industrialists for use directly in the production process. Banks merge or coalesce with industries and monopolies arise. These monopolies are not static or in harmony. They represent yet another level of the class struggle in our times.

The first reading introduces one aspect of monopoly capital. It is capital in its money form as owned and used by banking interests. This finance capital can be used as investment in areas for production. The second reading refers to capital that is tied to and used directly for production expenses. It is controlled by industrialists who are concerned primarily about the management of capital in production.

Johanna and Robert Brenner, in their article on "The Right Wing Offensive and the Working Class," investigate how the political Right attempts to manipulate crisis in the capitalist economy. Their article analyzes the political Right Wing and its relationship to the working class. The rise of the Right presents problems related to workers' consciousness in an economic crisis. This reading outlines the sharp challenge that working people's organizations must face today.

The articles in this session show that tensions between classes will not be resolved by improving the system. Rather our system of production is maintained and expanded by economic forces and political power in such a way that a struggle between capitalists and workers is inevitable. Exploitation is not simply the conscious and intentional decision by the ruling class to oppress workers. It is the basis of capitalist organization.

The readings which follow will help us analyze factors generating class struggle in our times and what we can expect from the ruling class as well as the working class. With new dimensions to the class struggle exposed, we are challenged to look at our own participation in this continuing struggle.   ■

Contradictions Within Finance Capital

by Larry Mellman

Finance capital, the merger of bank and industrial capital, is characterized by the struggle between its two aspects. . . .

Transnational capital is a highly-developed form of finance capital. It is the international money-capital of the foremost financiers of leading imperialist nations, headed up and dominated by the U.S. Wall Street grouping. While the industrial financial capitalists of the imperialist nations are rooted in domestic production with multinational extensions of this productive process, the leading financier-imperialists have consolidated into *transnational* grouping. They freely trade on one another's stock markets, industries and banks and invest in one another's countries and possessions. Transnational capital, the international money-capital of this financial cartel, flows freely around the world in search of maximum profit. While invested in the process of production, it is not tied to specific locations, regional or national. . . .

What or Who is Wall Street?

Wall Street is . . . a section of finance capital dominated by the Rockefeller (Chase Manhattan-Metro/Equitable Life-Oil monopoly)-Mellon (Gulf, Alcoa)-First Boston (John Hancock Life, etc.) grouping. This grouping also includes Kuhn, Loeb (investment bankers and original owners of Manhattan Bank which later merged with Rockefeller's Chase National) thus linking up major railroads and other main Wall Street investment bankers such as Goldman, Sachs, etc. But since this section of finance capital is dominated by the Rockefeller interests, we refer to it in shorthand, as Wall Street, or simply Rockefeller. This section of finance capital is primar-

Larry Mellman is a journalist living in Chicago. The above was excerpted from an article in *Proletariat*, Vol. 2, No. 1. Copyright © 1976 by Workers Press, Chicago, IL. Reprinted with permission.

ily concerned with the *application of money-capital*, as opposed to the National Association of Manufacturers (NAM) section, which is primarily concerned with the *application of capital to production*.

As for the house of Morgan, it is a part of the Wall Street financial world, now subordinated to the domination of the Rockefeller grouping.

For a long time, J.P. Morgan meant Wall Street; the Rockefellers were upstarts. But this is no longer the case. The Morgan financial (i.e. banking) empire was eclipsed, especially since World War II, by the Rockefeller-Mellon-Boston grouping. This happened mainly because of the shift from steel (the base of the Morgan empire) to oil (the base of the Rockefeller empire) as the most critical source of profit and power. As oil superseded steel, Rockefeller superseded Morgan.

According to Victor Perlo in *The Empire of High Finance*: "Between 1901 and 1953 production of steel increased 7½ times while production of oil increased 34 times. In 1909, steel companies accounted for 30.8 per cent of the assets of the 100 largest industrial companies; oil companies for 7.4 per cent. Forty years later, (in 1948), *these proportions were almost reversed*, oil having 28.8 per cent and steel 11.9 per cent of the assets of the 100 largest companies."

Also, the Morgan financial network was historically based in Western Europe and Great Britain. But the Rockefeller apparatus was built upon a truly global oil and kerosene marketing system developed as early as the turn of the century.

As the Rockefeller grouping consolidated its stranglehold upon the world of money-capital, Morgan was thrown back upon its industrial underpinnings, drawn back toward the other pole of finance capital, the National Association of Manufacturers. Consequently, the vast Rockefeller-Wall Street section has become progressively internationalized, extending the influence and power of its transnational money-capital.

How Is a Huge Company Like General Electric Different from Transnational Capital?

Undeniably, General Electric is the eighth largest corporation and is a cornerstone of the Morgan grouping. GE is *multinational* in the sense that it exports *productive capital* in the form of plants, etc., to a large number of other countries. But Wall Street *money-capital* is part of the Rockefeller-dominated *transnational* financial cartel. It flows freely, can invest anywhere, and is nowhere tied down — except temporarily — in the productive process, from whence it is yielded enriched and freed to move on. But the productive capital of the multinational corporation is tied down in a string of plants, all of which must be kept running.

This points up a contradiction between the productive and money forms of capital. General Electric, General Motors, Boeing, *et al.*, are all in the same boat vis-a-vis this contradiction. The daily squeeze of the deepening world crisis of imperialism creates the need for more and more money-capital to ride out the crisis, until productive capital, transformed into commodity-capital, can be reconverted into money-capital. But the imperialists' market is constantly shrinking. More and more capital sits, stagnates as commodity-capital, losing value as it sits.

It is clearly an objective contradiction of imperialism. In order for industrial giants to survive, let alone to expand and compete, more and more money-capital must be available to be applied to production. The NAM section of finance capital can't convert its tied up productive-and-commodity-capital into money-capital necessary to re-invest in production. This needed money-capital is controlled by the Wall Street section, which can choose to lend it wherever it is to *its own* advantage (maximum profit). Politically, this produces the situation in which the National Association of Manufacturers seeks policies that would force Wall Street money-capital into NAM industrials and not into German, Brazilian or Japanese industrials. On the other hand, Wall Street needs political policies that allow it to roam freely across the globe, maximizing its money-capital, needed to keep the capitalist system going. The only real solution is to free up more markets and it is at that point that the interests of the two opposed sections of finance capital converge.

What Is a Multinational Corporation, and What Is a Transnational Corporation?

During the period of mercantile imperialism, which corresponded to the pre-monopoly stage of capitalism, the capitalists of the more advanced countries, for example Britain, using their organ of violence, their state, (especially their armies and navies), conquered and occupied foreign markets, e.g. Egypt, India, the North American colonies. Holding these colonies in bondage with military force, the capitalists carted off raw materials (e.g., cotton) and carted back commodities (e.g. cloth) which they sold to these captive markets.

Lenin showed, in *Imperialism*, how, as capitalism developed, it threw off greater and greater quantities of money, giving rise to the financial domination of the banks. Pre-monopoly capitalism was transformed into monopoly capitalism — modern financial imperialism. "On the threshold of the 20th Century, we see the formation of a new type of monopoly; firstly, monopolist capitalist combines in all capitalistically developed countries; secondly, the monopolist position of a few very rich countries, in which the accumulation of capital has reached gigantic proportions. A 'superabundance of capital' has arisen in the advanced countries." This demands the export not of commodities, but of capital itself.

Capital can be exported in two forms — in money form, as loans for the development of industry, or as industry itself, the building of plants and means of production. . . .

The multinational corporation is a result of the export of capital in its productive form, the building of a chain of productive apparatuses in the colonial world, e.g., General Motors plants in Latin America and South Africa. On the other hand, the export of money-capital resulted in the domination and control of the productive apparatuses of *other nations*. With the increased domination of the banks and financier section of finance capital, and the consolidation of the imperialist financial cartel under the domination of Wall Street, transnational capital emerged: Money-capital manipulated by the transnational grouping, tied not to nations, but only to the field of highest return.

These two forms of investment are fundamentally different. The multinational corporation requires the production, circulation and sale of finished commodities and reinvestment into production. This demands, in the face of recurrent crises, constant and increasing reserves of money capital to continue producing. The transnational corporation is directly concerned only with the expansion of money. This can only occur in production, but the ownership and maintenance of the productive capital is in *other hands*. The multi-national corporation produces commodities, the transnational corporation invests money-capital and circulates others' commodities. . . .

The transnational corporation presently takes two main forms: The primary form is the financial institution itself, namely the bank and insurance company. They accumulate more and more money-capital, and by their financial power, dominate and control production. The banks are the primary agencies through which transnational capital flows in search of maximum profit. The other main form of the transnational corporation is best exemplified by the oil and grain monopolies.

The international oil monopoly, headed up by the Rockefellers, historically owned the major extractive apparatus of the world's oil industry. As transnational capital was consolidated and the neo-colonization of the colonial world proceeded, the world witnessed the "nationalization" of the oil industries of the various neocolonies, especially in Latin America and in the Middle East. What had occurred was the phenomenon of transnational capital stepping back from any *direct* connection to the process of production. The headache of maintaining the productive apparatus was turned over to the comprador (native/local) bourgeoisie. The Rockefeller oil monopoly allowed this because it controlled the major means of *circulation* — the pipelines, oil tankers, refineries — and clearly dominated the world market. The great leap in the price of oil was not the result of the increased value of oil. It was the result of the consolidation of control over the circulation of the world's oil supply by transnational capital.

Similarly, six major corporations control the circulation of the world's supply of grain: Continental, Cargill, Cook, Dreyfus, Bunge and Garnac — known as the "big six." These transnational corporations influence the economic life of entire nations. Continental alone handles *one-quarter* of *all the grain traded among the world's nations!* A U.S.-based corporation, Continental sells South American and Italian rice to Cuba, is the Australian government's exclusive agent for selling Australian wheat to South America, etc.

Cargill, Inc. (Minnesota-based) received a $2.5 billion loan from the Overseas Private Investment Corporation (OPIC), a U.S. government subsidiary, to build a new crushing plant for the firm's Brazilian subsidiary, Cargill Agricola. Said a representative of the American Soybean Association, "Our government shouldn't be financing this kind of thing . . . I don't see any way for the expansion of the processing industry in Brazil to help the United States." (*Washington Post*, 1/2/76)

The *Post* article goes on to say, "the extent to

69

which Cargill, or other grain conglomerates can be termed 'U.S. firms' *or associated with any particular country is questionable*. Bunge among the largest six firms, is involved in commodities, finance and shipping on every continent. *It is virtually stateless*, with all the stock held by a holding company called Los Andes, in Curacao, Netherlands Antilles.

"Tradax Inc., Cargill's Geneva-based overseas financing and trade arm, is probably one of the world's largest grain companies in its own right. It has been in Geneva since 1956 and now has offices in 14 countries . . . Tradax buys grain from Cargill at American ports and markets it to governments, flour mills, feed processors and food merchants. Today, it is believed to be the largest privately owned American company. But its reach extends far beyond the United States.

"Cargill's list of interlocking relationships with governments and businesses all over the world goes on and on."

Of extreme importance is that these corporations neither grow grain nor sell processed products (retail). They are agents of circulation on a global scale, transnational in the truest sense. Removed from production, they begin with money-capital and end with it, immeasurably expanded. They form an important aspect of the international financial cartel whose sole aim and activity is the movement and expansion of transnational capital.

What Is "Capital Formation" and How Does This Bear on the "Capital Crisis"?

What we are describing when we talk about a capital squeeze and capital formation is the objective situation described by Marx and Lenin. More and more capital becomes tied up in the form of constant capital and in production. However, because of the shrinking market it becomes difficult to realize the desperately needed money-capital. The Wall Street section of finance capital can supply additional money-capital up to a point, but only to the extent that its money-capital is being expanded in production somewhere. Thus, the Wall Street section must invest where the conversion of productive-to-commodity-to-money-capital is being completed. It can then reinvest its expanded money-capital in other productive processes. But if its money is invested where it is not being expanded, it must move on.

For Wall Street, too, is caught in a bind. The Wall Street section of finance capital must bail out the productive capitalists of the National Association of Manufacturers in order for the system to continue functioning. As the crisis worsens, and the process of circulation faces greater disruptions and stagnations, more and more money-capital is needed, and must be provided. If Wall Street goes elsewhere for maximum

profit, investing in Japanese or Brazilian production in order to expand money-capital, the National Association of Manufacturers section, for example General Motors, cries foul if that money-capital is not invested in General Motors-Brazil. The situation is thus aggravated by U.S. plants in foreign countries (rooted in the productive capital back home) competing with "local" production for the investment of money-capital. The National Association of Manufacturers fights to force this investment into its own industries. Wall Street fights for freedom and fluidity of movement for its money-capital, and an international situation which favors it — neocolonialism and detente.

It is a contradictory situation for both sections of U.S. finance capital. Wall Street needs more maneuverability to amass the vast amounts of money-capital required to prop up the world imperialist system. But NAM members hurt so badly they have little choice but to force the Wall Street section immediately to invest in them. Therefore they demand cold war policies, stepped up arms production and massive government contracts. They need the funneling of Wall Street's money-capital into their own industries.

Of course, the only solution for both sections of finance capital is the re-opening of closed markets — hence fascism at home and war against the socialist camp. But at the moment, Wall Street is still opting for greater maneuverability. It is the objective situation that makes war inevitable. At present, the Wall Street section favors detente. But the deepening crisis must eventually forge an identity of interest between these two sections. . . . ∎

The National Association of Manufacturers

by Lennie Brody

Founded in 1895, the National Association of Manufacturers (NAM), which had been merely one of many trade associations, became a national force when it became the spearhead of the anti-labor movement at its convention in 1903. At this convention, members boldly declared their intention to stamp out the trade union movement; as one speaker proclaimed, "Organized labor knows only one law, and that is the law of physical force — the law of the Huns and Vandals . . . Its history is stained with blood and ruin."

Using vigilantes, NAM members smashed union halls and broke up strikes. They conducted a massive campaign for the open shop and attacked the struggle for a shorter work day as "communistic." In fact, anti-communism was their main ideological weapon in attacks on the labor movement. Also, their bribery of congressional representatives to support their policies is a proven fact.

The Department of Justice, under Attorney General Palmer, was run as an appendage of the NAM. On the night of Jan. 2, 1920, 10,000 workers, mostly union activists, were grabbed from their homes and from the streets and thrown in jail.

The same capitalists who controlled the NAM founded the U.S. Chamber of Commerce, which worked very closely with the NAM, particularly in an anti-labor, anti-communist vendetta.

In the 1930s the NAM was the strongest pro-fascist grouping in the United States, and openly supported Hitler. Former president of the NAM, H.W. Prentiss, stated that, "American business might be forced to turn to some form of diguised fascist dictatorship." The NAM financed many fascist groups such as the

Lennie Brody has been a political activist in the Civil Rights and anti-war movements and is affiliated with the Communist Labor Party. The above was excerpted from an article in *Proletariat*, Vol. 2, No. 1. Copyright © 1976 by Workers Press, Chicago, IL. Reprinted with permission.

American Liberty League, the Crusaders, and the Sentinels of the Republic. It opposed every strike as a "communist plot," using local police, vigilantes, clubs, poison gas and machineguns. It has been estimated that U.S. industry spent $80 million on 100,000 spies per year, who were thought to have penetrated every one of the country's 48,000 local unions.

The scope of the NAM's propaganda was unbelievable. It was described as follows in a 1936 NAM report:

• Press Service: Reached 5300 weekly newspapers.

• Cartoon Service: Sent to 2000 weekly newspapers.

• Daily Comic Cartoon: Appeared in 309 daily papers with a total circulation of two million readers.

• Monthly Factual Bulletin: Sent to every newspaper editor in the country.

• Foreign Language Press Service: Weekly service translated into German, Hungarian, Polish and Italian, printed in papers with a total circulation of almost 2,500,000.

• Radio: "The American Family Robinson" — a program heard from coast to coast over 222 radio stations once a week and over 176 stations twice a week; and foreign language programs in six languages over 79 stations.

• Leaflets: A series of 25 distributed to over 11 million workers.

• Posters: Over 300,000 for a series of 24 for bulletin boards in plants throughout the country.

• Films: 10 sound slide films for showing in plants.

• Billboards: Over 60,000 ads.

• Pamphlets: Over a million copies of seven pamphlets distributed to libraries, colleges, business executives, lawyers, and educators.

This is only a partial list for one year.

In 1947, when the Taft-Hartley Act was passed, Representative Donald L. O'Toole of New York stated that, "The bill was written sentence by sentence, paragraph by paragraph, page by page, by the National Association of Manufacturers."

After World War II, the NAM continued its connections with right-wing, pro-fascist groups. The founder and leader of the John Birch Society, Robert Welch, was a former director and vice-president of the NAM.

Three former presidents of the NAM have served on the Birch Society's national council. Of these three, W.J. Grede, one of the guiding lights of the Society, is currently (1975) an honorary vice president of the NAM. The NAM also has connections to the right-wing Americans for Constitutional Action and the Young Americans for Freedom. . . .

Politics is a concentrated expression of economics.

The developing economic crisis, which is affecting the NAM grouping more than Wall Street, has led to a struggle around detente. The NAM needs a resumption of the cold war and the arms race, and the large government defense contracts that go with it.

Because of the NAM's direct connection with the productive process, it has in the past, and continues today to push vicious anti-labor policies. It is waging a campaign against striking workers getting food stamps, and against collective bargaining rights for public employees and for their right to strike. The

NAM opposed the "common situs" picketing bill for construction workers and was a key factor in getting President Ford to veto the bill. It opposes the "Equal Opportunity and Full Employment Act" which would establish the government as an "employer of last resort" to eliminate unemployment. The NAM opposes current unemployment insurance policies and claims that in some cases workers are getting more than when they were employed and that workers should pay taxes on these benefits. The NAM advocates streamlining equal opportunity and anti-discrimination policies — in reality taking out what little substance remains in these policies. It opposes health insurance for workers who lose their benefits when they get laid off.

The NAM also opposes any strengthening of anti-trust legislation. It opposes the "National Employment Priorities Act of 1974" which forces businesses to notify the government about plans to shut down factories and allows the government to decide if the closing is warranted. This legislation stems from the massive layoffs and plant closings which occurred as the economic crisis began to deepen.

We can see that currently the NAM is the most outspoken group within the U.S. bourgeoisie for the policies of war and fascism. However, because the NAM industrialists must go to Wall Street for their big money, and Wall Street has such tremendous economic power, the policies of Wall Street, on the whole, will predominate. But, the same economic crisis affecting the NAM grouping is also pushing Wall Street towards a war against the socialist camp and fascism for the United States. ■

The Right Wing Offensive and the Working Class

by Johanna and Robert Brenner

In the last few years, the organized Right Wing has become a real political threat. The Left has generally understood this development as a backlash against the gains of the '60s made by specially-oppressed sections of the working class — women, people of color, gay people. It is in this sense that we speak about the "New" Right. The right-wing movement does have some new organizational features: It has increased its financial base through computerized direct mail fund-raising techniques and has developed a single-issue electoral approach. But what is really new about the Right is that it has begun to enter the mainstream of U.S. politics. Around certain single issues such as tax cuts, government spending, abortion, gay rights, and affirmative action right-wing policies have found broad support.

In the forefront of this conservative thrust are those classes and groups that have historically been attracted to the Right — small businessmen, managers, independent professionals like doctors, small town and rural people, religious fundamentalists, etc. The activists and organizers for right-wing politicians and programs come overwhelmingly from these groups. But these groups alone do not have the numerical strength to determine the very real shift to the Right that has occurred in the American political scene and especially in the Democratic Party during the '70s. This rightward drift could not have happened unless substantial numbers of working class people had given at least passive support to these policies. It is this support that poses the real threat of

Johanna and Robert Brenner are leading members of Workers Power, an organization of revolutionary socialist activists with branches in four cities: New York, Los Angeles, Detroit and Oakland-San Francisco. This article first appeared in earlier form as a pamphlet by the Los Angeles branch of Workers Power in 1979.

the Right today. And it is this question — why is there greater acceptance of conservative alternatives in the working class? — that we must answer in order to develop a strategy that can meet the Right's challenge.

The analysis that begins and ends with "backlash" is not enough. First, it implies that reaction to the gains of the '60s is inevitable, without saying why. Second, it treats working-class consciousness at a purely ideological level. That is, it treats working people's ideas as fundamentally emotional and irrational. "Backlash" implies an unthinking, reactive response. Third, the "backlash" approach has led many leftists to see the right-wing offensive as a capitalist conspiracy in which the working class is fooled by the onslaught of capitalist propaganda into scapegoating sections of the class for their own problems. This analysis implies that racism and sexism (for that is what scapegoating is all about) are only a matter of prejudice. It forgets that racist and sexist ideas are rooted in a real material oppression which benefits the capitalist class, mainly. For racism and sexism are two major barriers to working-class unity and therefore support capitalist class power. Oppression also confers relative advantages upon one section of the working class (white male workers) at the expense of another section (people of color, women).

In what follows, we will try to go beyond "backlash" to understand why some working people are, for the moment, open to right-wing policies and programs. We will try to show how workers' politics today are rooted in and conditioned by two material aspects of their experience: 1) the capitalist crisis of the '70s and the accompanying employers' offensive against workers' wages and working conditions; 2) the disorganization of the workers' basic weapons of defense — especially the trade unions — in their effort to fight against the capitalist class.

CAPITALIST CRISIS AND EMPLOYERS' OFFENSIVE

The 1970s manifested a severe crisis in the world capitalist economy. In 1965 the average rate of *profit* (after taxes) in the United States was 10.1 per cent; by 1972 that rate had fallen to 5.4 per cent. The average rate of *growth* of the economy as a whole has been under 3 per cent during the '70s, as compared to more than 5 per cent between 1961 and 1966. In order to maintain profits, the employers have launched an all-out attack to drive down the wages and increase the pace of work. By 1979, spendable income for the average family of four had fallen to its lowest level in 15 years. Working people have less money to spend than they did in 1965.

The fact that corporate profits have been kept up by squeezing workers should not, however, lead us to think that the world capitalist economy is no longer in trouble. Maintaining profits by driving down workers' income on a world scale provides temporary relief, but it only aggravates the underlying structural problems of the economy: Low levels of capitalist investment, low productivity, stagnation. When working people's buying power shrinks, investment in productive assets declines, because fewer goods can be sold. Without investment, productivity lags, goods remain expensive, and unemployment grows. As unemployment grows, purchasing power shrinks,

forcing further cuts in production and then more unemployment. We are now experiencing (late 1979) a new phase in this downward spiral which brought recession in 1970-71 and especially in 1974-75 (the worst recession in post-World War II history). To make matters worse, the high profits which corporations report have been countered by inflation. Even though profits appear high, in fact capitalists have not been able to restore the rate of return on capital investment to the level they enjoyed in the 1960s. During the '60s, after tax profits averaged 8.2 per cent of capital investment; during the 1970s after tax profits averaged 4.5 per cent.

At work, speed-up has become a way of life. Even the unionized sectors — auto, teamsters, telephone, post-office, etc. have been hard hit. The 100 car per hour assembly line at General Motors' Lordstown plant, the MTM (Methods-Time-Measurement) "productivity" plan in West Coast grocery, the Kokomo Plan in the Post Office, excessive forced overtime in the Bell Telephone System — all these are just some examples of the employers' offensive to squeeze more labor from the workforce. The rank and file has moved, sometimes sharply, to counter the attack. But, *so far*, these efforts have been defeated — with the partial exception of the coal miners' strike. Meanwhile, the established trade union leadership has largely stood by in the face of the employers' onslaught, and at times has acted to derail the rank and filers' struggle — (as, for example, in the auto upsurge of the early '70s, and in the recent West Coast grocery strikes).

Twenty-five years of post-war prosperity, combined with the McCarthy-like attacks on the Left, created the conditions for the bureaucratization of the labor unions, the elimination of radicals from the trade union movement, and an almost total break with traditions of militant struggle and rank and file organization. The combination of capitalist crisis on the one hand and the weakness of working-class organization on the other, has meant that a collective response to the employers' offensive appears to many workers impossible. Nonetheless, finding some way to maintain the standard of living becomes necessary as the total pie shrinks. The capitalists' share of it seems beyond reach. In trying to defend themselves, working people have tended to turn upon each other — each section trying to improve its conditions, if not always consciously, by taking something away from another section of the class. In this situation, the existing divisions within the class (by industry, by race, by sex, by public or private sector), become the basis for individual workers' strategies for survival. People use existing divisions — white vs. black, men vs. women, "American" vs. "foreign" — to organize and exert power against each other, not the capitalists. As working people act on the basis of these divisions, the ideas that fit and justify their actions become more and more powerful. These are the ideas of the Right.

THE "NEW" RIGHT

We put "New" in quotes because in many ways the organized Right Wing of today is not *new* at all. The core of the movement is a network of activists, organizers and wealthy individuals in interconnected extreme right-wing organizations, operative since the 1960s. For example, Phyllis Schlafly, leader of Stop ERA, is a member of the John Birch Society, the American Conservative Union, and Young Americans for Freedom, all well-established extreme right organizations. Young Americans for Freedom (YAF) was founded in 1960 by Howard Phillips who now runs two new right-wing organizations, the Conservative Caucus which does grass-roots organizing for causes such as opposition to OSHA (the Occupational Safety and Health Administration) and Stop ERA, and the Committee for the Survival of a Free Congress, which raises money for right-wing candidates. Joseph Coors, one of the big money donors to new right campaigns such as the anti-ERA drive, is in the John Birch Society and the National Right to Work Committee, one of the oldest anti-union organizations. These older, established, extreme right organizations have been given new strength by Richard Viguerie, who sits like a spider at the center of this right-wing web. Viguerie is part of the new face of the Right. He runs a direct mail fund-raising operation. Through use of computerized mailing lists carefully built up over a period of years, Viguerie helps the Right tailor its propaganda and fund-raising calls to specific concerns. Through the mail operation Viguerie has brought thousands of dollars in small contributions to right-wing campaigns.

Besides its greater financial strength, the Right of the '70s differs from the Right of the '60s in terms of its tactics. In particular, it has begun to launch single-issue campaigns that make it possible to draw support from groups that would not support its whole program. In this way, the Right can have an effect far beyond its real base. An example is the Right to Life movement. Many right-wing organizations contribute personnel and money to Right to Life organizations. But in building the Right to Life movement, the right wing has been able to make an alliance with the Catholic Church, vastly increasing its political strength. It is estimated that at least one-third of the funds for the Right to Life organization are contributed by the Catholic Church. Yet, many Catholics actively supporting the Right to Life movement would not agree to other parts of the right wing's program.

The single-issue approach and a sophisticated fund raising operation have no doubt helped the extreme Right. But the Right hasn't won all across the board. The campaign against the Panama Canal treaty, for example, fizzled dismally — despite the fact that Viguerie's direct mail operation was used to organize funds and solicit letters to the White House, and despite the fact that one of the Right's most glamorous figures, Ronald Reagan, headed it up. In fact, there is little support for most of the Right's virulent anti-communist foreign policy. It is only when the Right focuses on certain issues — taxation and government spending, abortion, gay rights, women's rights — that it has had important victories. For example, in Dade County and Eugene, OR over gay rights; in Congress with the Hyde Amendment denying Federal funds for abortions; in California with the passage of Proposition 13. On these issues the Right has found broad support among the American population, including significant numbers of working-class. Why is this support there?

CAPITALISM AND CONSCIOUSNESS

The connection between the economic crisis and working people's openness to certain right-wing programs lies in the double-edged character of workers' experience under capitalism. Capitalism, as a system, shapes workers' consciousness in two diametrically opposed ways. To guarantee their survival, working people can adopt either competitive, individual strategies or collective, class strategies. Capitalism creates the basis for the development of class strategies. But at the same time, capitalism also initiates a dynamic toward individualistic strategies.

Marxists and socialists have tended to emphasize the first dynamic — collective action by workers. The capitalist economy is organized around competition between capitalist producers. To compete successfully, capitalists must accumulate, must make a profit, or otherwise be driven out of business. In order to maintain profits, capitalists will push to cut costs, including the cost of labor. So, the effect of competition is to make clear the direct conflict of interests between capitalists and workers. The length of the working day, the speed and pace of work, payment for labor, the introduction of labor-saving technologies, etc. — matters which determine the very survival of the workers — are a matter of conflict between workers and capitalists. Thus, capitalism creates the necessity for workers to struggle against their employers to survive.

At the same time, the capitalist economy creates conditions conducive to workers' organization. A society of proletarians and capitalists is also a society in which production is social, not individual.

Production is accomplished by a capitalist who brings laborers together to produce cooperatively (with means of production owned and supplied by the capitalist). This collective character of the labor process creates the conditions for workers to communicate, get together. This cooperation in production can be turned into political cooperation — collective organization over and against the boss at the point of production, around the wage, conditions of work, etc. Cooperation on the shop floor can be extended — on the basis of the *real interdependency* of workers in production — throughout the economy. Workers can expand their organization to other factories in the same industry, creating trade unions. From the industry, the collective struggle can expand to the class as a whole — to the struggle of the class of workers vs. the class of employers; and from the struggle against the class of employers to the struggle against the capitalist state. Of course, the historical process need not occur in this step-by-step manner — and usually doesn't. The point is that economic and political struggles are inter-related and both grow out of the real cooperation and interdependence of workers in society. The collective aspect of workers' experience under capitalism forms the basis for the development of class struggle, class consciousness, and ultimately, the revolutionary movement.

There is another side of workers' experience: Workers must provide for their own survival. But they do not own the means of production (land, tools, machines, etc.) which would allow them to produce what they need for themselves. So, workers must sell their labor power and must find a capitalist willing to buy it. In the labor market, workers are forced directly into competition, one with the other. If the worker's world of production is defined by interdependency and cooperation, the worker's world of the labor market is defined by individuals and competition. From this point of view, society is not one of two conflicting classes each attempting to guarantee its survival at the expense of the other. Instead, society is made up of millions of individuals, each relying only on himself or herself, each alienated and separated from the other, each attempting to guarantee survival at the expense of the other. That workers are sellers of labor power competing with each other in the market is a fact of life every bit as real as their cooperation in production. This can lead workers to be cynical about their ability to organize collectively. Then, individualistic strategies for survival seem the only possible ones. How many times do people say: "It's a dog eat dog world; you have to look out for number one."

Competition between workers as sellers of labor

power has broader consequences. When workers see themselves primarily as sellers of labor power, then they are open to acting the way capitalists do. The profitability of the firm can appear as important to the worker as to the capitalist. So we get, for example, auto workers supporting the auto companies when they demand relaxation of pollution standards. Or steel workers supporting tariffs on foreign steel to support the monopoly prices of U.S. firms. In the competitive war of all against all, it can appear very rational for workers and their employers to "join up."

The point is that capitalism as a system presents a contradictory reality. It cuts two ways, all the time. It pushes workers toward collective strategies *and* toward individualistic strategies for survival.

THE ROLE OF CRISIS

Marxists, of course, have emphasized the ways in which capitalism orients workers to develop class consciousness. Moreover, we have argued that there is an aspect of capitalism that makes it *necessary*, in the last analysis, for workers to develop *collective rather than individualistic* strategies *if* they are to survive. Capitalism is a system of economic crises. Economic crisis leads in the direction of class consciousness because economic crisis intensifies the conflicts of interest between workers and employers. In times of prosperity, when profits are up and investment is up, employment expands, so there tends to be less downward pressure on wages. In crisis, however, profit margins dwindle, investment funds dry up, and employment shrinks. Now the capitalists, facing declining profits, must squeeze more work for less pay out of the work force. Workers' standard of living goes down and working conditions rapidly deteriorate. Falling profits cause intense competitive pressure among the employers, and this leads to an employers' offensive against the workers. In the face of this, the idea that capitalists and workers have common interests is revealed to be false. To survive, workers are forced to organize against the employers.

In the long run, capitalist crisis will face working people with the choice either to fight or be crushed. But only in the long run. Socialists have often assumed that crisis will almost automatically force workers to organize. This assumption has misled many of us. For example, since the '70s there has been a progressively worsening crisis in U.S. capitalism. The Left waited expectantly for a workers' upsurge, encouraged in the early '70s by wildcat strikes in post-office and trucking, big strikes in the mines, in longshore, in the auto plants, the spectacular rise of public employee unionization. But by and large these did not produce any lasting militant organization. And since that time, many sectors of the working class have become demoralized.

The Left has been disoriented by this turn of events. Prepared to organize workers who would be ready to fight in militant upsurges, expecting a shift to the Left in the political spectrum, socialists were unprepared for what in fact happened: A decline in worker militancy and a political shift to the Right. While it is true that crisis creates the conditions for the emergence of workers' self-organization, crisis itself cannot produce organization. Needs and interests do shape consciousness. But the link between our experience and our ideas is *action*, *practice*. So, it is practical to entertain the idea that the boss is our enemy, practical to see that capitalists are responsible for economic crisis — but only on one condition — that we act in terms of that understanding, consistently and successfully. If it seems that there's no chance to fight the boss, no chance to fight the capitalist system, we begin to look for scapegoats. It is difficult to see the world in terms of bosses versus workers, if there seems little chance for acting with other workers against the bosses. If we need to fight, but no one is fighting, if we need to stand up to the boss, but the union is weak, if we need to fight capitalism but there is no revolutionary movement, it becomes difficult for our needs to form the basis for anti-capitalist ideas. No matter how much it may be in our interest to fight, if a fight appears impossible, then the need to survive forces us to come up with other strategies.

EMPLOYERS' OFFENSIVE AND WORKERS' DISORGANIZATION

This is the key, in the current situation, to workers' openness to right-wing ideas. It seems to numbers of workers that the only practical ways to struggle to survive are individualistic (and ultimately self-defeating) ones. Why doesn't an anti-capitalist alternative exist? Over the past 30 years, working class organization, especially the self-organization of the rank and file workers, has been very much weakened. At the same time, the trade unions have come under the control of enormous parasitic bureaucracies, alienated from the members and standing now as a barrier to workers' militancy. Unions are the natural, necessary instrument of workers' defense against the employers. But the unions, to the extent they remain controlled by the bureaucracy, will not effectively take on the employers. Workers, having come to rely on the trade union officials, instead of themselves, find that their unions will not fight.

Things were not always this way. In the 1930s, working people organized to get industrial unions. To achieve this they were forced to wage a bitter and broad struggle. They formed organizations that went

across craft lines, breaking with the conservative AF of L, and across industry lines — as workers from one industry struck in solidarity with those in others. They connected employed workers to the movements of the unemployed — to win the unemployed to their cause and prevent them from being used as scabs. They fought against the state which over and over again intervened on the side of the bosses through the courts, the police, the national guard and the army.

The objective conditions that workers faced in trying to defend themselves against their own employers demanded that they move beyond organization at the shop floor level. The condition for success was the development of broad, class-wide organization that could bring the combined force of the workers to bear against the combined forces of the employers and the state. The working class responded and created such a movement. In doing so, the workers had to break with the overwhelming majority of union officialdom which sought, time and again, to keep the struggle within the narrowest framework and to confine it to legal methods. In this process, the organized revolutionary Left was able to play a key role, because of its understanding of the nature of capitalism, of the trade union bureaucracy, and of the state. This was perhaps best revealed in the Left's leadership of the three great general strikes of 1934 that "broke the ice" so to speak, preparing the way for the CIO organizing drives: Toledo Auto-Lite, Minneapolis Teamsters, San Francisco Longshore. In all these instances, victory was achieved through

Unions are big business. Why should truck drivers and bottle washers be allowed to make decisions affecting union policy? Would any corporation allow it?

—Dave Beck (1949)

Diploma
Ritz
Dave Beck
School of
Union Democracy

uniting diverse sections of the class, especially the unemployed with employed workers, in confrontation with the state authorities. The same was true of the great organizing drive which brought an industrial union to auto, culminating in the great sit-down strikes of 1936-7.

From the end of the 1930s and the beginning of World War II, through the '40s, '50s, and '60s, workers' organization and activity declined. The famous "deal" between the bosses and the bureaucrats arose in its place. The reasons can only be briefly sketched here. (1) During the war, government contracts with guaranteed high profits created the basis for the rapid development of the union bureaucracy and "stable unionism." The employers granted union recognition in exchange for the no-strike pledge and wartime wage controls, policed by the new labor officials; (2) the rise of McCarthyism led to the vicious purge of communists, socialists and other militants from the trade union movement; (3) relative labor peace was achieved through a trade off between union officials and the corporations. Union officials took more and more control over bargaining from the workers and built an apparatus to isolate worker militants and to break organization among the rank and file. In return, employers allowed the officials to "deliver the goods" to the workers in contract bargaining. Trade union officials were able to "win" a rising standard of living for unionized U.S. workers out of the enormous corporate profits

of the war and post-war period. With the standard of living increasing — and especially where they were able to maintain some shop-floor organization as an immediate protection against the employer — workers saw little need to take on the task of organization. This was left to the union officials, who centralized control, kept local levels of leadership in line, and organized along the most narrow, business-unionism lines. In other words, the union bureaucracy was able to maintain its position because it appeared to be doing its job. The workers for their part came to rely on their union officials, because it seemed to be the practical thing to do. Organization, at least beyond the level of the shop floor, did not appear to be necessary to protect their interests.

But relying on labor bureaucrats sapped the strength of the working class. The unionized work force has shrunk; organization of the rank and file within the unions has eroded.

Trade union bureaucrats have left growing sectors of the work force out of the union movement. Organizing the unorganized is arduous and takes the active support of the already organized. Union leaders were not interested in mobilizing their own rank and file membership to help organize other workers — their own rank and file might get out of hand. They also were not interested in risking their treasuries on organizing drives that might be unsuccessful. They preferred sweetheart contracts from employers that guaranteed them more dues paying members without

much fuss and bother. The result: By 1975 only 16 per cent of all full-time women workers were organized in trade unions, compared to 31 per cent of all full-time male workers. Only 24 per cent of the total work force (men and women non-farm workers) were union members in 1975, compared to 33 per cent in 1955.

Up through the '60s, the fundamental weakness of a trade-union movement organized by union bureaucrats was masked by the expanding economy. With the return of economic crisis, the unions' weakness was revealed. No longer a powerful movement, but in many ways an ossified bureaucratic shell, the unions have fallen like ten pins under the employers' attack. In contract after contract, supposedly powerful unions like the United Autoworkers and the Teamsters have failed to protect workers' standards of living and working conditions, proving that the unions are only as strong as the organized militancy of the rank and file, who had abdicated their role at this point.

During this time, the capitalist class did not sit still. The employers made big efforts to get around the one remaining area where the workers had strong organization — the shop floor. Essentially, what we have seen in the last two decades is a tremendous re-organization of capitalist production methods specifically designed to weaken the effectiveness of shop floor organization and a tremendous tightening up of capitalist political organization to isolate shop floor militancy.

The companies have used the law, the courts, and the legislature to whittle away at workers' power. These have hamstrung workers' ability to act directly to solve their problems by passing and implementing anti-labor Acts, such as Taft-Hartley in 1948, which outlawed the secondary boycott. Almost every contract now virtually outlaws strikes within the term of the contract. The grievance procedure channels shop floor conflict to a safe and long judicial debate. When strikes do break out, workers these days must almost inevitably face injunctions against mass picketing plus direct police action to protect scabs.

Employers have used technology to eliminate or lessen their dependence on labor. Two examples are in agriculture, where mechanization has followed hard on the heels of the organization of the United Farmworkers; and in ports where the employers made enormous investments in mechanized equipment which can unload whole ships, employing only a few people, to break the hold over the labor process won through years of struggle by the Longshoremen's union.

Corporations have re-organized production. A major example here is General Motors. In the late '60s, GM introduced General Motors Assembly Division (GMAD) in which assembly plants located all over the country are flexible enough to shift model production. When a militant assembly plant goes out on strike, its production can be shifted to other plants in other parts of the country. This happened, for example, with the Norwood, Ohio Local, which struck for 11 months in 1972, while other plants worked overtime to produce Norwood's quota. In this way, GM can sustain a long strike at one plant without any real losses.

Employers have developed their own organizations to collaborate and support each other in strikes. The old tactic of whip-sawing, in which one company was struck and others allowed to run in order to take on the companies one at a time, no longer works when the capitalists develop solidarity.

Employers have used their ability to operate on a world-wide scale to undercut workers in the United States. During the whole post-war period, U.S. capital expanded outward from high-wage, unionized areas to low-wage, non-unionized areas — to Europe, to the South and Southwest United States and to the Third World — to exploit cheaper labor there. With the onset of crisis and the declining rate of profit in the '70s the "runaway shop" movement accelerated. And corporations have been using these world-wide operations to blackmail better organized workers. They threaten to close down production if workers won't pay the price. They cry that "foreign competition" will force them out of business unless labor costs go down. A classic example of this strategy is the steel industry. Steel companies have used plant closures and the fear of more to come due to less expensive imported steel to force steelworkers into accepting the Experimental Negotiating Agreement (ENA). ENA effectively guarantees the companies that steelworkers will not strike.

In summary, the trend of post-World War II history has been that the employers have become more and more organized and powerful, while the workers have become less and less prepared to fight.

If we look back to the 1930s, we can see that this impasse is not permanent. In that period also, working class response to the employers' offensive of the Great Depression was by no means immediate. Between 1929 and 1933 under conditions far worse than the current crisis, U.S. workers were relatively quiet under the blows of the capitalists: Starvation wages, inhuman working conditions, long and toilsome hours of work, and especially high unemployment. Then, too, working people found themselves disorganized and separated, and the struggles were few and far between. However, beginning in 1933, there was a qualitative breakthrough. Militant, rank and file upsurges in a few places sparked a massive upheaval. Almost at once, the possibility for collective action was realized. Working people moved from little organization to a massive rank and file movement. By 1934, several U.S. cities had been rocked by General Strikes, and industry after industry was hit by militant upheaval. Hope lies in that the situation of the working class can change *qualitatively* very quickly.

THE MATERIAL BASIS FOR RIGHT WING IDEAS: THE TAX REVOLT

For the moment, workers feel class action is impossible; but some kind of action is necessary to defend their living standard from the employers' offensive. So there is the temptation to organize around divisions which unite one section of the class against another — company vs. company, craft vs. craft, race vs. race, sex vs. sex. The right-wing consequences of this type of strategy is most clear in the so-called "taxpayers revolt." Here, both the short-run rationale of capitalist strategies and their connection to right-wing ideas are most clear.

Proposition 13 and the "tax revolt" reveal workers in the private sector attempting to improve their situation at the expense of workers in the public sector and those who are dependent on public services. The huge development of public services — health care, welfare, higher education, increased unemployment benefits, etc. — was based on the tremendous economic prosperity of the post-war period. On the whole, the costs of these services came out of workers' wages. With the onset of crisis, two things have happened. First, real wages are declining, so workers can no longer afford to support expanded public services; second, in order to restore declining profits, there has been a shift of the total tax burden onto the working class. Meanwhile, between 1966 and 1976, the corporate share of total taxes paid declined from 23 per cent to 13 per cent.

The rate of taxation for workers has almost doubled, while that on capitalist profit has declined. In 1953, taxes took 9.2 per cent of workers' income; by 1974 taxes took 16 per cent. In 1953, taxes took 43 per cent of corporate profit; by 1974, 31 per cent. (The corporate tax rate is inflated by government figures; most economists estimate that the effective rate in any year is much lower. However, the figures given here illustrate that the trend has been steeply downward.)

The increasing share of public services that workers have been forced to bear is the result of two things. First, there has been a conscious policy to cut corporate taxes. To keep up the rate of profit, the government has lowered business taxes through laws such as investment tax credits and accelerated depreciation allowances. Second, inflation automatically increases the tax rate on wage incomes. For example, inflation amounted to 50 per cent in the years 1968 to 1975. That means that a family with $15,000 in 1975

and $10,000 in 1968 had the same real income, the same real purchasing power in both years. But the rate of taxation of $15,000 is double that of the rate of taxation of $10,000: 9 per cent vs. 4.5 per cent. So that a family has actually suffered a 5 per cent cut in their standard of living due to taxation even if their money wages kept up with inflation.

The effect of inflation on increasing the tax burden is especially evident in the Proposition 13 campaign. Originally property tax was an instrument for making property owners rather than working people pay for state services. But since World War II, higher working class incomes and the drive by workers for security from landlords have created a home owning boom. In 1940, only 41 per cent of all living units were owner-occupied. By 1975, 65 per cent were owner-occupied. In areas of population growth such as California, the general inflationary pressure in the economy has created a tremendous inflation in housing prices. As the market goes up, so do assessments. Assessments represent potential, not actual income. Yet, as assessments go up so do property taxes. Workers' income of course has not kept pace. Property taxes have become a very visible source of workers' declining standard of living.

The point is that taxation really hurts working people, who cannot afford to pay. The liberal opponents to Proposition 13 who chided people for their lack of generosity in supporting it, and those radicals who insisted that "no cuts" was in itself sufficient to fight 13, were unable to get support because they failed to address this problem.

Working people were looking for an answer. Proposition 13 provided one. The alternative would have been to make the corporations pay, to shift the tax burden where it belongs. But this kind of reform takes a political offensive, a real organizing effort. Who would take this on? The Democratic politicians scurrying to reduce corporate taxation to prop up profits and stave off economic disaster? The trade union officials whose whole strategy toward the crisis has been to go along with the corporations' demand that we protect their profits first to get the economy going? None of the institutions which supposedly represent workers' interests were able or willing to fight for this alternative. This left working people with the other alternative: Join with the capitalists to cut back on government services. So in the Proposition 13 campaign we had the spectacle of Howard Jarvis, lobbyist for the California Real Estate industry, leading a "popular revolt." Business has reaped the major part of the benefits of Proposition 13 — an estimated $4.6 billion out of the total $7 billion cut in state revenues. But even though it meant a $4.6 billion giveaway to corporations, working people overwhelming supported Proposition 13 — because they too will benefit, in the short run. In the longer run, of course, the spending cuts will hit workers in the private sector. The income gains made by limiting their taxes will not anywhere enable them to buy all the services the state now provides free — schools, libraries, garbage collection, sewage disposal, recreation areas etc.

DIVISIONS IN THE WORKING CLASS

The program of tax cuts and spending cuts also finds support because government spending for social services is based on a redistribution of income within the working class. Welfare, health care, unemployment benefits, are used by the unemployed, or the underemployed, and paid for by employed workers. These services have expanded tremendously in the post-war period. Added to these basic services, although completely inadequate, are the poverty-program services — special training programs, free child care, scholarships for higher education, etc. Oppressed people, and especially people of color, are the unemployed and the underemployed in this society. In 1978, the unemployment rate for black men was 11.6 per cent, for Hispanic men 7.6 per cent, for white men 4.5 per cent, for black women 13.7 per cent, for Hispanic women 11.3 per cent, for white women 6.2 per cent.

The expansion of basic services, and especially the poverty program, were won through their struggle. They were part of the gains of the movement of the '60s. The Right Wing fought against these from the very beginning. But during the '60s they could not find a mass audience. Why?

First was the continuing prosperity. Even the existing rate of taxation produced greater state funds on the basis of rising incomes, and increasing tax rates were not so burdensome on working people.

Second, the militant struggles of the blacks and other oppressed groups combatted the assertion of white male privilege. The strength of their organization put at least the public expression of racist and sexist ideas off limits. At the same time, their powerful movements, culminating in the Black Panthers and the League of Revolutionary Black Workers set an example of what can be gained by militant collective organization. And they won the admiration of younger workers, helping to break down racism and sexism.

But from the late '60s, the situation changed. The squeeze on wages got worse. And the militant movements of the oppressed — isolated from the rest of the working class and viciously attacked by the state — were largely halted. Attacked by the capitalists and no longer pressured by mass movements of the oppressed, white workers were much easier to organize against government spending for programs that benefit and are absolutely necessary to the survival of people of color. Now, as white workers move to defend themselves, at the expense of people of color, they tend to adopt ideas that make sense of this. Ideas such as, "blacks don't want to work," etc., are the false, racist stereotypes that are deeply part of U.S. culture. What has changed is the material situation. It is not just racist ideas that have led sections of the white working class to racist action; it is their action, which is racist in its effect, whatever its original intent, that has strengthened their acceptance of racist ideas.

There have been similar developments around jobs. With the onset of economic crisis, the job market has shrunk. Not only has unemployment climbed, but there are fewer good jobs to go around. White workers have responded by trying to re-establish their monopoly of the best jobs. The Bakke case came to represent affirmative action and preferential hiring — the instruments through which this monopoly had been broken. The Weber case directly challenged the rights of oppressed people to have a share of the few good jobs that exist. Whites, including white workers, have adopted "reverse discrimination" as their rallying cry — a slogan that would have seemed unmentionable 10 years ago. Anti-ERA sentiment flows from the fact that the ERA has come to symbolize the threat that women will now compete with men for jobs. Working class support for kicking out undocumented workers is part of the same thing. A "capitalist" strategy for survival leads directly to racism and sexism.

THE CRISIS OF LIBERALISM

From this point of view we can understand why liberalism has failed so dismally in the '70s, why the Democratic Party has moved to the right, why the supposedly liberal "veto-proof" Democratic Congress and a Democratic President elected in 1976 have passed bill after bill benefitting business. The liberalism of the '60s aimed to cushion the worst abuses of capitalism — unemployment, poverty, inequalities between classes in education, medical care, etc. — through state services. This was accomplished primarily through taxation of the working class — not capitalist profits. In conditions of prosperity, liberals were able to do this. But if liberal programs depend on prosperity, they also depend on capitalist profits. So, it is entirely logical that in a period of economic crisis the Democratic "friends of labor and the little man" are doing everything they can to restore profits. This includes of course, reducing taxes on corporations. This is a world-wide phenomenon. In the recent period, "social democratic" and labor governments in Germany, England and elsewhere have taken the lead to secure the conditions for capitalist profitability —

not only by cutting government services, but by directly freezing wages. Because of the employers' offensive, the working class cannot afford to pay and is resisting taxes. But to maintain or expand social services there is only one other place to get government income — corporate profits. Since liberals are unwilling to attack profits, they have no political alternative to offer workers.

So the "liberals" have moved to coopt the programs of the Right Wing. From Jerry Brown in California to Carter in Washington, the "new liberals" of the Democratic Party are conservatives, trying to beat the Republicans at their own game. They proclaim "fiscal responsibility" (i.e., slashing social services) and attack "big government" (i.e., firing public workers).

The fight against the firings and the cuts will require a fight to make the corporations pay. Just as the working class will have to refuse to pay for the crisis by cutting back their standard of living, they will have to refuse to allow the least well-off in the class to suffer so that capitalist profit can be protected. The liberals and the Democratic Party will not lead this fight. They will continue to capitulate to the Right Wing, in this way strengthening the Right Wing.

One area of right wing politics appears at first to be completely unconnected to strategies for economic survival. This is the attack on women's reproductive rights and the attack on gay rights. Anti-abortion and anti-gay politics do not flow directly from any material conflict, any defense of economic privilege. But they are nevertheless bound up with the economic crisis. The link is through the defense of the nuclear family. The affirmation of gay life-styles and

women's right to choose whether to have children, both challenge the nuclear family. Both gay rights and women's right to choose deny that either men or women must accept as natural or inevitable the adult sex roles defined by the nuclear family: "Men are breadwinners who support a woman and their children; women are dependent on men for their support in return for which they raise children and take care of men." While neither the gay movement nor the pro-choice movement defines itself as attacking the family, the struggle for the right to choose (on abortion) and for gay rights seems to bring the nuclear family into question.

Once again, if we look back to the '60s, the Right Wing was organizing against the women's and gay movements. But in fact, many people, including working people, responded positively to these movements, or at least tolerated them. The women's movement was able to win out, over against the Right. Why is it that now people are rising to the defense of the family?

The family, as we know it, is organized to assure male dominance. Women are oppressed by traditional sex roles, and male sex roles put tremendous strains on men themselves. The family, as people experience it, is hardly enjoying great success with so many families breaking up.

On the other hand, the family, with all its weaknesses, is one of the few institutions in capitalist society in which people can have *non-competitive*, inter-dependent, relatively supportive relations. They are not competing with each other on the market, but are trying to make a go of it together. As the economic crisis deepens, and when working class collective action does not develop, intense competition between workers tends to break up their solidarity. The world outside the family becomes more and more a "war of all against all." In this situation, the family can become much more important to people. Here they feel they can find some support, some solidarity and trust; here they feel that everyone has to work together because they are dependent on each other.

The idea that the nuclear family can fill these expectations is a romantic one. Still, without other alternatives people are forced to rely on it. So desperation about the loss of the family as a shelter from the world of competition can make the "threat" to the traditional nuclear family seem like something that must be fought.

THE WAY FORWARD

The capitalist crisis and the employers' offensive have formed the basis for the right-wing drift in the working class. But, at the same time, these factors are creating the conditions for the re-emergence of class

"AN ATTACK ON ONE WILL BE ANSWERED BY ALL"

WORKERS CONFERENCE
AGAINST BRIGGS/PROPOSITION 6

action and class politics for the first time since the 1930s. In this period of economic crisis individual strategies for survival cannot work. Tax cuts and spending cuts are not eliminating "bureaucratic waste" or hurting only the poor. The spending cuts are further depressing workers' standard of living. The schools and public libraries, parks and museums, trash collection and road maintenance programs are all being cut along with welfare. Suppression of gay people, the denial of abortion to the poor, defeat of the ERA will not keep women out of the labor market or prevent the disintegration of the family. Forcing people of color to bear the brunt of unemployment and eliminating affirmative action programs will not stave off unemployment for whites. Job opportunities for whites will continue to shrink because the capitalist economy is stagnating.

The exclusion of people of color from the unionized and better paid jobs only creates a scab labor pool for the employers. In the 1970 teamster wildcat, the Los Angeles beer drivers strike in 1978 and in the 1978 West Coast teamster grocery strikes, employers recruited from among the unemployed to break the strikes. Ads in the newspapers and on radio directed especially to people of color promised immediate high paying jobs with "equal opportunity employers." Striking teamsters learned a bitter lesson about their failure to organize against job discrimination against blacks. Similarly, immigration controls are used not to keep undocumented workers out but to create a cheap unorganized labor force for the employers. In Los Angeles, the retail clerks' union recently organized a plant and won a union election. The employer called in the immigration service which arrested the undocumented workers employed there and broke the union.

As workers are pushed into conflict with their employers, the disaster of strategies based on the oppression of one section of the class by another will be made clear. Moreover, the crisis is showing workers, for the first time in decades, that they must challenge union officials' collaboration with employers. While there are places and moments when workers have moved to struggle against their employers, the working class is not yet in mass motion. As we saw from the history of the early Depression, this situation could continue for a time. However, where struggle does occur, workers can and will move very quickly to new forms of activity and new ideas.

What makes the 1970s different from the 1950s is that capitalism is no longer "delivering the goods." The system is not functioning like a smoothly-running machine, as though it were the natural order of society, unshakeable and inevitable. Vietnam and Watergate have undermined confidence in the unselfish righteousness of the American "mission" and the incorruptibility of our politicians.

In this situation, what keeps working people resigned to their lot is the feeling that they are powerless to change things. Cynicism and desperation are twin reasons for their attraction to right-wing politics and programs. They opt for a Proposition 13 and budget cuts for lack of anything better. In doing so, they act against other sections of the class; and this action further connects them to right-wing politics and attitudes. Still the process of workers' acceptance of full-blown right-wing politics — as opposed to specific right-wing policies — has not gone very far. And it is being constantly counteracted by other forces. Consciousness, today, is mixed and confused, and subject to swift transformations.

Under present conditions, therefore, workers can quickly open up to socialist politics, to the degree that they can begin to struggle in their own interests. These days, even the most routine contract negotiations run up against vicious resistance from the employers, determined not just to prevent gains but to take away advances made in the past. The union officials either capitulate or, when forced by the rank and file, call a strike. Then they do everything they can to control the strike and keep it within safe, and losing bounds. On the street, workers learn two things: First, union officials cannot be trusted, the rank and file will have to organize themselves; second, they cannot win without militant tactics — refusing to accept injunctions limiting their pickets, which means defying the courts; pushing to spread the strike to other workplaces in their industry; organizing support from workers in other industries, building their picket lines with supporters from the community, from other unions. These were the lessons so quickly learned by the mine workers in their recent heroic struggle.

TOWARD A RANK AND FILE MOVEMENT

Rank and file organization within the unions is now in its formative stages, providing an opportunity to break through the feelings of powerlessness and cynicism that dominate workers' approach to the world, and to overcome divisions within the class. Once in struggle, acting on class solidarities, workers become open to anti-racist and anti-sexist ideas. In fact, the search for allies makes links with other groups in struggle natural avenues for organization. As the crisis deepens, the opportunity for socialist politics, as opposed to right-wing politics, increases. By relating to and helping to strengthen rank and file organizations we can build a left current in the working class based on the organization of rank and file militants. A left current would put forward strategies for action that unify the class: Organizing the unorganized and supporting the struggles of specially oppressed groups.

Thus, for example, the fledgling rank and file organization, Teamsters for a Democratic Union (TDU), has already moved to support the struggle of oppressed people and to educate its membership on the need for class unity. The TDU emerged out of the fight around the national trucking contract of 1976. Since then, it has grown largely on the basis of local struggle — sometimes wildcat strikes — almost always waged in opposition to the official leadership. On the basis of their experiences in struggle, TDUers have seen the desperate need to break down racist and sexist divisions in the class. In the Bay Area, the TDU chapter took a position opposing the anti-gay Proposition 6. Los Angeles TDU leaders have actively supported the Coalition Against Police Abuse. At its 1978 national convention TDU endorsed ERA and was one of the first labor groups to take a stand against Weber.

A militant rank and file current will also contribute to re-development of the movements of the specially oppressed. In the 1960s, while the majority of the working class stood passively by, the oppressed sections of the class organized. But despite their militance and elan, these sections could only go so far without the support of the rest of the class. Ultimately their gains were halted, even partially reversed, and their movements disorganized. Now, oppressed communities are suffering most severely. In response there has been motion — fights against Bakke, against cuts in specific community services, against police abuse, against immigration restrictions, against the denial of government funds for abortion, for gay rights, for the ERA — but not yet on the scale of the '60s. These groups remember that during the '60s their movements were isolated from the rest of the working class. This fact, whether clearly understood or vaguely felt, has produced a pervasive sense of powerlessness. The organization of the rest of the class, especially its unionized sectors, in their majority white and male, can help to overcome this isolation and to rebuild these movements.

Since oppressed people are a high proportion of unorganized workers, a strategy for the rank and file movement in which unionized workers take responsibility for organizing the unorganized will be an important way to build links between white male rank and file workers and the rest of the class. The organization of the oppressed is key to the development of the rank and file movement. Through organization, the oppressed help close off to white workers the strategy of saving themselves at the expense of the weaker sections of the class. Because they make right-wing strategies less possible and because they show what can be won by collective strategies, the organization of the oppressed helps move other workers toward class organization and away from the Right.

We need to link the organizing activity of workers against their employers to the organizing of oppressed people. The key to a successful fight against the Right is the development of workers' struggle against the bosses. But the development of workers' struggle against the bosses depends in part on the ability of workers to unite the class. By concentrating our forces and by working together, the Left can help make workers' self-organization more practical. We can involve ourselves in and lend support to rank and file organization. And we can use our connection to other arenas of struggle to bring support to rank and file organization from oppressed communities. In turn, we can use this practice to break down the racist and sexist politics within the working class, to unify the class through its own activity. ■

Group Exercise

This exercise is designed for a two-hour period and is divided into three sections: Discussion of readings, 30 minutes; "Which Side Are We On?" role playing, 45 minutes; and concluding discussion, 45 minutes.

I Discussion of Readings

Begin the session by taking 30 minutes to discuss the readings. Discuss those elements from the readings that were new and those sections that raised questions. Try to be as specific as possible in your discussion in relating the readings to local struggles or issues that reflect an awareness of class struggle in our times and its many dimensions.

II "Which Side Are We On?" Role-Playing

This role playing exercise should continue for about 45 minutes. Everyone should participate in the exercise.

Here is the setting: Because your group was known to be studying social analysis, you have been called to an emergency meeting at your local parish. A strike has been called by the majority of workers at Widgetmakers Inc., a transnational manufacturer with a factory in your city. In less than three months, four workers have lost their hands due to faulty equipment. Organizing around these accidents has touched off a series of demands. While the union leadership was uncertain about calling the strike, the rank and file ordered it. Your social analysis reflection group has been called to help the church come to some decisions about who to support in the strike. A major shareholder, who also serves as chairperson of the Board of Directors of Widgetmakers Inc., is a member of your church and one of the major contributors. A large majority of your parishioners work in the factory. Both sides are looking to the church for a response.

Your social analysis reflection group comes together to meet and hears the following positions presented at a public hearing:

Workers' Demands

- Replacement of faulty equipment: Accident rate in the factory is increasing due to outdated and ill-repaired machinery.
- Extension of medical disability insurance: The families of the four workers who were disabled are not receiving adequate benefits on which to live.
- Development of a child care facility near the factory to benefit those women who are working at the factory.
- Disability for those women on pregnancy leave.
- Health benefits to cover abortions for workers and their families.

Chairperson of the Board and Major Stockholder

- In comparison to other divisions of Widgetmakers Inc., profits for this particular factory are down.
- With decreased profits, outdated machinery cannot be replaced due to cost factor.
- Increased costs for running this factory, i.e. upgrading of machinery or increased health care for workers, could lead to the closing of the plant.
- "I am morally outraged that the workers would include the question of benefits for abortions. We are not dealing here with serious workers, but with those who do not value human life."

Chamber of Commerce Civic Club

- We want to publicly thank Widgetmakers Inc. for their interest in our community as indicated by their recent contribution of shrubbery to the city park.
- We want to thank Widgetmakers Inc. for their contribution to the Hospital Auxiliary, indicating their concern for health care.
- We want to initiate a weekly evening of bingo for workers and their families as a way of strengthening the family. (It should be noted that the night suggested for bingo is the same night that the Widgetmakers union meetings are held.)

Press

- In our reporting of the workers' movement, we have noted an increased militancy from workers. We have felt this to be more news worthy than the accidents suffered by the four workers who are now disabled.
- We have noted that the pro-life group has several women in it whose husbands work at the factory and appear to be satisfied with current conditions.
- We have noted the presence of several new workers who have taken a leadership role in organizing other workers. They appear to be better educated.
- Yes, it is true that we carry weekly advertisements in our paper for widgets and other gadgets made by Widgetmakers Inc.

Worker

- She affirms the demands of the workers outlining in detail conditions and the weekly earnings of workers, many of whom take home a little over $150 weekly for 40 hours of work.
- She indicates how attempts to dialogue with management and the Board have failed.
- She notes a decreasing production rate and increased lay-offs.
- She admits that at times she has bought widgets made in Taiwan because shrinking real wages prevent her from buying the merchandise she has helped produce.

Corporate Information Center

- A spokesperson indicates that the owners of this widget factory are closing down U.S. operations and moving abroad.
- Data are provided showing that all workers' demands across the nation have been denied by Widgetmakers Inc. this past year, even though labor agitation has increased.
- Data are given showing that profits for Widgetmakers Inc. were up 83 per cent from widgets produced abroad, while only up 13 per cent for those made in the United States.

Local Banker

- Capital is not available through his bank for upgrading equipment for a factory whose profits are down. That would be a poor credit risk.
- During the strike, loans against workers will be foreclosed in the event that payments are not met.

Workers' Support Committee

- A group of other office and assembly workers from other factories in the city have joined the strikers in their demands.
- They indicate that the strike comes at a time when a growing number of workers throughout the city are becoming frustrated with low wages and increasing prices.
- They have taken up a collection for the families of the workers who have been disabled. They are asking your church for a donation.

Pro-Life Group

- We must dismiss all the workers' demands because of the request for abortion benefits and the day care program, designed to destroy the nuclear family.
- We believe that women should not be working in the factory, but should be home.
- In the event of strike violence, we believe in maximum penalties for disrupting the life of the factory. In the event of the loss of life through violence, we believe in the death penalty for those responsible for the crime.

Having heard these positions, you are now asked to meet for 45 minutes and to collectively draft a one-page report so the church can formulate a response to the strike. Begin your discussion by focusing on the workers' demands and responses from various community groups, outlined above, which you have just heard.

If time does not permit the actual writing of a one-page statement, an outline of points and issues should be completed. Also, note questions that remain or other questions that you would want to ask various persons from whom you have heard testimony.

III Concluding Discussion

Following the role playing exercise, take some time to discuss the following questions:

1 What did I learn about my values while formulating a response to a concrete issue like this?

2 Was I able to identify two clear sides in this labor strike? How did I identify the sides and/or alliances at work in this instance of class struggle?

3 Was I able to take a clear position between two sides? Why or why not?

4 What was my advice to the church? Was I tempted to take a position of reconciliation? Did I want to dialogue? Did I try to steer the church away from the conflict? What theological assumptions were informing my decisions and responses?

Through these exercises and readings we have seen that class struggle in our times is a complex phenomenon. The correlation of forces surrounding a given workers' struggle is important to analyze to determine the best tactics and strategy for moving forward. If time permits, or as an additional exercise, group members may want to examine a local issue, a local labor dispute or the activities of a local right-wing group and attempt to analyze them from a class perspective. Begin by identifying the various actors from the different social sectors. What is their class position? Whose interests do they serve? What contradictions are evident between their class backgrounds and the alliances they form?

Exploring the Alternatives

Session 4 examines the political choices facing us in this historical moment: Socialism — a qualitatively different economic and political system from capitalism — or some other alternatives that, in our view, leave intact the oppressive nature of the capitalist order.

Today, socialism is in construction in well over half the globe, in societies ranging from highly industrialized to pre-industrial. But the construction of socialist societies, like any other societal construction, proceeds by the resolution of contradictions. Because social revolutions are essentially volatile and, at any specific moment, inconclusive, we cannot embrace idealistic or utopian views of revolutionary change. A socialist revolution in one country cannot be used as a blueprint for change in another, or in another period. Each socialist construction will evidence the particularities and problems of its historical and cultural context. Neither will fundamental change come without mistakes, setbacks or struggle.

Essential to the development of the preceding sessions and of this one is a basic understanding of political economy, a concept with which most of us are unfamiliar. As Engels, writing in *Anti-Duhring,* described it: "Political economy, in the widest sense, is the science of the laws governing the production and exchange of the material means of subsistence in human society." A. Leontiev, an international economist, explains: "A scientific analysis of social development shows that definite laws operate in what at first glance appears to be a chain of disconnected phenomena. This being the case, social life can be studied with no less success than the development of nature."

The goal of political economy is to overcome the compartmentalization of knowledge as it is offered by the academic social sciences. Political economy works to re-establish unity in our understanding of social reality by helping us to *relate* historical, economic, political, social and cultural aspects of experience and analysis.

It is from this perspective, from a more holistic view of society, that we examine socialism here as the alternative to capitalism. A second understanding will also be helpful for us: The basic distinction between and relationship of socialism and Marxism.

Socialism is a system which replaces capitalism with a socio-economic order based on cooperation instead of competition. It organizes production so that labor is not an alienating activity. Since socialism stresses worker ownership, participation in planning, and decision-making — self-esteem and a sense of belonging are integral parts of the process. But socialism, as an historic project, offers no blueprint. For this reason, the key to establishing an alternative to capitalism lies in our ability to imagine and our capacity to act collectively to bring it into existence.

Marxism, as a world view, espouses historical materialism which, as a tradition, has many contending perspectives within it. Its premises and analyses lead logically to a total critique and rejection of capitalism. Other systems of thought which may reach similar conclusions pay little attention to historical analysis, or to the need to be integrated into a movement seeking an alternative to capitalism. The uniqueness of the Marxist tradition lies in taking up these three tasks and this establishes its connection with the movement for socialism. The Marxist perspective is the dominant perspective in the history of the world socialist movement.

Making sense of the world today requires that we understand that the reasons people (and countries) act as they do are rooted in the historical materialist analysis of society. The two readings for this Session help us to focus on this kind of analysis. The first reading,

"Overcoming the Myths: The Political Economy of Socialism," is by Kathleen Schultz. She examines some of our own assumptions about socialism and helps to clarify a few basic concepts of socialist political economy. The article gives an overview of the fundamental features of socialist societies and provides a backdrop for further study and discussion.

Myths such as those examined in the initial part of the article are often based on legitimate concerns or fears of people in the United States — including those of religious conviction. These fears can be replaced with new facts, with historical insight, with broader understanding. Toward that end, Schultz describes four basic features of socialism — social ownership, workers' power, laws of socialist economic development, and socialist values and the participatory process.

The second article, by Joseph L. Hardegree, "Illusionary Alternatives to Capitalism," places in perspective some major political tendencies of the current period, discussing their implications for social change. The author considers various individualistic incremental and structural change alternatives, including: Personalistic and pietistic religion, the human potential movement, pacifism, liberal reform, populist and social democratic movements, and fascism.

In assessing these various alternatives, the author includes a brief historical note, an examination of the class basis including the strategic and tactical class interests served by each, and reference to the specific ideology, whether subtle or overt, of each tendency.

Hardegree also examines the phenomenon of revisionism within the socialist movement — which has significant ramifications for progressive people in the United States who are searching for effective political action. The Left will be grappling with revisionism for some time to come, and the impact will be felt by all progressives working for social change, even those who are not in the socialist movement.

Since many progressive Christians are attracted to various political movements which are here characterized as reformist, populist, social democratic or revisionist in ideology, it is imperative that we examine the inherent pitfalls of these movements. Our study proposes that the question "Which Side Are We On?" must be answered either "capitalism" or "socialism," but not some illusionary middle ground.   ■

Overcoming the Myths:
THE POLITICAL ECONOMY OF SOCIALISM
by Kathleen Schultz, IHM

"Socialism" is an unpopular concept for many in the United States today. It has been so for over 30 years. The McCarthy era resulted in the equating of "socialism" with "un-American."

But around the world, and in the United States prior to the '50s, socialism has a proud tradition. It has always been a challenge to those economic systems which, to survive, must periodically destroy the lives of a substantial number of people within them. Traditionally, socialism has represented to many a way to build a better life and a more just society. During the Cold War period, however, U.S. foreign policy required that people be engineered to "get behind" the American system. And socialism became "un-American."

Today, when people are realizing that the present system is oppressive and an alternative must be sought, more and more are re-examining socialist history and socialist ideas. In the process we uncover myths which some of us have believed all our lives—myths which have often stifled the struggle for justice.

Frequently based in fear, these myths build on fundamental distortions and misunderstandings, preventing a critical assessment of socialism as a political-economic alternative to capitalism. The first part of this article challenges us to overcome six of these myths.[1]

Secondly, since socialism is a legitimate and urgent agenda item today among U.S. Christians, an understanding of the fundamental features of socialist political economy is prerequisite to informed exchange and evaluation. The concluding part of this article outlines four basic concepts vital to this understanding.

Kathleen Schultz is National Executive Secretary of Christians for Socialism in the United States. She is also active in the Detroit Alliance for a Rational Economy (DARE), Latin America solidarity work, and in an alternative group in the Immaculate Heart of Mary Congregation of women religious (IHM).

MYTH NO. 1 — *"Socialism is necessarily anti-religious."*

Why many people believe the above statement is understandable. The well-known Marxist critique of religion, the historical record of some socialist governments and most interpreters' understanding of Marxism's philosophical basis make traditional socialist attitudes toward religion sound ominous.

What is not so well known, however, are the various challenges to the anti-religious tenets of Marxism that have been raised in recent years within socialism itself. It is now widely agreed that original Marxist sources are ambiguous on the question of religion. It is clear that varying historical situations and certain trends and discussions within Marxism have given rise to radically different interpretations of Christian faith and the role of religion.

Socialism and atheism do not necessarily go hand in hand. One need only look at socialist countries like Cuba and Viet Nam, where religion is practiced with deep fervor and reverence. In those socialist countries where religion is seen as an enemy, the institutional churches have historically been associated with the owners and the oppressive classes. The Christian churches have sided often with the political and economic rulers, or at least have not spoken out or acted on the side of the poor.

But today, for many Christians, their faith is a liberating force, moving them to struggle for freedom and self-determination. Faith does not make them passive or submissive. It motivates them to stand with the poor and oppressed people and to work for a more just society. In countries like South Africa and El Salvador Christians are taking stands against oppression and for human rights; commitments which are most unpopular with the ruling regimes.

Some Christians, believing the capitalist system is not compatible with Christian values, say they are socialists because they are Christians. They believe that Jesus was clearly on the side of working people and the oppressed, and against the ruling classes who

Elizabeth Catlett

each individual or each family unit. It may be preferable to hold in common many of the objects needed for daily living.

In a socialist society the social appropriation and control of economic surplus, and some cooperative owning are profoundly reminiscent of the most authentic and revolutionary signs of the early Christian community: "The whole group of believers was united . . . no one claimed anything for his or her own use, as everything they owned was held in common." (*Acts 4:32*)

MYTH NO. 3 — *"Socialism sounds dreary — a cheerless routine."*

Part of the negative response of the U.S. public to socialist countries comes out of our society's consumer ideology. We have grown accustomed to an advertising barrage of choices and styles — from clothes to sexual mores — choices which have not always enhanced our dignity or happiness even if they were possible to acquire after the needs of the average family are taken care of.

We forget that socialism has come about, for the most part, in developing countries. The seeming austerity of life in socialist societies is related to the goal to overcome scarcity and provide for the basic needs of all. Life is disciplined in these countries — the discipline of daily sacrifice necessary to survive and to keep human values in perspective.

Surely, people in socialist countries share in the same "cheerless" routines as we do, with regard to our regular household tasks, child-raising and community responsibilities. But the idea that there is no joy or recreation in socialist nations is unfounded. Every home in these countries may not have a television set, but art at the community level, neighborhood sports, music and drama all involve people as active participants. Rather than depending on being entertained, people tend to develop their own creative and physical abilities.

In actual fact, socialism can even result in more leisure and human creativity since people do not have to "moonlight" to make ends meet, or be forced to work overtime. In a society where jobs are secure and more meaningful, where buying luxury items or "gadgets" is not a sign of success or status, people can benefit from both their work and community service as a means of individual fulfillment plus the building of a new society in which all can share.

MYTH NO. 4 — *"Socialism destroys individual initiative and creativity; people won't work if they can't get ahead."*

Even now, not many of us work to "get ahead." Most of us work just to get along — pay the bills, have food, shelter, a short vacation, maybe a few luxuries. The hope of fantastic profits doesn't get people to work in the morning; necessity does.

dominated and exploited. Socialism, these Christians believe, stands as a vision for the future.

MYTH NO. 2 — *"Socialism means I couldn't have any personal property."*

The "abolition of private property," an important socialist principle, does not refer to the personal property that each of us owns. The private property that is to be owned in common is only that which involves using the labor of others to produce goods and services only profitable to a small class of owners. When this property is owned in common, profits will be controlled by workers and the community, and used for the benefit of the whole. Such property includes factories, banks, farmland holdings (thousands of acres), and apartment buildings.

When this private property becomes the property of the people, controlled by people's organizations, it will produce more personal property for all. Even now there is enough wealth produced in the United States for all to have decent housing, adequate health care, needed transportation. The problem under the wage-labor system in capitalism is that wealth is privately owned and distributed unequally.

Our stoves, refrigerators, clothes and homes will remain ours under socialism. We don't use them to exploit the labor of others for profit. But on the other hand, in the socialist society, when the commodity production needs of the economy no longer require it, ownership of some goods will not be thrust on

Would all inventions stop if people couldn't make windfall profits on new ideas? Very likely not. Most creative people enjoy what they do, and in a socialist society, there will be an added social motivation to invent. All the people will benefit, not just a few corporate marketers. There are also opportunities for advancement in a socialist society because socialism is not a welfare state. People do get paid for their work, and they are also adequately cared for if they can't work.

Imagine, then, a society in which people produce necessities under safe working conditions, being paid a decent living wage, and having free access to education, health care, recreation. Wouldn't we be willing to work in such a society?

In many ways, in a socialist society the truly human dimensions of work are restored. No longer primarily a means toward personal acquisition, work becomes creative self-expression, a societal contribution by the individual to the people's needs and aspirations. Under socialist conditions, work can once again enhance human freedom, a notion which is very much part of a Christian understanding of work as selfless stewardship and service.

MYTH NO. 5 — *"Socialism is un-American."*

The struggle for socialism in the United States has been part of American history since the 1880s. This struggle is no more "foreign" than the struggle against British rule in 1776 or the fight against slavery. Wherever there is injustice, the American response, at its best, has been to struggle against it. The struggle for social security, for trade unions, for community control of schools — all of these evidence the spirit of U.S. people seeking greater equality and democracy.

Since the freedoms and other goals which are the foundation of this nation are not always manifest in our daily lives, the struggle for socialism goes on — a conscious movement toward a new economic system which guarantees fundamental rights: To a job, decent housing, education, health care and the freedom to dissent. This certainly is more in keeping with the humane aspects of the American tradition than accepting domination and injustice.

In fact, we need to ask some critical questions about the "American way" which is supposedly better than socialism. From the beginning, this "American way" has benefited a significantly small minority. This is true both within the United States itself and at the global level. In the United States, the distribution of wealth is almost identical with the distribution of wealth in India. The difference is that in the United States the economic pie is much bigger and so the results of this maldistribution are not quite as visible. Further, with this wealth goes much of the control over the country's resources, industry and public services — a source of continuing profit based on the exploitation of working people.[2]

And at the international level, the history of capitalist development reveals the same pattern of benefit for a minority based on exploitation of others. Despite increased foreign private investment, loans from Western governments, increased collaboration with the World Bank and the presence of the multinationals, the external public debt for 96 developing countries by the end of 1976 was $227.4 billion (a 23 per cent increase over 1975, which was a 20 per cent increase over 1974).[3]

In short, to love our country and our people does not mean that we must support the capitalist economic system which exploits the people and resources of other countries and leaves many of us with our futures mortgaged for all our lives. The economic system does not equal the country; that system can be changed.

MYTH NO. 6 — *"Socialism is undemocratic; free enterprise is democratic."*

Today, no existing socialist country measures up to the full vision of socialist possibility. Some socialist countries seem to be totalitarian and to deny freedoms. Many need to strengthen and extend full democratic participation. Often the freedoms which are limited in these countries are primarily those of the minority which formerly owned and governed the society. If that small elite were left totally free, it would do all in its power to undermine socialism and return the system which gave it wealth and power.

Basic socialist freedoms have to do with fulfilling fundamental human rights — to food, education, health, housing, employment and dignity in old age. The rights to private property and individual ownership are not emphasized out of all just proportions by the structure and values of socialism as they are under capitalism.

"They say to get elected to public office in America one must be rich. Well, my friends, I'm rich. I'm very rich."

Because of the human freedoms it supports, it suffices to say that far from being undemocratic, only socialism has the possibility of being truly democratic. Under socialism, the great majority of people have a voice in the economic decisions that control their lives.

Today, in the U.S., many "free enterprise" practices actually guarantee the right of a small economic minority to exploit many people. And it is clear to most of us that our "free elections" are basically controlled by those rich enough to pick and publicize candidates acceptable to them.

In the end we must ask: Who is free in the United States, and for what? If we want to work effectively for the ideals of the country and for Gospel values — freedom, truth, compassion, justice, equality, community — can we ever do so in an economic and political system that structures inequality and puts profits before people?

THE POLITICAL ECONOMY OF SOCIALISM

We can only examine the political economy of socialism in an historical framework, within the specific contexts in which socialist systems are in construction. The particularities in each instance determine the speed, the priorities and the problems encountered in a society striving to overcome contradictions in the wake of capitalism. As Marx once described it:

> What we have to deal with here is a . . . society, not as it has developed on its own foundations, but, on the contrary, just as it emerges from capitalist society, which is, therefore, in every respect, economically, morally and intellectually, still stamped with the birthmarks of the old society from whose womb it comes.[4]

The problems and possibilities in the transition to socialism are subjects for continuing study by those committed to the historical struggle for global liberation. While a detailed examination is not possible here, we can briefly outline the basic features of the political economy of socialism. We first look at the distinguishing characteristics of socialism and at the political pre-conditions for its emergence. Further, we can delineate the laws of socialist economic development and outline some of the social-cultural values apparent in everyday life and social institutions in socialist societies. These fundamental features of socialist political economy give us a working description of the socialist alternative and allow us to assess its potential for human liberation.

SOCIAL OWNERSHIP

Socialism is a social system and mode of production based on the collective (or public) ownership of the means of production. This requires the abolition of private ownership of the means of production, which allows one individual or class to exploit the labor of another person or class. Social (or public) ownership of the means of production is a way to overcome both the alienation of labor and the class divisions in a society.

This definition excludes such economies as Sweden's, in which 93 per cent of industry remains in private hands. Progressive taxation and extensive welfare benefits do not produce socialism. Only that society in which the means of production belong to the whole of society is socialist.

A familiar phrase which aptly characterizes socialism is "from each according to ability, to each according to labor." Since the means of production belong to the whole of society, every worker receives from the fund for social consumption, goods and services corresponding to a given quantity of work. Thus, with the exception of that amount reserved in the public fund for the expansion of production, replacement of machinery, for administrative expense, for schools and hospitals, etc., every worker receives from society what each has given to it. Socialism allows for a more equitable distribution of the social product.

But socialism is not a situation of absolute or utopian equality. Unjust differences in wealth can persist under socialism, due to both the scars left by capitalist "development," and the fact that socialism can proceed only gradually to eliminate the injustice of distributing consumer goods "according to the amount of labor performed" and not according to needs.[5]

People are, in fact, not alike: One is strong, another weak; one is married, another is not; one has more children, another has less, one is in good health, another disabled, etc. Because of these real differences, Marx concludes that socialist distribution (according to work) will not mean full equality. Only unequal distribution, i.e., according to needs, will accomplish this, a task left to communist development.[6]

Socialism and communism are alike in that both are systems of production for use based on public ownership of the means of production and centralized planning. Socialism grows directly out of capitalism; it is the first form of the new society. Communism is a further development or "higher stage" of socialism.

Socialism is the first step in the process of developing the productive forces to achieve abundance and changing the mental and spiritual outlook of the people. It is the necessary transition stage from capitalism to communism.

Nevertheless, the course of development of social-

ism tends toward greater equality since what each receives will depend not on wealth inherited under capitalism but on how much one produces. Inherited wealth will become socially owned wealth. Socialism makes a dramatic reversal of the logic and priorities of capitalism and opens the door to the possibility of full human equality.

WORKING PEOPLES' POWER

Socialist transformation can only occur with the transfer of political power from the capitalist class to the working class. While the taking of political (state) power by the working class is not sufficient for the economic establishment of socialism, it is the fundamental pre-condition.

Questions about the nature and power of the state in the process of socialist revolution are thereby closely bound with the entire process of socialist transformation.

Before socialism is firmly established, a new state faces grave dangers. The first threats are direct attempts by the defeated capitalists to reclaim their positions of power. But also problematic are the mechanisms and policies used in economic planning and administration under capitalism, which now must be transformed to a socialist character.

Questions of the role of the market, the use of material incentives, the organizational forms related to control of production and distribution, the relation of the state to the actual producers of society — all must be concretely examined and measured in their effect in overcoming class divisions and the alienation of labor. What is decisive for socialist transformation of both productive and social relationships is the class in power.

LAWS OF SOCIALIST ECONOMY

The central purpose of socialism is to overcome the "blind laws" of capitalism — profit making and capital accumulation — that operate "behind the backs" of those who live under capitalism, and to subject the economy to conscious social control by working people. This, of course, does not mean that limits to what can be accomplished do not exist. Practical limitations such as the size and skill of the labor force, the supply of raw materials, available tools and equipment, the development level of communication and transportation — all of these will set constraints on what can be accomplished.

Therefore, socialist development and economy requires attention to two interrelated and interdependent aspects of planning: The political decision about the goals to be met, and the objective limits of what can be accomplished. In other words, the conscious selection of a course of development must take into account the existing objective constraints,

95

including those created by conflicting interests among various sectors of the population.[7]

On the whole, socialist economic development will tend toward planned and proportionate development of the national economy.[8] It will tend toward ending the commodity nature of labor power through democratic control by workers over their work process and products. Finally, it will tend toward using the principle of distribution according to work to increase the productivity of labor, and in this manner, the process of socialist accumulation. This in turn speeds the socialist transition to communism, and the reconciliation of the diverse interests of the state, the collective and the individual.

The laws directing the economic development of socialist society serve the socialist goal of achieving full equality. To achieve this goal is at once a possibility and a necessity. Given the condition of a planned economy and the planned increase in productive capacity, basic scarcity can eventually be overcome and, in the process, the traditional divisions between working people can also be overcome. These include the divisions based on sex, race, and national origin, the differences between town and country life, and between mental and manual labor. In addition, the waste of global wars, militarism, and ecological destruction will be overcome or greatly limited.

SOCIALIST VALUES IN EVERYDAY LIFE

The values that undergird socialist societies are implicit in an analysis of capitalism itself, for socialism reverses the order of capitalism, an order based on inequality, alienation, racism, sexism, irrationality and imperialist expansion.[9]

A fully socialist society would be characterized by equality — equality in sharing material benefits of the society, in decision making, and in society's encouragement to develop one's full potential. Work would cease to be a mere means of "making a living" and become a more creative part of life. Arbitrary distinctions by race and sex which under capitalism are the social basis for particular forms of oppression, for dividing working people and tracking many into limited opportunities — will end. The irrationality of production for profits would be transformed into the rationality of production to meet social needs. The unequal and expansionist relations of imperialism would be replaced by a cooperative global ethic based on recognition of mutual responsibility and interdependence.

In such a society, people would have *security* — material, physical and psychological and be *equal* — genuinely equal in condition, not just in the opportunity to succeed in an unequal society. While sexual, ethnic, racial, national and regional differences would and should — like individual differences — continue to exist, material inequalities among these groups and, even more, patterns of social relationships which embody superiority/inferiority would be abolished.

In such a society, *mutuality* — community, cooperation, solidarity — would replace alienation as the basic mode of social existence. Finally, in the socialist society, once a material basis is secured, people could live together in *peace*, settling disagreements among themselves without resort to interpersonal violence.[10]

This vision of socialism clearly suggests the embracing of fundamental human values — justice, equality, cooperation, democracy and freedom. And the socialist society must establish and sustain these values within its basic structure and institutions — the common ownership of social resources for the benefit and service of all.

To do this, socialism requires a process. To describe this process is, in many ways, even more difficult than to define the goals of a socialist society or the values it seeks to inculcate. Perhaps most fundamentally, socialism means democratic, decentralized and participatory control. In short, it means that people make the decisions that affect their lives.

A participatory process in socialism requires equal access for all to the material and cultural resources of the society. This access is based in the abolition of private property as well as in the redistribution of social wealth. But participatory socialism also calls for socialist men and women to eliminate the alienating and destructive forms of production, consumption, education and social relations. It requires the elimination of bureaucracy and unnecessary hierarchy, to be replaced by a self-governing, self-managing people with directly chosen representatives, subject to recall and replacement.

In short, socialist goals and values that affirm ". . . the free development of each [as] the condition for the full development of all" and the socialist process of participatory democracy are necessarily tied together.

SOCIALISM: AN HISTORICAL PROJECT

While the four major aspects of socialist political economy can be separately described, none of them functions in isolation. Socialist political and economic democracy is a hard-won historical victory, and the transition to socialism in a given country and on a world scale most likely will not develop along a singular path.

Nothing so clearly demonstrates this as the contradictions visible today. Within socialist societies, the achievement of socialist democracy remains a serious concern since it is increasingly clear that a democratic political superstructure does not automatically emerge once power is taken and a socialist economy established. Growing bureaucratization in some countries suggests that all rights won by working people under capitalism must be preserved and extended under socialism.[11]

Not only are there contradictions within socialist societies but also among socialist nations. These take their sharpest form in ideological struggle and hegemonic rivalry, in military build-ups and mutual threats. Recently, we have even seen the armed invasion of one socialist country by another.

Because of such apparent contradictions, one Marxist economist argues that "none of the 'socialist' societies" today "behaves as Marx thought they would." Paul Sweezy suggests that the result has been a deep crisis in Marxian theory of post-revolutionary societies.[12]

Whatever theoretical path is taken to explain such problems, it is important to emphasize that there is only one global economic system — not two. This means that any nation which now attempts an economic transition to socialism while the world economy is still under capitalist hegemony, must do so under all the constraints that this imposes.[13]

Socialism is an historical project; one which requires a people to be subject (not object) of their history, to grasp the facts and conditions of their situation and to set in motion the process leading to change and liberation. But socialism is also subject to the pressures of human mistakes and historical conflicts.

The struggle for socialist political and economic democracy will involve continuing experimentation in many areas, especially in the relations between the state, political parties and mass organizations. In Cuba, the Committees for the Defense of the Revolution (CDRs) and the Peoples' Power Assembly (Poder Popular) represent mass, relatively decentralized forms of control over economic and social institutions. In Yugoslavia, Workers' Councils function as forms of self-management at the social and economic levels.

Communist parties of most Western European countries argue for multiple, autonomous parties and mass organizations, and for the need, also, of developing forms of direct democracy. On the other hand, the Soviets and East Europeans hold that a single leading party and a strong centralizing state are compatible with and often required for democracy in political and economic life.

As this examination of the essential features of socialist political economy illustrates, tension will be inevitable. In particular, tensions will exist between the socialist goals of rational planning and the achievement of human liberation, as well as between the principles of centralization and decentralization.

These tensions can only be worked out through a process of struggle and innovation. They cannot be resolved in advance by "trade-offs" worked out in theory. The establishment of socialism will not bring an end to pain or difficult choice. This is why the historical project of constructing socialism requires the best of human imagination and collective will. Capitalist hope is only for marginal and temporary improvement. Socialist hope, on the other hand, seeks the reversal of capitalism's priority of profit before people. It is a vision worth fighting for. ■

1. Adaptation and expansion of "Can a Christian Be a Socialist?: Myths and Facts About Socialism and Christianity" prepared by the Detroit Chapter of Christians for Socialism, 1978. Distributed by CFS in the U.S., National Office, 3540 14th St., Detroit, MI 48208.
2. See "The Myths of Capitalism" by McCulloch, Toland *et al.*, as revised and updated in *Must We Choose Sides?: Christian Commitment for the '80s* p. 59, published by the Inter-Religious Task Force For Social Analysis, 1979.
3. "The Myths of Capitalism", *op. cit.*, p. 58.
4. Karl Marx, *Critique of the Gotha Program* (Part I.) in *Marx-Engels Reader*, Robert Tucker (ed.), 1972, Norton and Co., Inc., NY, p. 387.
5. See Lenin on Marx's understanding of socialism as the first or lower phase of communism. In *State and Revolution* in Collected Works, Vol. 25, pp. 456-474.
6. *Critique of the Gotha Program, op. cit.*, p. 388.
7. Adapted from "China: New Theories for Old" by Sweezy and Magdoff (eds.), *Monthly Review*, Vol. 31, No. 1, May 1979.
8. See *Textbook on Political Economy: A Beginner's Course* by A. Leontiev. Proletarian Publishers, P.O. Box 40273, San Francisco, CA 94140.
9. See the introduction to "Visions of a Socialist Alternative" in *The Capitalist System*, Edwards, Reich and Weisskopf (eds.), 1972 edition, Prentice-Hall, Englewood Cliffs, NJ, p. 520.
10. See introductory essay by James Campen in *Socialist Alternatives For America: A Bibliography*, Resource Materials from the Union for Radical Political Economics (URPE) Vol. 1, Spring, 1974, pp. 8-15.
11. See M. Johnstone's article "Socialism and the Democratic Exercise of Political Power" in *Socialist Revolution* #35 (Sept.-Oct. 1977).
12. Paul Sweezy develops this thesis in "A Crisis In Marxian Theory" in *Monthly Review*, June 1979, pp. 20-24.
13. William K. Tabb in *In These Times*, Nov. 7-13, 1979, p. 22.

Illusionary Alternatives to Capitalism

by Joseph L. Hardegree, Jr.

> . . . for there must be factions among you in order that those who are genuine among you may be recognized.   (I Cor. 11:19, R.S.V.)

One of the things I learned while driving a taxicab in the early 1970s was that 99 per cent of my customers were convinced something was wrong with our country and that significant changes needed to take place. They differed, usually along class lines, over what was wrong and what should be done, but the feeling was almost unanimous that we were living at the end of one era and at the beginning of another.

Today, things are even worse. Our problems are accumulating faster than solutions are being implemented. Even the richest and most powerful are, in the words of Matthew Arnold, "swept with confused alarms of struggle and flight." When major oil companies bring us reassuring or chiding advertisements about our need for faith in capitalism, they do "protest too much," and reveal that even capitalists are uncertain and insecure about the future.

In the midst of this come many suggestions about what to do. But most of them make promises that cannot be fulfilled by the means proposed and will likely bring about consequences that are quite different from those intended. Hence, alternative suggestions for the creation of a better future must be carefully and critically analyzed.

The underlying assumption of this article is that Marxian socialism is finally the best and most complete answer to the question of our future. It came to be so partly by recognizing the limitations and difficulties of the other alternatives examined. The critique expressed is from that point of view. Primarily, this means applying a class analysis to each political

Joseph Hardegree is an ordained Disciples of Christ minister currently in the doctoral program in "Religion and Society" at the Graduate Theological Union in Berkeley, CA. During recent years he has been a taxicab driver, a union officer and an editor for *Radical Religion*.

perspective. Whose interests are represented? Who is likely to support it and who will oppose it? Does it have the net effect of uniting a majority of the people around a common and worthwhile set of goals or does it only appeal to a few while alienating large numbers of oppressed people who should be allies in the struggle?

People generally support major change in society for one or more of the following reasons: First, is the suffering experienced from direct, material oppression. Slaves want to be free, the exploited want justice and those who are demeaned seek to be treated with dignity and respect. Something basic in our humanity makes us rebel at harsh, cruel and unfair treatment from other people.

The second reason is a similar resistance to "spiritual" oppression, usually called "alienation" today. Karl Marx defined alienation under capitalism as a separation of workers from their work, the separation of people from one another (both as individuals and as classes) and the separation of each of us from our basic humanity.

Separation from work means that the modern industrial process, with its division of labor and capitalist ownership of the means of production and finished products, robs the individual worker of a sense of identification with and control over the products of her/his labor. Thus, work has become almost universally an alienating instead of a fulfilling process. Separation from one another grows out of the class divisions engendered by the capitalist economic system and the general competitive nature of that system. Separation from our own humanity is the end result. Almost all of our work and much of our lives tend to be a constantly *frustrated* search for real meaning.

People grow tired of experiences and relationships that restrict and distort their opportunities to live loving and meaningful lives, even if direct physical oppression is absent. A political/economic system that turns people into competitors and casts most experiences into modes of profit or loss and winning or losing takes away something very important: The chance to be genuinely human to one another instead of oppressors and oppressed. In the long run, this kind of oppression is as deadly as the more direct, material forms.

A third reason why people opt for change is moral commitment combined with rational analysis. This often expresses itself as a concern for justice. It is not difficult to see that many of the world's economic and political arrangements are grossly unjust. For example, why should Third World countries have to

stop growing food to feed their own people in order to grow cash crops for export to the developed nations? What justifies the suffering resulting from capitalist ownership of the land, when it is based on transactions about which the vast majority of the people had no knowledge?

Another example is that capitalism requires a constantly expanding economy. Every major capitalist corporation must grow or die; such is the dynamic of the system. Since resources are limited, how can a political economy that demands unlimited growth be maintained?

For these and many other reasons capitalism no longer makes sense. It oppresses people materially and spiritually. It exploits and increasingly destroys natural resources which must be carefully used and preserved if there is to be a human future. A concern for these factors, separately or in combination, underlies the various alternative strategies for change being examined here. They help form a common bond that can unite us in our attempts to make necessary changes in our society and all of the societies of the world.

But how people analyze the problems and the solutions, how the rationale for change is experienced and understood, will be a chief concern as we examine the various alternatives.

INDIVIDUALISTIC CHANGE ALTERNATIVES

A very broad category of "solutions" to the problems of a sick society, greatly encouraged by capitalism, can be called *individualistic*. Each person is expected to work out his or her own *private* adjustment, or personal liberation. Such solutions posit that little has to change in one's outward circumstances in order for liberation to be achieved. For them, significant change takes place within the individual and perhaps in interpersonal relationships.

While individualistic solutions acknowledge that people are alienated — from themselves, from other people, from their work and from life in general — these solutions place the burden of responsibility upon the individual. Hence, people are often made to feel guilty about their alienation, the cause of which they are powerless to control. They are frequently told that if they cannot cope, something must be wrong with *them*.

One of the greatest hoaxes perpetrated by the propaganda forces at the command of our present political system is the notion that the basic cause of most of the problems each person has to face is some flaw (or collection of flaws) within her or his individual human character. The positive expression of this is that if each person will rid her/himself of certain misconceptions, everything, or most things, will be made alright.

This individualistic approach does, of course, contain an element of the truth. The individual human factor is important and the individual must assume personal responsibility for dimensions of the process of liberation, including the decision to stand against oppression in all its forms. But by far the largest cause of human suffering is the social behavior shaped by the dynamics of our capitalist political economy. Not only does this system produce its patterns of misery, in "Catch 22" fashion, it also creates a misunderstanding of them. Its victims are made to believe that they or some other group of victims are the cause of the problems. And when *individualistic* solutions are pitted against *social* problems most individuals will be crushed by the one-sided conflict. The walking wounded among us and within us testifies to this every day.

INDIVIDUALISTIC AND SEPARATIST RELIGION

The first, and by far, the most widespread of individualistic solutions is to seek comfort in individualistic religion, both in its pietistic and personal-

istic forms. Pietistic religious belief and practice urges people to seek consolation in another spiritual dimension where all of the material suffering and spiritual alienation that they experience in their present circumstances is overcome. Personalistic religious belief of a more "liberal" stripe places the answer in inner peace, psychological adjustment and compassionate interpersonal relationships. The difference between pietistic and personalistic forms of religion is largely a matter of class. Pietistic and "escapist" forms of religion usually attract the poor and oppressed. People with higher class status gravitate toward the personalistic, which is a less escapist and more accommodationist form of religious practice.

Both forms espouse elements of truth. Biblical religion properly understood sees us in relation to a more profound reality which includes but goes beyond the immediate and concrete. Further, it does insist on the importance of one's inner personal attitude and commitment, and on being just and loving in personal relationships.

But Christianity and Judaism, rightly understood, stand adamantly opposed to allowing our understanding of God, our personal faith or our personal relationships to be avenues of escape from genuine social responsibility. A great challenge to individualistic religion is presently being offered by "liberation theology" which recovers the biblical message that

God is involved in the overthrow of oppressive social, political and economic structures. But it is still, unfortunately, a minority movement.

Individualistic religion tends to lead to an acceptance of the status quo, no matter how unjust and oppressive. From the standpoint of those in power who benefit from a destructive social and political arrangement, this quiescent response is highly advantageous. Religious folks like these are no threat to stability.

Advocates of individualistic religion argue that it creates a new kind of person who, in a very small way, begins to change the system from "within" by living a more moral life. If enough people are converted, so the argument goes, then the political/economic order will begin to reflect the higher ethical values of those who have accepted religious faith. Unfortunately, this argument fails to take into account the complex and powerful social forces that shape consciousness and motivation, let alone the class forces which hold the present order in place.

Every political/economic order is constantly working to create people who "fit in" with the system. Invariably, the production of the kind of people the system needs overrides the "conversions" of some to a higher morality, unless their conversion includes a commitment to change the system directly. When the system does adopt a particular religion, as when the Roman Empire became "Christian" under the emperor Constantine, the religion adopted must accommodate itself to society, not the other way around.

Rather than accommodating people to the system, separatist (or utopian) religion rejects established institutions in favor of a separate culture and society. As much of life as possible is kept within the church — settling disputes, marrying, schooling, and socializing. In some ways, this describes Christianity early in its history. This model has been embodied in notable religious movements throughout history, including the monastic and anabaptist tradition. In the 19th Century, there was a special flowering of utopian societies. Today, some "intentional community" religious groups are attempting to recreate this pattern, considering themselves to be quite radical politically.

A separatist religion does pose more of a threat to the system than an accommodationist one. It stands as a clear and present judgment against the larger society and by its very existence suggests the possibility and need for social change, but as an all-encompassing strategy for change, it proves inadequate. If it becomes a threat it will be directly repressed. If it is not a threat it will be safely marginalized on the edge of the larger political economy upon which it remains dependent, whether it wants to be or not.

HUMAN POTENTIAL MOVEMENT

The human potential movement, which has mushroomed in recent years, shares many of the virtues and drawbacks of individualistic religion. From one perspective it can be seen as a positive reaction to the depersonalization and alienation which advanced capitalism breeds, even among those who are to some extent its material beneficiaries. The loss of emotion and energy, the subordination of personal satisfaction to achievement and competition, as well as personal experience of racism, sexism and classism have caused deep psychic pain. Often these wounds are passed on from generation to generation in the form of seriously distorted capacity for feeling and acting, for tenderness and anger, and manifest themselves in a denigrated sense of personal worth and value.

To the extent that various psychotherapies and growth experiences help restore basic human capacities, they are to be affirmed. In significant respects, the human potential movement is pioneering in areas which directly challenge the mechanistic, medical model of health and promise to offer a more holistic understanding.

This personal growth perspective in most of its manifestations, however, does not directly address the larger socio-economic reality which is the cause of so much oppression and suffering. Those who look to the human potential movement for guidance regarding the overall strategy for human liberation will find themselves settling for personalistic, individualistic solutions which ignore the basic economic and political sources of oppression.

In fact, some of the more hedonistic aspects of this movement even serve to erect barriers to acknowledging the material suffering of others, especially among those out of relatively affluent backgrounds who form "separatist" personal growth circles. The people it attracts do not desperately need to change the material world. They generally have the financial, class and status resources to shelter themselves from the harsh realities of the economic system. The perversion of personal growth solutions reaches its ultimate when it is used to justify a world of hot tubs, ski weekends, and Porsche autos while most of the world has not enough to eat and is fighting bloody revolutions for the sake of a decent human existence.

The future we seek should be one in which personal self-realization is indeed possible but it will be in the context of the realization of human community. Thus, as a strategy for social change, the human potential movement is an illusionary alternative.

PACIFISM

The end of one era and the beginning of another makes for a tumultuous time. "Wars and rumors of wars" increase as the social/political contradictions of the old order grow more acute and the *ancien regime* uses everything in its power to try to prevent the new order from taking over.

War fundamentally offends human sensibility. By its very nature it is destructive. Most of the time, those who actually fight in wars are relatively "innocent" regarding the political issues involved, but are drawn into the armies by the forces of constraint and the ideology that are so easily manipulated by the various classes. Since in virtually all of human history, including the present, there have been class divisions, the history of war is almost universally a chronicle of poor people fighting and dying on behalf of the rich and the powerful.

Under such circumstances it is not at all surprising that many people opt for pacifism as a way out. Problems, they think, could be solved much more easily if killing were ruled out as an alternative; everyone would be much better off. Some would argue that pacifism should be discussed as a social movement rather than an "individualistic" change alternative. It is included here because of its similarity to religion in its demand for a personal conversion to a particular lifestyle.

An analysis of pacifism is complicated by the fact that not all who claim to be pacifists deserve the name. "Pacifism" of convenience frequently springs up whenever there is an inter-class struggle. This takes the attitude that oppressed people should be pacifistic in their rebellion but that the "establishment" has every right to use the armed might of the police and army to put down all "disturbances."

Apart from this, however, many sincere pacifists are aware of the contradictions of capitalism, do not seek privileges and sometimes even give up their privileges to commit themselves to a life of poverty and service to help change the world. Such commitment is admirable, and for those of us who live in the mightiest armed camp in history, pacifism can be a compelling form of resistance.

However, the primary problem with pacifism as a strategy for social change is that it places the goal of *peace* before the process of achieving a just society. There is not now, nor will there ever be, peace without justice.

The road to peace lies in the establishment, on a world-wide basis, of a fair system of ownership of work and distribution of goods within a truly democratic political system. That road must necessarily pass through the "territory" of those who wish to maintain or re-create the unfair system we now have. Like happiness, peace is never achieved directly, but flows from the development of a classless and liberated society across the whole earth.

Even though pacifism grows largely out of an intellectual analysis and moral commitment for change, it tends to make no analytical distinctions between the various wars. The struggles of a nation to throw off foreign domination, such as our own Revolutionary War, was different from the march across Europe by Nazi Germany in the 1930s. One has to consider who is doing the fighting and what they are fighting for. The revolutionary uprisings of an oppressed people have a legitimacy that imperialist aggression does not, and ruling classes in the capitalist system (or any system) are not basically changed by a pacifist movement. Three outstanding pacifist political movements of the 20th Century have been Gandhi's rebellion against British rule in India, the U.S. Civil Rights Movement led by Martin Luther King, Jr., in the 1950s and '60s, and the Farmworkers' struggle for unionization under the leadership of Cesar Chavez. All three had worthy goals, strong leadership and a measure of accomplishment. None of them, however, resulted in a fundamental alteration of the political/economic system. Their achievements and noble aspirations must not obscure this truth from us.

Pacifism presumes that war and killing are the greatest evils possible. The argument against this is that certain forms of oppression are worse than the rebellion and struggle against them. A brief war that ends slavery, for example, is better than slavery enduring over a long period of time.

Pacifism is useful as a tactic, as shown by the Civil Rights struggle in the United States. But to make pacifism an absolute can lead to acquiescence to the forces of oppression, particularly where class struggle has taken the form of armed confrontation. Real social revolutions in the 20th Century — as in all centuries — have only occurred where people have been willing to struggle directly with the armed might of repressive forces.

INCREMENTAL CHANGE ALTERNATIVES

A second category of illusionary alternatives is comprised of those *movements* (as opposed to individualistic solutions) which attempt to make alterations within the present system without changing the fundamental dynamic of capitalism itself. The strategy is to ameliorate the harsher contradictions, to lessen the extremes of poverty and wealth but to maintain all of the basic "benefits" of capitalism.

Liberal Reformism: The largest social tendency committed to incremental change is "Liberal Reformism." The class base for liberalism is predominantly the middle to upper-middle classes who enjoy some benefits from the system as it is but are still sensitive to the suffering of the more oppressed, and are aware as well of the threats to the well-being of all from ecological damage and nuclear war. This stratum also includes those labor union officials who may be motivated by a genuine concern for working people but who are too privileged to appreciate the need for systemic change.

Liberal reformism, therefore, is largely an intellectual/moral concern of those who do not suffer a great deal of material oppression and are, to some extent, unaware of the political/economic roots of their spiritual alienation.

The main reason liberalism has appealed to so many is that reformism is not always illusionary. Most periods of human history do require working within the system to improve it. Capitalism, in its early years, was a liberating advance over the political economy of feudalism. Even now some social progress is still possible under capitalism. For example, some European countries have done a much better job than the United States in taking care of the basic material needs of their citizenry even though they retain a basically capitalist political economy.

A negative factor supporting the liberal position has been the constant effort on the part of the media and educational institutions to portray socialist societies in the worst possible images. Because a true picture of socialism, its achievements as well as its problems, has seldom been made available to the U.S. public, honest and concerned people have been psychologically and intellectually induced to believe that liberal reform is the only viable option for change in our society.

Additionally, a progressive section of the ruling class is usually liberal, believing that it is better to make some changes on behalf of the oppressed in order to retain the system as a whole. Since the socialist alternative would take away their wealth and power and distribute both much more equitably, they prefer giving up a little for the sake of keeping the rest. It was said of Franklin D. Roosevelt, for example, that "he saved his class" by instituting certain reforms within capitalism.

Liberalism assumes class differences can be ameliorated within capitalism. Liberalism assumes a "harmony of interests," arguing that in the long run everyone benefits from the present system and any reforms that are made within it. This is where the argument is joined between liberals and Marxian socialists. Socialists argue that the system does not operate for the benefit of all and that reforms usually do little to redress the imbalance between the capitalist class and the workers and the poor.

A good example is Medicare and Medicaid. Medical care has improved only modestly for the lower classes in recent years but government subsidy for doctors has gone up dramatically. The average medical doctor's income has increased at a rate that far outstrips inflation during the past 20 years even though it already was several times the average income for the population at large by 1960.

The U.S. health system needs a drastic overhaul to make it available to everyone on an equal basis. It also needs to emphasize prevention of disease as well as cure for the sick. The cost of health needs to be borne by the system as a whole and not tied in any way to a class-divided, individual income structure. Neither should health care be an opportunity for super wealth by any of its practitioners. But because changes like these either limit or actually interfere with the incomes of doctors and the medical establishment, and would upset the present system, they will be fought to the bitter end by most health professionals, supported by most sectors of the ruling class. As a result, the various "reforms" offered by the mainline politicians hardly touch the real problems of health care.

On an international level, the various "aid" programs to poor countries were almost entirely a combination of loans and subsidies for the purchase of U.S. goods, the setting up of U.S.-based businesses and the shoring up of the military power of each "aided" country's government for the sake of putting down rebellions and revolutions among the people.

Looking at the tax burdens and the tax breaks in the United States today we can easily see who are the direct recipients of governmental monies. Far more "aid" goes to big business and the owning and upper managerial classes than is given to ordinary folks. Some of the benefits of this "sharing of the wealth" with the wealthy do "trickle down" to the rest of us. Airport construction grants and airline subsidies make it possible for more people to fly in airplanes but the overwhelming beneficiaries of this "aid" to the airline industry are big business and the upper-middle to wealthy classes.

Highway construction subsidies allow most of us to travel more by car but the direct transfer of government funds goes mainly to the large construction firms which make good profits even while maintaining a work system that lays off its workers on a periodic basis. Add to this the way that government funds help lock our whole society into a system of transportation that is hopelessly wasteful and irrational. Mass transit gets token subsidies while big oil, the automobile companies and large highway construction firms roll merrily along. And when a corporation like Chrysler gets into trouble we find the government providing direct subsidy and insisting that workers accept huge paycuts by way of sacrifice to keep their hard-to-get jobs.

The list of examples is endless but the point is clear: Class divisions are not overcome by liberal reforms. Indeed, liberal reformism as a political tendency is in retreat. A majority of U.S. citizens now know that patching up the system has not and cannot solve the problems of our society. Conservatives are trying to capitalize on liberalism's failure by championing a "return" to a capitalism that shows no concern for anything but business. Many former liberals are showing their true class interests by joining forces with this neo-conservative element.

Liberal reformism tends to treat symptoms rather than causes. There is no better example of this than the welfare system. At the present time, capitalism "takes care of" people out of work or otherwise unable to fend for themselves. But we are propagandized to believe that people on welfare are lazy cheats

taking advantage of the hard working people. Meanwhile, almost every political leader talks of an "acceptable" unemployment figure of 4 per cent to 6 per cent and every business enterprise must trim its employment rolls to the minimum to stay competitive. Genuine full employment is not desired by the capitalist system because it would make it harder to keep wages down and/or hire people for new enterprises.

Another dynamic of liberal reformism is that it encourages the fragmentation of problems into single-issue politics. This "scattering" of reform efforts keeps people from dealing with the interconnections and fundamental contradictions of our society.

Being a "liberal" or "conservative" advocate of capitalism is no longer a real alternative because liberalism's failure is, in effect, capitalism's failure. Liberalism has been unable to overcome the contradictions in capitalism. To believe, however, that liberalism's failure means there is no hope for a humane and well-functioning society is to give in to a destructive mythology carefully cultivated by capitalism's ideological apparatus. This is not true. There are grounds for optimism and hope even if liberal reformism has turned out to be an illusionary alternative.

Populism: A relatively radical political movement arose in the 1880s and 1890s representing primarily the interests of farmers who were being brutally exploited by the banks, railroads and wholesale buyers of farm products. It was called "The People's Party"

and members became known as the "populists." Since that time several other appeals to rural folks and the "little people" have been termed "populism."

Populism has come to mean, therefore, a direct appeal to poor people, whereby a certain amount of anger is expressed against big business, high finance and an uncaring government, but with little or no basic analyses of class struggle and the contradictions of capitalism.

Tom Watson from Georgia was a leading populist from the 1890s to the end of World War I while Huey Long of Louisiana, and George Wallace of Alabama later led "populist" movements for a brief time.

Populism grows out of direct material oppression along with large measures of alienation but lacks the general analytical concern necessary to give it a deeper grounding and a wider vision. It manifests the grievances of some of the oppressed without combining them into a broader social commitment. It represents a militancy against certain powerful interests of a society (who inevitably deserve the attacks mounted against them) but is not a threat to the political/economic system in itself. In some ways, populism seeks to bring into a stronger position within capitalism the "little people" who have been relatively ignored in the political/economic process.

Another basic flaw of populist movements is that they are built on the *perceived* fears and direct threats to the people with no critique that might penetrate to a more profound understanding. The practical political effect is that the very people who ought to be united in a struggle against a common oppressor find themselves divided. Racism, for example, has often accompanied populist movements. Oppressed and vulnerable white workers have felt threatened by black workers who are in an even more desperate situation. In this regard, there is a thin line between populism and fascism. Watson, Long and Wallace each felt right at home with the Ku Klux Klan during certain populist stages of their political careers.

All political movements seeking serious change must mobilize the righteous anger of the oppressed. But to be truly liberating, anger must be combined with serious analysis and the broadest social vision. Because populism tends to limit itself to expressions of anger only, it invariably follows one of three paths: It dies out; it turns into fascism; it becomes absorbed into the more developed politics of Marxian socialism. Unless it follows the third path, it is an illusionary alternative. Most of the time it does not.

Fascism: Fascism is a very real option for a capitalist society in its death throes. First introduced in Italy after World War I, it achieved its greatest power in Nazi Germany. Continuing today in certain Third World countries, it is also a serious threat in the United States.

There are many aspects of fascism. Early ideologists such as Giovanni Gentile in Italy emphasized the infallability of one strong-willed political leader. An absolute loyalty to Mussolini or Hitler was based on the idea that only a dictator "can get us out of the mess we are in."

The base for fascism is the lower middle classes. Not being able to identify with the working class, they find themselves in dire circumstances as monopoly capitalism drives out small businesses. In Germany, fascism not only appealed to such people, it made a practice of giving many of them some measure of responsibility and authority that they felt they had lost.

A major psychological component of fascism in the 1920s was the cynicism and despair felt by most young people in Europe after World War I. The devastating effect of war on the whole notion of bourgeois liberalism was virtually universal, giving rise to a "lost generation" of creative artists and the nihilistic morality of fascism.

The most important aspect of fascism is its ability to manipulate the fears and frustrations experienced by the masses when their society is falling apart. Fascism seeks to identify small groups which are vulnerable and then heaps on them all of the blame for everything that has gone wrong. In Germany, the Jews were the primary target but communists, socialists, and homosexuals also suffered imprisonment and death. A similar phenomenon could happen in the United States where campaigns of varying size have already been mounted against blacks, gays, women's liberation groups and the welfare poor.

Yet another major aspect of fascism is its ideology of wounded national pride. War hysteria is easy to whip up when leaders can point to a real or imagined enemy. Fascism also helped rejuvenate the economies of Germany, Italy and Japan, at least temporarily, through massive military build-ups prior to World War II. Even though a growing war machine combined with the manipulation of a nationalist inferiority complex invariably leads to destruction, fascism deliberately goes even farther to maintain a constant war mentality.

One probably does not have to argue very forcefully to convince many U.S. citizens who are middle aged and older of the illusionary nature of fascism. Younger people are a different matter, however. From time to time public opinion polls among youth indicate a surprising amount of "admiration" for Adolf Hitler as well as much confusion about the meaning of World War II. The "punk rock" phenomenon has fascistic overtones beyond the actual Nazi insignias favored by these alienated young people and those who are willing to make money promoting its decadence. At the very least, these trends mean that fascism has not been thoroughly discredited for all time.

Recent trends in U.S. society indicate that a turn to fascism may well be underway. A military-industrial complex much larger than the Krupp empire in Germany before World War II plays a powerful role in governmental decision making. "Insults" to our national "pride" are quickly seized upon and magnified by the media. As one segment after another of the social fabric begins to fall apart, more calls for a "strong" leader are heard. As Nazi groups and the Ku Klux Klan get more media exposure, the fires of hatred are fanned with increasing intensity.

Most of the illusionary alternatives discussed in this article will never really get off the ground. However, they will attract people for a time and serve to distract them from more credible solutions or burn them out, barring further involvement. Fascism is different. Most signs indicate it is growing in momentum in the United States. Several countries have turned fascist in recent years, some with the assistance of the CIA, and fascism is the only way that a declining capitalist system can hang on. Indeed, it is highly unlikely that capitalism will survive without moving in a fascist direction. The issue is whether change will take place in a socialist direction or a fascist one. Therefore, an anti-fascist, as well as pro-socialist, struggle is called for.

In the late 1930s, a great deal of effort went into the creation of a "United Front Against Fascism." Many left groups today are attempting to develop a similar movement here. It is very clear that fascism needs to be taken seriously.

On the other hand, fascism is not likely to develop in this country under that name. The various U.S. "Nazi" parties are unlikely to attract the same kind of following as did Hitler in Germany. Nor will such "traditional" hate groups as the Ku Klux Klan and the John Birch Society get very far. They have been around long enough to be discredited in the minds of most.

Instead, fascism's best chance will be to develop one step at a time under the guise of "necessity." The class *most* interested in the development of fascism, the one that provides the power and resources to make it work, is the capitalist ruling class. A majority of this class comes to see that the most repressive and iron-handed measures are *necessary* to "preserve" the present class arrangements.

Because fascism develops as the last desperate strategy of a dying capitalism, it is included here as the most extreme possibility for change "within" the system. It could just as well, however, be characterized as a basic alternative to the present system and be included in the next section. Fascism introduces such qualitative changes, even in capitalism, that the system is fundamentally altered.

STRUCTURAL CHANGE ALTERNATIVES

There are, of course, some movements that seek neither individualistic solutions nor try to reform or "restore" capitalism to save it. They see a need for a basic alteration — a new arrangement for society. When this option is considered, two basic sets of questions must be asked:

1. Do present circumstances truly call for a revolutionary change in society? Has capitalism run its course? Is it time to move beyond capitalism, to the socialism that appears to be the next logical step for historical development? Will socialism be genuine progress for humanity?

2. If we live in circumstances of revolutionary possiblity/necessity, what alternatives to the present system will provide genuine liberation and what alternatives will (if undertaken) prove to be illusionary? The argument so far has been that individualistic alternatives and working within the capitalist system are both illusionary. Now the question becomes: Are certain strategies for moving beyond capitalism also illusionary?

Social Democracy: The strongest competitor to Marxian socialism is its cousin, social democracy. Social democracy was the first "revisionism" of Marxism. Marx and Engels always insisted that the ruling class of capitalism, like all ruling classes, would not give up its power, wealth and privileges without fighting to keep them. All of the democratic practices of the advanced capitalist countries such as the United States and England (which, flawed as they are, are still an achievement) would melt away when the ruling class had to fight for its life, no matter if a socialist alternative had been democratically voted in by the people.

A corollary to this was that a great part of the political process that already exists within capitalism is not nearly as democratic as claimed. The "equality" of all people in a capitalist democracy has to be realistically evaluated. The wealthy are much better able to enjoy the various democratic freedoms and exercise democratic power than the poor.

In 1898, Eduard Bernstein, a member of the German Social Democratic party, argued that Marx's understanding of the political road to socialism was in error and needed to be revised. In particular, he claimed that Marx had misunderstood the role that democracy would play to alter the economic contradictions within capitalism. Bernstein believed so fervently in the democratic process that he overlooked the reality of continuing class struggle within capitalism. He declared that socialism was not a goal but a "process," meaning that parliamentarianism is always best, no matter what its socio-economic outcome.

In the ensuing controversy among the socialist par-

ties of Europe, Bernstein's theory came to be called "revisionism," meaning that he had so revised the original work of Marx that his (Bernstein's) theory could no longer be considered a variation of Marxism. At the same time, he struck a responsive chord among an emerging group of socialist party politicians in Germany and elsewhere. "Social Democracy" came to be the name for an attempt to combine some features of socialism with a reformed capitalism.

Social democracy, therefore, is presently identified with such countries, groups and personages as Denmark and Sweden, the British labor movement, Willy Brandt in Germany and the late Golda Meir in Israel. In the United States, the Socialist Party had from the beginning a social democratic faction and from the leadership of Norman Thomas on (beginning in the late 1920s) this faction held control. This tendency is also represented today in the United States by such groups as the Democratic Socialist Organizing Committee (DSOC), the Citizens' Party, and the newspaper, *In These Times*.

The criticism of social democracy by Marxian socialism includes a reaffirmation of Marx's and Engels' original contention that capitalism will not go away peacefully when voted out. The military coup in Chile, which overturned the legally-elected socialist government of Salvador Allende is offered as the most recent bit of evidence to support this contention. It is in this light that contemporary developments in the United States look so ominous. Both police agencies and the military have recently been given sophisticated training and new weapons to be used against the people of this country when it becomes "necessary." The official reason given is "to put down riots and civil disturbances," but it is naive to think that such instruments in the hands of a threatened ruling class would not be used against the people should they opt, by a democratic decision, for a socialist future.

A second criticism of social democracy is that its best achievement so far — welfare statism — is *not* socialism, even though it supercedes other alternatives within capitalism. It settles for taking care of people in an elitist way that ultimately dehumanizes them. "The dole" is not socialism, no matter how broad a scale on which it is distributed. Socialism is sharing in the work, the rewards and the responsibilities for creating the future, in the workplace, the community and in the society as a whole. Social democracy's best possible future lies in a more humane capitalism. When called "socialism," it gives that movement a bad name. Socialists should not seek as a goal in the United States the creation of a system like Sweden's, even though it would be preferable to that which the capitalist class would like to force upon us.

A third criticism is aimed at the class basis of social democratic leadership. It is easier to make compromises with the present system when one's economic position is relatively privileged, which is true of most social democrats. Social democrats also often see themselves as playing a mediating role between workers (whom they consider "backward" politically) and the ruling powers, content to affirm a social vision which never has to come to pass as far as they personally are concerned. The revolution can be endlessly postponed because they are not suffering in an immediate, material way.

Finally, social democratic countries like Sweden share in the rewards of the capitalist/imperialist system. They are able to provide large welfare benefits at least in part because of the exploitation of the poor nations of the world by the developed nations. If a worldwide system of economic equality existed, the social democratic combination of capitalism and social welfare would become far less tenable.

It is likely that social democracy will be a strong competitor to Marxian socialism, especially in the United States, where the feeling that everyone — including the most powerful — will go along with whatever is voted in predominates. The legacy of anti-socialism in this country is still very strong. The temptation to solve our problems either through larger doses of welfare or the callousness of fascism instead of through a liberating transformation to socialism will be difficult to resist. At the same time, the obvious bankruptcy of the social democratic alternative manifested in a country like England will continue to be used as an ideological weapon against the alternative of real socialism.

Anarchism: Marxian theory holds that the "state" is the instrument of power for the ruling class. The entire state apparatus, from the direct force of the military and the police to the ideological "superstructure" of the legislature, the courts and the educational system, has but one essential purpose: The maintenance of power by those who already have it. This is as true for the socialist state which operates on behalf of the working class as it is for capitalism, where the state functions on behalf of the bourgeoisie.

After the working class takes power, Marx argued, there will emerge through an evolution *within* socialism (the whole reason for socialism is to bring this process about) a classless society in which there will be no need for one class to rule over or oppress another. Lenin called this development the "withering away of the state." Such a concept did not foresee the end of a need for the coordination of goods and services. Instead, it meant a police force and an army would no longer be necessary so that the coordinating institutions could use them to wield oppressive power.

None of this was expected to happen overnight. There would be a period of transition called "socialism" or the "dictatorship of the proletariat" in which the old remnants of capitalism would gradually be eliminated and a new kind of human being, committed to cooperative rather than selfish values, would begin to emerge.

Anarchism agrees with Marxism in its analysis of the state as an instrument of force and oppression. But it differs from Marxism in that anarchists believe that the existing capitalist state should be brought down as soon as possible by whatever means are necessary; then the people will begin to work for the immediate creation of a stateless society based on purely voluntary principles.

In other words, Marxian socialism insists upon a transitional period in which the working class can create conditions under which the oppressive instruments of class rule are not needed. On the other hand, anarchists believe that the state can be destroyed in one move and there is no need for an intermediate step of a workers' state. Marxian socialists contend that the anarchist theory, if put into practice, would create a power vacuum of which the worst elements of the present bourgeoisie would take advantage, ushering in a state even worse than that provided by present day capitalism.

Anarchism's appeal rests on the frustration and anger people feel toward the government under capitalism. The U.S. government *is* generally unresponsive to the needs of the people and *does* serve the interests of the rich and powerful much more than it does the rest of us. The despair of many former political activists over the possibility of getting something done through the "normal" political processes grows more widespread every day.

A number of significant events in U.S. history are tied in with anarchism. The famous Haymarket Affair in 1886 in Chicago made world-famous martyrs of several prominent anarchist leaders. The International Workers of the World (IWW) known as the "Wobblies" developed fairly early into an anarchistic direction. Nicola Sacco and Bartolomeo Vanzetti were anarchists as was Emma Goldman, a prominent feminist who lived during the early part of this century.

In practical political affairs the only political activity that makes sense to anarchists is to be disruptive and destructive of the system. They cannot *plan* the next step after the present system is defeated. They have no positive program except for the hope that the people will organize themselves voluntarily. Their hopes, therefore, for the future are utopian and illusionary.

Panacea Movements: From time to time in U.S. history there have emerged one-dimensional movements which claim that a single adjustment to the political economy will lead to a substantive change for the better. Several of these "panacea" movements were popular in the late 19th Century. One of these was the unlimited coinage of silver or the printing of paper money which, by producing an inflationary rise in prices, would allow debt-ridden farmers to pay off their mortgages with cheap money. This naive crusade reached its highest point in the Democratic Party's presidential campaign of William Jennings Bryan in 1896. Henry George, in his book, *Progress and Poverty*, first published in 1879, advocated the establishment of a "single tax" on land as a method for a broad redistribution of wealth. George attracted enough of a following to make a strong run for the office of mayor of New York City in 1886.

More recently, several economists have put forth panacea suggestions. Robert Theobald and others argued in the 1960s for a "negative income tax" to establish a basic economic stability for everyone. All who did not earn up to a certain level would be paid the remainder by the government. Its primary advantage was to be the abolition of the welfare system. It would serve as a more direct, less costly, transfer of income to the poor.

Louis Kelso, co-author with Mortimer Adler of *The Capitalist Manifesto*, has suggested elsewhere a scheme to transfer a significant measure of ownership of large companies to their employees, making them capitalists as well as workers. This would result, he argues, in a return to workers of a larger percentage of the wealth produced by their work as well as control over their enterprise. A variation of this idea has recently been put forth in "socialistic" possibilities that could be exercised by investment policies of the major union pension funds which have now reached large dimensions.

Proposition 13 in California is another example of a panacea movement, although not as straightforward as those just mentioned. Proposition 13 and its kind combine an appeal to middle class economic interests with a huge tax savings for big business. While state surpluses created by inflation have delayed the financial impact of Proposition 13 in California, the likelihood that this alteration of the tax system is going to have a long-term beneficial effect is nonexistent.

The various panacea movements do not take into consideration the alienating results of capitalism, the periodic crises (recessions/depressions) or a number of other contradictions. Additionally, all of these ideas have one thing in common: They do not propose to make any serious inroads on the class position of professionals and managers. It is among such people that panacea movements flash across the horizon for brief moments in history, mildly diverting everyone from the real struggles that cost much more than such movements suggest.

PROBLEMS WITHIN SOCIALISM: NEW FORMS OF REVISIONISM

As was indicated earlier, the assumption of this paper is that the only non-illusionary alternative is Marxian socialism. A history of some of its exciting possibilities has already emerged in socialist revolutions around the world. These positive achievements include both advances toward a more just distribution of material wealth and less alienating forms of human interaction. This does not mean that all problems have been solved in socialist countries or that all problems will ever be solved. Not only will it take time to eradicate the destructive inheritance of late capitalism, there will surely be new contradictions to deal with as history unfolds. At the same time, socialism must be basically liberating for our time for it to be justified. The gains for humanity that it brings into being must exceed the cost it takes to achieve it.

The most complicating factor for the development of socialism that has taken place so far is the fact that socialism has only been attempted in countries that had not developed industrially. Socialism has been able to implement industrialization probably more quickly than capitalism under the circumstances of the 20th Century. Certainly countries like the Soviet Union, Cuba and China have been able to do more in

issues, however, include the following:

• Have some socialist societies "restored capitalism" by relying on material incentives to spur production instead of the "moral" incentives of a commitment to the revolution?

• Have socialist societies in some cases allowed the creation of a "new class" of bureaucrats with different forms of power and privilege but frighteningly similar to the old capitalist ruling class?

• Has a form of "socialist imperialism" arisen where large socialist nations are more interested in exploiting small nations for their own benefit (whether socialist or not) rather than supporting a liberating socialist revolution in those countries?

•Has the development of a genuine democratic political process been taken seriously by socialist countries? To what degree have ordinary men and women been brought into the decision-making processes at all levels: Work place, community and national? Is the "withering away of the state" itself an illusion or is it still a real possibility?

Cynics argue that such revisionism is inevitable, that all attempts to create the "new kind of person and society" are doomed to fail. It is the Marxian socialist conviction that this is not so. Whether or not Marxian socialism itself is also an "illusionary" alternative depends, at least in part, on the kind of socialist commitment people are willing to make. Which side are you on and what are you going to do about it? ■

this regard than comparable "undeveloped" countries within capitalism's orbit. At the same time, having to industrialize has created problems for these countries in trying to implement their socialist visions.

Not everything done in the name of Marxian socialism is necessarily good or desirable. This brings us to our final illusionary category: Socialist revisionism.

"Revisionism," as has already been explained, was originally used to characterize the theories of Eduard Bernstein and social democracy. In another sense, however, it has come to mean any alteration of basic Marxian theory that gets off the track of a liberating transformation of society. This is not the same thing as change in Marxian socialist theory. The difference is between change that brings the revolution closer to its goals and change that interferes with the achievement of those goals.

The question of revisionism is further complicated by the fact that Left political parties are prone to label as "revisionist" any theory in disagreement with their own. It becomes the whipping word used to cut off further debate on any subject.

This misuse of the term must not obscure the fact that there have been fundamental ways in which Left parties and socialist countries have deviated from desirable socialist practices and goals. Left parties and socialist revolutions can go wrong. It is this problem that legitimizes the use of the term "socialist revisionism."

It would be partisan at this point to take a position on the various controversies where "socialist revisionism" is currently being charged. Some of the

Group Exercise

Discuss the readings for this session for half an hour using the following questions as a guide:

1 What other popular myths about socialism come to mind? What objectively-based fears are being expressed in them? What historical developments or conditions gave rise to the consciousness expressed, and what class interests are served by each?

2 In what ways do liberal reformism, populism, social democracy, anarchism and panacea movements ultimately help to sustain capitalism and perpetuate the problems they seek to solve?

3 In your opinion, is fascism a possibility in the United States? If so, what can be done to prevent it?

Assign the following roles to members of the group: A liberal reformer, a populist, a social democrat and a pacificist. (Additional roles could be assigned depending on the size of the group, e.g., a practitioner of pietistic religion, a person involved in the human potential movement, an anarchist, person(s) advocating a single (panacea-type) solution to U.S. societal problems, etc.) Each of the group members is to try to respond to the situations listed below as though they were operating according to the ideology of their assigned political perspective.

Other members of the group are to critique the solutions offered by each and point out the similarities and differences, successes and failures they see. Those doing the critique should keep two questions in mind as they analyze the programs offered by the role players:

1 Whose class interests are best served by each program in the long and short run?

2 Does the program offered actually solve the problem given?

Following the role play, the entire group should spend some time discussing what a critical solution to the situations might have been if none presented by the role players makes sense. Spend about an hour and a half on this entire exercise.

THE SITUATIONS:

• The OPEC nations have just doubled the price of crude oil.

• The Soviet Union has just sent arms and advisors to Marxist revolutionaries in Quasiland, and the revolutionaries are about to overthrow a government which has been friendly to the United States.

• The public schools in your city are segregated, economically bankrupt, and the quality of education has proven to be quite inferior.

• A large industrial factory in your city, employing 8,000 workers, is closing down and moving operations to a city in the Southwest United States.

• The secretaries in a large company in your city are trying to form a union, and a number of the leaders have been fired by the company.

Note: Before your group adjourns, take a moment to preview the Group Exercise at the end of Session 5, to assure adequate preparation for the next meeting.

The Socialist Movement in U.S. History

W.E.B. DU BOIS

MOTHER JONES

EUGENE V. DEBS

WILLIAM D. HAYWOOD

DANIEL DE LEON.

Picheta

Most earlier writers of U.S. history systematically excluded peoples of color and women from the books and articles that were supposed to tell us about our past. Fortunately, a new generation of scholars and popular writers is now producing materials, full of information and insights, which uncover this valuable history. This has generated a sense of pride and purpose, as well as a deeper understanding of the problems and possibilities that must be dealt with, among those once denied their history. Not only is the feminist movement, for example, much larger than it was 15 years ago, but people involved in feminist struggles today have a great deal more information from which to draw strength than was previously available.

Unfortunately, this new trend in the writing of history has not developed evenly. While myriads of books and articles have been written about labor unions and socialist political movements, most history textbooks have largely ignored them. Additionally, no general or popular work has integrated the various aspects of this story.

One of the major reasons for this is the class nature of our educational institutions and the popular media. The dominant financial interests in our society are best served by a history that glorifies the capitalist value system of rugged individualism and those who have attained wealth and power. When working people, labor unions, rebels, revolutionaries, and socialist political organizations are mentioned at all, their roles are usually de-emphasized or they are portrayed as foolish or misguided.

A second reason stems from two important features of the 1950s: A widespread prosperity within the white middle class (partly the fruits of U.S. profits at the expense of the poor nations of the world), plus a major effort to suppress all anti-capitalist and anti-imperialist organizations. These two factors virtually eliminated all voices of dissent. "Communists" were talked about in the most frightening terms in the media although few people actually knew any communists or socialists or had any clear idea of what they stood for beyond the "destruction of the American Way of Life." But it was easy in those days to equate the "American Way of Life" with the temporary blessings of the white middle class.

The New Left, which emerged in the 1960s, had almost no connection with and little awareness of the major Left movements that had contributed so efficaciously to the development of U.S. history from the Civil War to World War II. The time has come to rediscover that history — a panorama of successes and failures, victories and defeats, lessons learned and lessons ignored and a variety of organizational and leadership patterns. We can ignore it only at our peril.

In every new surge of protest against the injustices of our economic and political system, there are many people who assume that a little bit of thought and a lot of enthusiasm will get the job done. Such a notion is totally unfounded. The old saying that those who do not know their history are doomed to repeat it is probably truest of all when applied to revolutionary political change. Serious work around fundamental change in our society requires intense study of the lessons of the past.

In this regard, it is ironic that some U.S. citizens know more about the history of Left parties in other countries, such as the Soviet Union or China, than they do about the Left in their own.

To rectify this, the first reading for this session is Joseph Hardegree, Jr.'s essay on the major Left parties in the United States. Within it, some may feel uncomfortable discussing the Communist Party in the United States (CPUSA). Partially, this comes from being brainwashed by the prevailing capitalist ideology. But the CPUSA is still very much alive, and since many people involved in the struggles for socialism have strong feelings one way or another about that organization, it deserves study and historical analysis. Further, many may feel that the Socialist Party and the Socialist Labor Party had their heydays so long ago that there is nothing we can learn from them.

Hardegree's essay points out that each major Left party has had strengths and weaknesses, achievements and failures, advances and declines. At present, no one party has emerged to attract the imagination of the masses in the United States even though the current worldwide challenge to capitalism is greater than at any time in the past. Given the need for an organizational form that will bring us together for the struggles that lie ahead, real success for such an organization depends on a willingness to learn why past attempts have failed.

The second article in this session is from *The Autobiography of Mother Jones.* Mary Harris Jones was a fearless labor organizer whose best work was with the coal miners during the last quarter of the 19th Century and the first quarter of the 20th. She helped lead many strikes, daring to organize under conditions of extreme danger and hardship. The presence on the battle lines of this elderly woman inspired many a worker to greater commitment.

For most workers today, the struggles are at a higher and more complicated level than those in which Mother Jones fought. But there are still places where even the fundamental right to form a union is objectively denied in this country by certain large corporations, such as J. P. Stevens. Also, in the Third World, a great many transnational corporations are engaging in labor practices that go back to the last century in their ruthlessness and barbarity. So Mother Jones still inspires, reminding us again of the need for courage and steadfastness when taking on an entrenched and powerful ruling class.

"Solidarity on the Embarcadero" is from *Labor's Untold Story* by Richard O. Boyer and Herbert M. Morais. This account of the general strike in San Francisco, around the establishment of the Longshoremen's union in the 1930s, is an example of a strong working relationship between "movement" activists and organized labor. It shows that power can be achieved when workers unite and the politics of class struggle are clear. ∎

Left Political Parties in the United States:

SOME HISTORICAL LESSONS

by Joseph Hardegree, Jr.

Every successful attempt at revolution in the 20th Century has been based on the ability of the leading group to learn the lessons of the past. It is always necessary to analyze what has worked, what has not worked and *why* to better educate and organize so that movement can be made towards substantive structural change.

Refusal or inability to learn these lessons causes any movement to stagnate or slip backward. Our ignorance of the shape and content of the struggles for socialism during the past 100 years can only condemn us to make the same mistakes and suffer the same defeats over and over again. During the 1960s, some assumed that we had nothing to learn from the past. Then, when it was discovered that real change was going to be harder than had been expected, many activists were too easily discouraged. Had the lessons of experience been cumulative instead of ignored, the '60s might have been much more productive.

The purpose of this essay is to provide a quick tour through the history of Left parties in our country, beginning with the period following the Civil War. The primary concern is to analyze some of the consequences of that history for people who have not had the opportunity to study it before. The lessons emphasized here are neither beyond debate nor are they the only ones to be learned. Our advancement in this analysis will depend on the degree to which we are stimulated to do more reading, pondering and discussing of Left history in this country and elsewhere.

Joseph Hardegree is an ordained Disciples of Christ minister currently in the doctoral program in "Religion and Society" at the Graduate Theological Union in Berkeley, CA. During recent years he has been a taxicab driver, a union officer and an editor for *Radical Religion*.

FROM THE CIVIL WAR TO THE TURN OF THE CENTURY

Both a labor movement and a utopian socialist movement existed in the United States during the first half of the 19th Century. The labor movement was generally small and scattered and its gains were few, primarily because industrialization was yet to take hold. Agriculture continued to dominate the economy and the South was still locked into slavery. Indeed, perhaps the most significant labor movement of that period consisted of the various uprisings, slowdowns and other rebellions and survival techniques sparked by slave groups in this country and in Latin America.

Many besides slaves saw the need for a different kind of society. A number of utopian socialist experiments were attempted, including some with a strong religious base such as the Shakers who began in the 1770s, the Amana Community, which eventually settled in Iowa, and the Oneida Community in New York which showed itself to be quite innovative in agriculture, arts and crafts. Under the leadership of John Humphrey Noyes, the Oneida Community developed "mutual criticism" sessions that were remarkably like the "criticism, self-criticism" practices of modern revolutionary parties.

Secularly-based experiments included an attempt in Indiana by Robert Owen to create a more socialistic version of his successful, enlightened-capitalism operation in New Lanark, Scotland. The celebrated Brook Farm, set up and supported mainly by a group of well-known writers such as Nathaniel Hawthorne, Arthur Brisbane, Margaret Fuller, Horace Greeley and Ralph Waldo Emerson was organized on the principles of Charles Fourier, a French writer whose theories (along with those of Robert Owen) drew both praise and criticism from Karl Marx and Friedrich Engels.

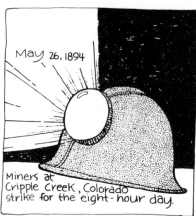

People's History May 29, 1824

Women weavers in Pawtucket, R.I. join first joint strike of men and women workers in the U.S.

January 14, 1879

The last of the Molly Maguires, labor radicals in the Pennsylvania coal fields, hanged.

May 26, 1894

Miners at Cripple Creek, Colorado strike for the 'eight-hour day.'

None of these attempts succeeded in developing a working model as an alternative to capitalism. But even if they did not inspire direct changes in the system, they did generate a lot of interest and contributed to the development of a socialist consciousness in their time.

The Civil War was a great turning point. It destroyed slavery and the semi-feudal political economy of the South and proved to be a great impetus for the development of capitalist enterprise in the North. A great many fortunes were made, a good number through highly devious practices. J. Pierpont Morgan, for example, bought some obsolete rifles from the War Department and then sold them back to the Army at a 600 per cent profit. Philip Armour amassed his fortune by buying meat and selling it to the government at more than twice the price. Morgan and Armour found it much more profitable to pay the $300 fee required to hire a replacement to serve in the Union Army so they could engage in these deals. In paying this modest fee, they joined such "robber barons" as Andrew Carnegie, Jay Gould, James Mellon and John D. Rockefeller.

High finance was not just the concern of a few crafty entrepreneurs, however. Basic industries in the North were greatly strengthened through governmental purchases for the war effort. During the Civil War and the period following (1859 to 1899), the value of manufactured products increased sevenfold. The Northeast, in particular, rapidly expanded its industrial capacity, creating the need to increase the labor supply quickly and dramatically. Most of the workers who came to fill this need were immigrants from Europe, often lured by promises of immediate prosperity. What they found was a chance to work long and hard hours (except during the periodic depressions that occurred) for a very low wage and the opportunity to live in overcrowded and generally wretched conditions.

During this time of rapidly developing, unfettered capitalism, vast fortunes were accumulated by the infamous "robber barons" who often secured their wealth by under-the-table dealings with corrupt government officials. At the same time, the great majority of the working class, including women and children, was being outrageously exploited by wages that barely kept them alive and working conditions that were almost unendurable.

As a result, working people began to organize to improve their lot. Although the rapid and harsh development of capitalism was the prime reason for organizing, there were many other contributing factors. The anti-slavery movement, which came to a climax with emancipation, projected a vision of a transformed society and for the first 10 years after the Civil War significant numbers of blacks and whites worked for some basic changes in the political and social order. The Women's Rights movement had originally been closely associated with the anti-slavery fight, and during much of the period under discussion Women's Rights leaders such as Susan B. Anthony and Elizabeth Cady Stanton identified their struggle for the vote with the general effort to improve the lives of working people.

After every political crisis in Europe another wave of refugees with political interests would arrive in the United States. Many brought with them the new socialist ideology that had been developing in their homelands. After the uprisings in Europe in 1848, the Paris Commune of 1871 and the anti-socialist law in Bismarkian Germany, refugees arrived who had not only an anti-capitalist ideology but also a direct experience of struggle.

These and other currents came together to form the most advanced workers' organizations of the period after the Civil War. The first of these was the National Labor Union (NLU). Under the leadership of William H. Sylvis, the NLU had neither a clear political nor a consistent tactical direction. Sylvis himself pressed for the inclusion of women and blacks in the NLU but was unable to make much headway before he died in 1869. The Knights of Labor, which picked up, in many ways, where the NLU left off, was more successful in uniting into one union men and women, black and white. Unlike the labor unions that later came to dominate most periods of organized labor's history up to the present day, both the NLU and the Knights involved themselves in broader social and political matters as well as the basic economic concerns of their members. Unfortunately, they were not clear or comprehensive in their political analysis.

Systematic investigation of the contradictions of capitalism and a significant strategy for overcoming them had not made headway in this country at that time. The problems were many and massive but what to do about them was not clear. This opened the door to a great many ideas of questionable validity although often of widespread — if shortlived — attractiveness.

One of the more appealing options to many frustrated and oppressed workers was anarchism. The general anarchist strategy was to be as disruptive to the system as possible. This naturally led to strong anarchist support for militant strike activity. It also frequently placed anarchist leaders in a vulnerable position before the police, even when, as was true most of the time, they were engaged in speech-making and organizing activities supposedly guaranteed by the Constitution. Perhaps the most significant moment in the history of anarchism in the United States came in the Haymarket Affair of 1886. Following a bombing incident, the Chicago police arrested a number of prominent anarchists, none of whom were near the explosion. Union members and progressive political people were virtually unanimous in the opinion that the anarchists were framed. Nevertheless, four of those charged were eventually hanged and one committed suicide in prison. For decades after, the Haymarket Affair seared the consciousness of the socialist movement as a glaring symbol of the injustices of capitalist society.

Anarchism, then as now, does not take the problems of political organization in the new socialist society seriously enough. Anarchism assumes that once the structures of the oppressive capitalist state are done away with, broadly-based, thoroughly democratic local groups will spring up and handle organizational problems in a voluntary manner. Most non-anarchists consider this idea utopian. The power vacuum created by the collapse of a government is far more likely to allow the worst elements to take over unless a strong leadership committed to progressive change is prepared to take charge. It is true, nevertheless, that the general anti-capitalist attitude of the anarchists made them an important force during the period after the Civil War when a progressive and unifying revolutionary theory had not yet taken organizational form.

There also appeared, at the time, a number of progressive social movements based on one grand idea, the implementation of which was supposed to solve all problems. The Greenback Party, for example, believed that the printing of more paper money would solve the problems of the indebted, mortgaged-to-the-hilt farmers. One of the central ideas of Populism was the unlimited coinage of gold and silver, a different version of the Greenbackers' theory. Henry George proposed a "single tax" on land as a way of equalizing wealth and managed to attract thousands to his ideas as well as his candidacy for mayor of New York City.

Less simplistic but to be classed in the general category of "panacea" suggestions was the vision presented in the novel, *Looking Backward*, by Edward Bellamy. While Bellamy sought to disassociate himself from the socialist movement, his novel projected a future society organized on many socialist principles. *Looking Backward* was one of the major literary events of the 19th Century.

In the midst of this widespread concern to solve some of the pressing problems brought on by adolescent capitalism, two organizations were created at about the same time. Both advanced the long-range struggle for socialism while simultaneously creating new problems. They were the Socialist Labor Party (SLP) and the American Federation of Labor (AFL).

Founded on Marxian principles in 1877, the SLP was the first generally successful party committed to a socialist revolution. For about 20 years (1880-1900) it was *the* leading Left organization in the United States. For all of its strengths and weaknesses, it led the fight until the Socialist Party came into being. The leading figure in the SLP was Daniel DeLeon, a brilliant theoretician but an eccentric, autocratic personality.

The Federation of Organized Trade Unions was founded in 1881. In 1886 its name was changed to the American Federation of Labor and, under the leadership of Samuel Gompers and his successors, it dominated the labor movement until the 1930s and the rise of the Congress of Industrial Organizations (CIO).

In his early years, Gompers was less explicitly anti-socialist, claiming an appreciation for Marx's *Capital* and engaging in some correspondence with Friedrich Engels. It was not long, however, before he broke with the Left and became the prototype "economist" union leader.

"Economist" is the term Lenin used to describe the

political position of advocating a sharp split between economic and political struggles. Indeed, the founding of both the AFL and SLP at about the same time marked both an advance and a retreat for working people in this country. On the one hand, each represented an advance in working class organization and consciousness. Both labor and the Left were temporarily stronger as a result. On the other hand, for the first time, the political Left and the trade union movement were clearly separated from one another. A labor union leadership emerged which repudiated a socialist analysis, focused labor's interest almost exclusively on bread and butter (narrowly economic) issues and moved away from any serious commitment to socialism. Instead of working to change the political/economic system for the benefit of all, organized labor under Gompers' leadership worked to get a larger share of the profits of capitalism.

This led labor down a predictable road. By looking after narrow economic interests only, certain skilled trades were able to move ahead of the majority of workers in matters of wages and benefits. These workers, sometimes called "labor's aristocracy," by and large became strong supporters of the capitalist system and the source of strength for what came to be an entrenched labor bureaucracy.

Indeed, many labor leaders eventually came to look more and more like successful capitalists themselves, with high salaries and comfortable life styles far removed from the rank and file they were supposedly representing. As some unions became more prosperous, it worried them less and less that certain contracts allowed them to cross picket lines of other unions.

This is not to deny labor's heroic role in the period under discussion. Individual unions, both within the AFL and outside of it, fought many tough battles. Company owners seldom showed any restraint in dealing with unionizing and strikes. The famous Homestead strike against Carnegie Steel in 1892, the Pullman strike of 1894 led by Eugene Debs and the earlier strikes in the coal fields of Pennsylvania (the Molly Maguires) resulted in hundreds of injuries and deaths, most of which were inflicted by hired thugs and even private armies of the companies. One took one's life into one's hands upon becoming a labor organizer or even just a union member back in those days.

Meanwhile, the SLP was introducing, for the first time, some of the enduring problems that have plagued the Left down to the present day. The most important of these was *sectarianism*.

It is difficult to avoid two basic mistakes in socialist political organizing. One is to lose all sense of direction, all theory and analysis, and merely follow the path of least resistance. This error is called *opportunism*. Opportunism can be practiced by any political activist or group — left, right, or middle — and is always a temptation to the Left, especially in a country that has strong "pragmatic" traditions and where it is easy to put someone down as being "overly-theoretical."

This is because of the problem of *dogmatism*. Dogmatism emphasizes a narrowly-defined theory to the exclusion of all other factors. A "correct political doctrine" takes precedence over everything else, including any real and organic relationship with the masses of people.

For revolutionary political success a delicate balance must be maintained. Being in solid touch with the activities and consciousness of the people is absolutely necessary. A firm grasp of theory, analysis and direction is just as necessary. The dogmatic error of sacrificing the masses in favor of "correct doctrine" and the opportunistic error of sacrificing proper theory by catering only to the current consciousness of the people are both wrong. Each is an over-correction of the other. Most pitfalls of Left political organizations tend to one or the other of these alternatives.

A dogmatic attitude usually leads to the practice of *sectarianism*. It is the essence of sectarianism to spend a great deal of time and effort struggling against other Left movements or labor groups. When correct political doctrine becomes the center of activities, all attempts to adjust to the needs of the moment are seen to be betrayals of the cause.

The SLP was a logical reaction to the lack of theory that had been exhibited by movement groups prior to its founding. But it became sectarian, especially in its relationship with the AFL. The SLP alternated between setting up its own separate unions ("dual unionism") and trying to take over the AFL ("boring from within") in a heavy-handed fashion. The SLP's ineptitude at the latter served to strengthen Gompers' militant anti-Left position. Rank and file members of the AFL felt alternately ignored and callously manipulated by the SLP.

By the middle of the 1890s, therefore, some of the continuing problems of the Left had already surfaced. The economic and political dimensions of workers' class interests were divided. A group of labor bureaucrats who were committed to maintaining capitalism rather than changing it had emerged. A Left party with strong sectarian tendencies and a vacillating policy towards organized labor had been formed.

Two other aspects of SLP organization deserve comment. Because its membership was mostly foreign born, many SLP members still had language problems. It was difficult for them to be politically effective outside of their own ethnic groups. It also made the SLP vulnerable to various forms of racism and chauvinism among members of the working class who were English speaking and/or "native born."

The SLP also suffered from a lack of democracy. DeLeon ran the party with an iron hand. Members often found it difficult to work within the narrow confines of his strict rule. The SLP developed strong leadership at the expense of, rather than in tandem with, democratic participation within the party.

Political advancement for any party (meaning that which leads to some measure of real liberation for a society) depends more on making the right move than it does on any particular organizational form. "Democracy," for example, does not always lead to such liberation. Some forms of democracy, as in ancient Athens or in the United States today, easily lend themselves to manipulation by demagogues in the marketplace or powerful figures in corporate board rooms.

A revolutionary party requires strong leadership, especially in the beginning. Usually a highly-disciplined, centralized structure is necessary, particularly when the party is being directly attacked by hostile forces. In the long run, however, the members of any revolutionary or progressive party, as well as the citizenry as a whole, must find a proper form for participation in a genuinely democratic political process. The formula seems to be: *Good leadership plus real participation by the people for the sake of doing that which is truly liberating.* DeLeon and the SLP failed to discover the proper formula.

By the end of the 1890s a great many socialists felt the need to form a new socialist organization. In 1901, several smaller groups which arose virtually simultaneously were merged to form the Socialist Party of America (SP). The SP was the leading Left party from its founding until the end of World War I.

FROM THE EARLY 1900s TO THE END OF WORLD WAR I

At the beginning of the 20th Century, corporate capitalism was still relatively competitive in spite of the monopolistic efforts of the "robber barons." The time was not yet ripe for an industrial system dominated by a few giants in each industry, a system that has largely prevailed in the United States since World War II and, more recently, has come to dominate world capitalism. But there were already signs pointing in that direction. In 1901 the U.S. Steel Corporation was the first company to be initially capitalized at over $1 billion. Business had become very big, if not quite the giant transnational conglomeration of today.

Meanwhile, the internal contradictions of international capitalism were beginning to lead to a world-wide crisis. The "open door" policy toward Asia instituted by the U.S. government in the 1890s had committed it to a role in international politics beyond its expressed designs on Latin America (previously spelled out in the Monroe Doctrine). The expanding needs of rapidly developing U.S. industrial power allowed for no other alternative. The developing industrial forces in Europe and the United States needed markets and raw materials. World War I was a logical result of this increased international competition.

The period in question was also a time of certain advances for labor, the Left and the Women's Movement. Most of the Women's Movement had become largely middle class and singly focused on the right to vote. But women were also emerging in the labor movement as a force with which to be reckoned. Mother Jones was already well-known as a labor organizer, especially for her work among miners, and Elizabeth Gurley Flynn was beginning to make a name for herself as an orator and organizer.

The black struggle produced a new leader in

W.E.B. Dubois, who helped found and give primary leadership to the NAACP (first called the Niagara Movement). Dubois challenged the accommodationist strategies of Booker T. Washington and set the stage for a new black consciousness and culture still growing today.

By the turn of the century, Native Americans had entered into a long period of colonial repression in their relations with the dominant culture. The U.S. government, through its Bureau of Indian Affairs, established institutions which seemed bent on eradicating Indian culture while keeping most Native Americans isolated and oppressed. Mexican Americans in the Southwest found themselves increasingly repressed by the flood of people of European ancestry moving West, while the Asian communities on the West Coast had, from the first day of their arrival, been subjected to severe economic exploitation and a virulent racism.

The AFL continued to grow under Gompers' leadership but it became even more anti-socialist and pro-capitalist. Gompers went so far as to join, for a few years, the National Civic Federation, an organization set up by big business to provide a chance for "business and labor to work together in their common interests."

The Socialist Party of America surpassed the SLP in influence from the very beginning. The SLP has continued its existence down to the present day although it has not been a serious factor since World War I. In contrast to the SLP, the SP developed a much larger constituency, most of which was "native born," although it did succeed in organizing numerous ethnic groups. The SP's organizational practice also was different — more in keeping with the town meeting democratic traditions of an earlier time in U.S. history. While the SP did not present any final resolution of how best to organize the Left, its democratic swing away from DeLeon's non-democratic style was a healthy move.

Many leaders of the SP were quite progressive on matters of racial and sexual equality but in the main the SP did not deal adequately with these issues. Some SP members and leaders on the West Coast (Jack London, for example) led the way in fanning up race hatred against the Chinese.

Whereas the SLP had concentrated its work in a few big cities, the SP involved itself in grass roots politics all across the country. Local elections were won in hundreds of cities and towns and some socialist candidates were elected to Congress. Ira Kipnis describes SP achievements in *The American Socialist Movement: 1897-1912* as follows:

> At the height of its power it had over 150,000 dues-paying members, published hundreds of newspapers, won almost a million votes for its presidential candidate, elected more than 1,000 of its members to political office, secured passage of a considerable body of legislation, won the support of one third of the American Federation of Labor, and was instrumental in organizing the Industrial Workers of the World. A study of the Socialist Party is essential if we are to understand such American developments as industrial unionism, national and municipal ownership of public utilities, socialized Christianity, restrictions on immigration, women's rights, labor legislation, municipal reform, and the general attack on privilege and corruption known as the Progressive Movement.

A great many clergy were members of the SP, the most prominent of which was the Rev. George Herron, a Congregationalist minister. Herron was a leading figure in the party, especially during its peak years of influence. Other socialists of the period were W.D.P. Bliss, who was instrumental in founding the Society of Christian Socialists in Boston in 1889; Vida Scudder, an Episcopal activist who taught at Wellesley College; Walter Rauschenbusch, the well-known theologian of the Social Gospel movement; and the Rev. George Washington Woodbey, a black minister, of the Mt. Zion Baptist Church, San Diego.

The perennial SP candidate for president was Eugene V. Debs, the party's most effective orator and best known figure. Debs came up through the ranks as a railroad worker, organizer and editor who led the great Pullman Car strike in 1894. He had a great sensitivity for the oppressed, well expressed in his famous statement before the judge who sent him to prison for his opposition to World War I:

> Your honor, years ago I recognized my kinship with all living beings, and I made up my mind that I was not one bit better than the meanest on earth. I said then, and I say now, that while there is a lower class, I am in it; while there is a criminal element, I am of it; and while there is a soul in prison, I am not free.

The SP was not able to solve the problem of how to relate to the labor movement. The major effort of this period was the establishment in 1905 of the International Workers of the World (IWW), the famous "wobblies." Some of the SP leaders instrumental in forming this greatest of all "dual unions," were Big Bill Haywood of the Western Federation of Miners, Mother Jones and Gene Debs. The IWW was the most serious attempt in U.S. history to create a political, revolutionary-oriented union. Unfortunately, it also quickly developed a simplistic ideology based on the panacea notion of the general strike. But the idea of "one big union" that cut across all restrictive barriers of caste and craft was sound, and nourished industrial unionism during a period when the craft-based AFL held hegemony in the labor movement. The IWW led many difficult strikes and

People's History

February 6, 1919
General strike in Seattle, Washington. 65,000 workers walk out in support of striking shipyard workers.

STRIKE

SEPTEMBER 22, 1919
Massive steel strike begins, involving 365,000 workers. Nearly every mill in the country is shut down. In the process, 22 workers are killed and thousands more wounded.

January 2, 1920
"Anti-red" Palmer Raids arrest 5,000 persons, jail 3,000. Hundreds are deported.
from U.S.A.

produced some authentic labor heroes, including the famous song writer, Joe Hill, who was executed in Utah in 1915. The charge was murder but many people across the country and overseas thought his chances of getting a fair trial were virtually non-existent because of his role as a labor radical. Joe Hill and others organized in regions of the country, especially the West, that the AFL had been loathe to touch.

World War I proved to be a turning point for the SP as it was for socialism and capitalism. Response to the war provoked a major division in the world socialist movement. On the one side were those who believed that the working class should express a greater solidarity with the workers of other countries than with the ruling classes of their own. Most appeals to patriotism were seen by this side as artful manipulation by the ruling classes to get workers to fight the wars that the ruling classes wanted to wage against one another. Debs, among others (including Lenin in Russia), interpreted World War I as a quarrel among capitalists in which socialists should have no part.

Others were unable to resist the appeals to national patriotism made in every country. Gene Debs, as a war resister, went to jail for his stand against the war and from his prison cell received almost a million votes for president during the 1920 election. By that time, however, the great days of the SP were over. It had reached its zenith in 1912 and was already in decline two years later when World War I began in Europe. Conservative and middle class elements had come to control the party, its working class base had eroded and its militancy declined appreciably.

The final SP crisis was brought about by the revolution in Russia in 1917. The emergence of Lenin and the Bolshevik party had two immediate consequences for the world socialist movement. It established the credibility of Lenin's organizational principles (call-ing for a tightly disciplined party of full-time "professional" revolutionaries) and frightened the leading capitalist powers into a frenzy of anti-socialist repression.

By 1920, the SP was largely an organization of doctors, lawyers, academics and clergy. Gene Debs no longer had much influence after he got out of prison in 1921 and he died just a few years later. Norman Thomas, a thoroughly middle class clergyman (who later collaborated with the government in a drive against the "reds"), replaced Gene Debs in leadership of the SP. The IWW also was not able to effect much after the war. While both the SP and the IWW continue to the present day, they exist without significant influence.

It was logical and healthy that the SP had introduced both a more democratic and less dogmatic theoretical commitment and organizational form than that practiced by the SLP. But in the long run, this did not prove to be sufficient either.

Following hard on the heels of the Russian Revolution and the end of World War I were the notorious Palmer Raids. Attorney General A. Mitchell Palmer rounded up for trial, imprisonment and (in many cases) deportation thousands of IWW's, SP members and anarchists. The time of *relatively* free and above ground organizing which the SP had largely enjoyed throughout most of its life was over.

FROM THE END OF WORLD WAR I TO THE END OF WORLD WAR II

The 1920s are characterized by the media as a wild and giddy era. In fact, those years marked certain gains for some people and the lifting of the puritanical restraints that had prevailed before the war. It is always a relief when a war ends whatever its causes and outcome. For U.S. capitalism, things never looked brighter. Most of the European capitalist nations had suffered serious setbacks in the war while U.S. capitalism came out of it relatively stronger than it went in. Just enough fortunes were being made in new industries related to the automobile and real estate booms to feed the myth of success being right around the corner for anyone willing to take a chance. Topping it off was the rapid growth of a new medium, the film industry, emerging out of Hollywood to provide amusement, distraction and fantasy for the masses, largely in support of capitalist ideology.

The larger cities in the North had received a steady stream of blacks from the South during the first two decades of the century and in New York City this led to the development of the Harlem Renaissance, a flowering of urban black culture. Black political consciousness was also growing, finding expression in Marcus Garvey's "Back to Africa" movement. The general lot of black people, however, showed little improvement. Race riots still occurred every several years and lynchings were common; the Ku Klux Klan experienced a new birth in both the North and the South.

During and immediately after the war, two major strikes — one among packinghouse workers and the other in the steel industry — provided a harbinger of things to come. Both were led brilliantly by a relatively unknown radical named William Z. Foster. The steel strike of 1919 involved over 350,000 workers and was finally defeated after a bitter struggle. But Foster was to play a leading role in the Communist Party (CPUSA) for the next 35 years.

Two communist parties were formed in the United States in the aftermath of the war. Both looked to the new Soviet leadership for approval and it was in response to Soviet pressure that they moved to form a single Communist Party.

The Bolshevik party, led by Lenin in Russia ("Bolshevik" is the Russian term for "majority"), had operated with a tight organizational pattern. Party members were expected to be "professional revolutionaries" for whom work was primarily for the sake of organizing and only secondarily a way of making a living. All other commitments took second place to the party's plans. The party was to have a firm theoretical center with a day-to-day tactical flexibility.

Compared to the ideological and organizational looseness of the SP, the tighter organization of the Bolsheviks presented an attractive alternative to U.S. socialists. They also had the glow of success in an actual revolution, something that had eluded U.S. radicals. The Bolsheviks had also found it necessary to struggle with a vicious police repression forcing them into a great deal of underground activity. The generally repressive methods employed by the U.S. government after World War I made it clear to the Left that a party organization was needed which could handle that kind of struggle.

Lenin was a writer for most of his revolutionary career and had produced a number of major theoretical works. He provided what came to be seen in the eyes of many as *the* successful distillation and update of Marx's works, with a strength and appropriateness that made his writing stand on its own merits. The translation of his essays into all of the major languages in the early 1920s influenced socialist movements across the world beyond measure.

More than anything else, the Russian Revolution stimulated the formation of new parties along Leninist lines all over the world. For the first time a major nation was embarking on a socialist journey.

In the United States, the CPUSA quickly became the dominant political force on the Left, a position it held from the 1920s until the "Cold War" period following World War II. Since World War II, of course, the CPUSA has continued to exist and has even shared in the rebirth of the Left dating from the 1960s. It is still larger than any of the "New Left"

parties. But the era of its hegemony on the Left and its influence on U.S. politics in general ended with the Cold War.

During the 1920s the CPUSA's relationship with the Soviet Union was primarily beneficial to the party. It was under pressure from abroad, for example, that the CPUSA instituted a serious attempt to organize among non-whites, especially in the black community. By the end of that decade there was a strong contingent of blacks in the CPUSA as well as a coherent theory of Black Liberation in this country. A similar attempt was made to encourage women to membership and leadership roles in the party, although achievements in this area, while real, were not as great.

The CPUSA rightly insisted that the majority of its membership be of working class origin or present circumstances. This was a conscious change from the practice of the SP and in keeping with Bolshevik experience. The party did not exclude professionals from its ranks and it did not neglect working closely with various professionals and their organizations but it made a clear stand on behalf of a working class focus for its membership and activities.

Probably the leading churchperson who was closely connected to CPUSA politics was the Rev. Claude Williams, a Presbyterian (originally) who worked with tenant farmers and across racial lines in the South and then organized among Detroit workers during World War II. The Rev. Harry Ward of Union Theological Seminary was a leading socialist during the 1920s and 30s who, along with his associate, Winifred Chappell, of the Methodist Federation for Social Service strongly supported both the Soviet Union and the CPUSA in most of its activities. Reinhold Niebuhr's well-known early socialism was primarily in support of the Socialist Party and against the CPUSA. Niebuhr later became a leading ideologist for the Cold War mentality of the McCarthy era although he disagreed with the methods used by McCarthy himself.

The CPUSA discovered almost from the beginning that it had to be a partially underground organization. It was politically dangerous for most party members to identify themselves as such.

By 1921, when the CPUSA was formed, it was no longer "legitimate" to advocate socialism. The government, most educational institutions and the mass media operated a huge propaganda mill against Marxism, socialism and communism. It became difficult for most people to gain honest information about a socialist alternative and vivid images of the "red menace" were effectively burned into popular consciousness.

From World War I right up to the present, the U.S. government has maintained agencies, committees, laws and a spy network aimed at destroying the Left or at least rendering it harmless. That the CPUSA and other Left groups have had to combine "underground" with open activities under these circumstances should not be surprising. Nevertheless, a price has been paid in terms of general effectiveness.

Throughout the history of the U.S. Left, there have been other party organizations active besides the three central ones described. One of the major ones came into being during the late 1920s as a result of a conflict between the policies advocated by Stalin and Leon Trotsky.

Trotsky and Stalin, both leaders of the Russian Revolution, had clashed over the question of whether the revolution had to proceed quickly into all countries of the world or whether the new Soviet Union might have to build "socialism in one country" for a while. Trotsky was an advocate of the former and Stalin the latter. Corresponding to this difference of opinion were Stalin's basically pragmatic approach and Trotsky's tendency toward dogmatism. After the break between Stalin and Trotsky (with Trotsky being exiled and later assassinated) a division on the Left occurred in the United States (as in most other places) between the "Stalinists" of the CPUSA and the "Trotskyists" of what came to be called the Socialist Workers Party (SWP). While the CPUSA was not without problems of its own, the main failing of the SWP has been its dogmatism and sectarianism. A primary criticism leveled by opponents of the SWP is that SWP members have spent a disproportionate amount of energy in polemics with the CPUSA and other Left organizations and not enough struggling directly against capitalism. For them there is, apparently, only one revolution — the perfect one — and whenever a country or party makes a mistake or follows any other path than that laid out by Marx or (sometimes) Lenin or Trotsky himself (as interpreted by the SWP), they have hopelessly betrayed the revolution.

The CPUSA itself has not totally avoided sectarian tendencies. Indeed, sectarianism has been a constant problem on the Left in the United States, from the time of the SLP until the present. But the Trotskyist parties generally established the paradigm for that particular tendency.

Throughout the 1920s the CPUSA repeated the SLP error of following a dual union strategy and did not make much headway with the labor movement. But the Depression in the 1930s presented a great opportunity for a different strategy and the CPUSA made the most of it. Its greatest achievement was the central role it played in the establishment of the Congress of Industrial Organizations (CIO). Pushing industry-wide unions, (contrary to AFL policy), and with a strong multi-racial base from which to work, the CPUSA contributed greatly to the CIO's success. Many (in some industries *most*) of the best CIO organizers were CPUSA members. The CIO fought some tough battles before victory came, one of the most dramatic occurring in the automobile industry, where a successful sitdown strike took place at the Chevrolet plant in Flint, MI. In that struggle the solidarity of whole families, with both women and men playing key roles, was a landmark effort of successful labor organizing. CPUSA members were centrally involved.

The CPUSA emerged as a champion of the rights of black people through their organizing efforts on behalf of the "Scottsboro Boys," a group of black teenagers accused of raping two white women while all were riding in a railroad freight car. One of the women later went around the country claiming the accused were innocent but, in any event, the possibility of young blacks being dealt with fairly in a racist southern court system was nil. When the CPUSA came to their defense it attracted world-wide attention and symbolized the CPUSA's commitment to racial justice, thereby helping to advance the cause of the party.

World War I marked the conclusion of Socialist Party influence, by bringing new pressures and contradictions to bear and by exposing some long standing weaknesses; World War II did the same for the CPUSA.

The inspiration and leadership the CPUSA received from the Soviet Union in the 1920s (and even into the 1930s) were largely beneficial. But as World War II loomed on the horizon the close ties with the U.S.S.R. came to be a nagging liability.

The Soviet Union was facing a dire threat from the West in the form of Nazi Germany. There was also the relatively well-known conviction among other Western governments that the best thing that could happen would be to let Germany and Russia fight it out to the destruction of both. For these and other reasons the U.S.S.R. anticipated (correctly, as it turned out) that it would have to bear the brunt of a war against Germany. Political unity at top leadership levels took on a critical urgency in the minds of Stalin and his advisors.

This led to some harsh decisions by the Soviet Union. One was the well-known Moscow purge trials, leading to the execution of some former leaders of the party. Even more confusing was the unexpected peace treaty between the U.S.S.R. and Germany (which was later correctly seen as growing out of the Soviet Union's need to buy time).

The CPUSA was caught in a bind in both of these developments. The purge trials had the look of the revolution devouring its own children. The official line of the U.S.S.R. prior to the treaty with Germany

had been a "United Front Against Fascism" — so eloquently put forth by Georgy Dimitrov just a few years before — a line which the CPUSA had enthusiastically supported. Overnight the line became "peace at any price." Between these two maneuvers — the purge trials and the reversal on relations with Germany — the CPUSA lost much of the credibility it had built up throughout most of the 1930s.

After Germany attacked the Soviet Union, the CPUSA immediately endorsed all out support for the war effort. Under the leadership of Earl Browder, the CPUSA abandoned virtually all concern for workers' rights and the struggle for socialism in favor of greater war production and military effectiveness. The CPUSA was even dissolved as a political party and reconstituted as an educational association. Strikes were opposed, no matter how serious the workers' grievances. Zeal for an allied victory became the only goal. Browder developed such a high level of enthusiasm for the party's class collaboration with the leaders of what later came to be called the "military-industrial complex" that it proved to be a disaster for the party as well as his own career within it.

At the turn of the century, Lenin became a vigorous opponent of the line put forth by Eduard Bernstein (a member of the German Social Democratic Party), who believed that socialist goals could be entirely obtained by working within a capitalist parliamentary system. Marx had argued, and Lenin agreed, that when capitalists are really threatened they will not give up control without first doing everything in their power to destroy those who were advocating socialism. Marx further believed that all democratic forms and civil liberties in such countries as the United States and England would be swept away by the capitalists in power before they would relinquish control.

Bernstein's theory came to be called *revisionism*, meaning that the fundamental, revolutionary theory was being "revised" to the point of crippling compromise. However, no one ever argued that Marxism was a sacred dogma never to be questioned or changed. The opposite is the case. Even the most dogmatic hold that there is a necessity for the growth and development of theory. It has been stated over and over again, beginning with Marx himself, that socialist theory must constantly be altered as different political realities and new experiences of political practice emerge. Theory and practice are both in constantly interacting evolution.

The CPUSA, responding to criticisms from the international communist movement, removed Browder from leadership after World War II and severely criticized as "revisionist" the path it had followed under him. But by that time the damage had been done. The party had lost support from without and within because of the purge trials and the turn about of the Soviet Union's relations with Germany. Because of its lack of a revolutionary leadership during the war, others dropped by the wayside. After the war, the party was extremely vulnerable and the forces on the Right were able to take advantage.

Moreover, even though Browder had been disgraced, "Browderism" continued to prevail. It is the opinion of most new party organizations that the CPUSA never did return to the militant revolutionary political position it had held in the 1930s. The "revisionist" position of working for socialism through electoral politics (with expectations that those with wealth and power will voluntarily give it up when they are outvoted), still seems to be the position of the CPUSA.

In a pattern similar to what followed World War I, it was easy for the leading forces of capitalism to whip up anti-Left hysteria post-World War II. Again a major nation, China this time, emerged as a socialist country. The U.S.S.R. was able to exert pressure in support of socialist revolutions all along its border in Eastern Europe (partly in response to threatening moves from the United States and its NATO allies) and seemed to be in a position to grow strong very quickly in spite of having lost 20,000,000 lives in the war. The United States once again emerged from the world war as a stronger imperialist power than before and sought to contain or defeat all socialist threats to its power and economic interests at home and abroad. The CPUSA faced its sternest test in its most weakened condition.

Shortly after the war, opponents of socialism within the CIO insisted that all of its member unions purge their ranks of communist office holders. Most unions did so; 11 did not. Of the 11, however, only two were of any significant size: The Longshoremen's Union on the West Coast and the United Electrical Workers. For the next 20 years, organized labor fell prey to anti-communist ideology. Its leadership even collaborated with the State Department and the Central Intelligence Agency to play an anti-communist role in the international labor movement.

Almost everyone is familiar with the Smith Act trials and McCarthyism in the late 1940s and early 1950s. The Smith Act sent most of the top CPUSA leaders to jail and McCarthy helped create a climate of hysteria that put even establishment liberals in jeopardy. The era of Communist Party dominance on the Left in the United States was over.

The CPUSA was a decided advance over the SP and much can be gained from studying its history in detail. But it is ultimately counterproductive for a U.S.-based Left party to over-identify with a foreign revolution. For one thing, revolutions are not trans-ferable from one set of historical conditions to another. Much can be learned from successful revolutions elsewhere, but every revolution has to be indigenous to the people, the history and the circumstances of the country in which it takes place. The CPUSA became more and more involved in defending Soviet foreign policy and less interested in carrying on a socialist revolution in this country. Today, at best, it is a progressive force in the labor movement but is no longer the influential Left party that it once was.

FROM THE 1950s UNTIL THE PRESENT

The 1950s marked the lowest point of Left activity in the United States since the Civil War. U.S. imperialism was at its height, bringing back home the super profits it gained from Third World countries, allowing for an improvement in the standard of living for many U.S. citizens, including workers with strong unions. A new "middle class" emerged which had its roots in the hard days of the Depression and was easy to convince that the new prosperity it was enjoying made the "American System" the best of all possible worlds.

Anti-communism was so strong that a whole generation grew up knowing virtually nothing about Marx, Lenin, socialism or the political and labor struggles working people had carried on so valiantly over the years.

The Chinese Revolution did not immediately have the energizing effect on the U.S. Left that the Russian Revolution had following World War I. The Chinese decided to concentrate on their own revolution (especially after the Korean War) and the U.S. government made it virtually impossible for U.S. citizens to visit China.

The net result was that the 1950s are almost a blank page in the history book of the U.S. Left. But things were not totally quiet.

The most important political event in the 1950s was the eruption of a new Black Liberation struggle. World War II had served as a catalyst for change in its use of non-white military personnel, usually either on the front lines or in menial, servant-like roles such as cooks, valets to generals, etc. Several riots ensued during the war period, including the well-known "Zoot Suit" riots in the Chicano community of East Los Angeles in 1943, which served notice that ethnic minorities were not happy with what was happening either. As non-white soldiers moved out across the world and, in many cases, died in the war, those who returned were less willing just to go back to the ghettos and endure the status quo.

Black struggles escalated after the U.S. Supreme Court ruled in 1954 that school segregation was un-

constitutional. In 1955 in Montgomery, AL, a black woman named Rosa Parks refused to give up her bus seat to a white. This sparked the Montgomery bus boycott. From this incident emerged the leadership of Martin Luther King, Jr., and the Black Church, and until the late 1960s, when the Vietnam war protest gained the ascendency, the struggles of black people were at the center of movement activity. A general consciousness of oppression ignited the uprising of liberation movements by all national minorities — women, gays, seniors, handicapped persons and others.

Progressive church people played a significant part in this rebirth of militancy. Black churches in the South were often the central staging grounds for Civil Rights activities in those dangerous times. The first "sit-ins" in 1959 were organized by delegates returning home from a Student Christian Movement conference. A great many religious leaders became involved in Civil Rights and Anti-War activities.

The Left was rejuvenated in 1962 at a meeting of the Students for a Democratic Society (SDS) in Port Huron, MI. Other student-based groups also were formed, including the Student Non-Violent Coordinating Committee (SNCC) and the Resistance, an anti-draft group. The Black Panther Party was founded in 1966.

These student organizations were able to provide a fresh impetus to the Left. The old Left was dormant; the "New Left" came to life. Because of the gap in consciousness and historical development of the Left throughout the 1950s, the New Left presumed there was nothing to be learned from the past. Therefore it plunged immediately into making many of the old mistakes afresh. To its credit, the New Left radicalized a significant portion of an entire generation and had a consciousness raising effect on the whole country. Its major achievement was changing the minds of the majority about the Vietnam war. It also

instituted life style changes that appear to have had a permanent effect on the culture, causing many to maintain a negative attitude toward the "rat race" of daily capitalism.

The war in Vietnam brought contemporary capitalism in the United States to its present crisis. In Vietnam, the cost of maintaining the world safe for capitalist investment began to exceed the profits from those investments. The consequences have become increasingly severe.

Today, every major institution in our society is in trouble: The Economy, Education, Health Care, Transportation, the Legal System, the Welfare System, etc. The "energy" industry is telling us that because of shortages we must both pay dearly for its supplies and suffer the destruction of the environment. Not since the 1930s has mass anger reached its current level. The opportunity and the need for a new leading Left political party has never been greater.

But the Left is still, to a great degree, in disarray. It has yet to bring the major forces of the movement together into one leading organization in the way the SLP, the SP and the CPUSA were able to do. As long as this situation exists, the struggle for socialism will have difficulty moving forward.

The New Left's most glaring weakness was its lack of a sense of history. It often assumed that it was the first generation which had grappled with capitalism. But toward the end of the 1960s several things happened. One of these was a rediscovery of Marx and the general socialist tradition, with a new excitement about China, thanks to a flood of information about that revolution. The revolution next door in Cuba played a similarly inspiring role. That the Vietnamese were carrying on a socialist revolution also took on increasing significance in the minds of those opposing the war.

A second development was that many students left

campus (or were expelled) for jobs in industry where they began to organize among workers. The recent rise in militant rank and file movements in the major unions is at least partly a result of the efforts of these former students.

The most important phenomenon, however, has been the rise of numerous organizations attempting to develop the successful Left party organization for our time. Even though none of these parties or pre-party formations has gained hegemony on the Left, a unifying party movement could well emerge in the 1980s. If such a party emerges, it will do so at least partly on the basis of learning some of the lessons indicated in this essay. Like all lessons, they are easier to state than to put into practice. But the following list should serve as a summary for discussion.

1. Labor and the socialist movement must be re-united. There can be no change in class relations with one or many organizations fighting for economic gains for its membership (and supporting only those changes in the law which assist such endeavors) and other organizations carrying on separate struggles for socialism.

2. Left organizations and progressive political activists need to carry on much more investigation of the histories of their predecessors, at home and abroad, to understand what really worked, as well as what did not work, and why.

3. Theory has to be firm enough to sustain the basic direction of the struggle but not so rigid as to become unquestioned dogma. As has been classically stated: Theory must support practice and practice must contribute to the reformulation of theory.

4. Democracy and the ability to make and implement decisions must be held together. A thorough reconsideration of political organization is called for. How can effective leadership emerge? How can party members and non-party members participate in the decisions that have to be made? The SLP was too authoritarian; the SP could not develop unity. There must be a way to combine the need for unity and leadership with the participatory inheritance of our culture. Finding that way is the present "party building" task.

5. An effective U.S. movement cannot tie itself to a foreign revolution even though it must learn from the successes and failures of all revolutions. When supporting or criticizing a foreign revolutionary party becomes the main task of a Left party in this country, it forfeits all chances for making a significant contribution to the U.S. revolutionary process.

A party should be deeply rooted in a given national historical context. The sources of revolutionary experience and theory are international as well as domestic but the revolution is always indigenous to a people if it is to be successful.

6. The problem of number four (above) should not deter us from the necessity of building a new leading Left party. Truly liberating and substantive change does not occur spontaneously. ∎

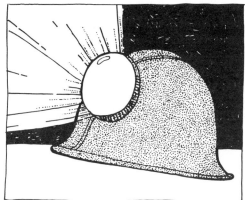

Victory in West Virginia
by Mary Harris "Mother" Jones

One morning when I was west, working for the Southern Pacific machinists, I read in the paper that the Paint Creek Coal Company would not settle with their men and had driven them out into the mountains. I knew that Paint Creek country. I had helped the miners organize that district in 1904 and now the battle had to be fought all over again.

I canceled all my speaking dates in California, tied up all my possessions in a black shawl — I like traveling light — and went immediately to West Virginia. I arrived in Charleston in the morning, went to a hotel, washed up and got my breakfast early in order to catch the one local train a day that goes into Paint Creek.

The train wound in and out among the mountains, dotted here and there with the desolate little cabins of miners. From the brakemen and the conductor of the train I picked up the story of the strike. It had started on the other side of the Kanawha hills in a frightful district called "Russia," — Cabin Creek. Here the miners had been peons for years, kept in slavery by the guns of the coal company, and by the system of paying in scrip so that a miner never had any money should he wish to leave the district. He was cheated of his wages when his coal was weighed, cheated in the company store where he was forced to purchase his food, charged an exorbitant rent for his kennel in which he lived and bred, docked for school tax and burial tax and physician and for "protection," which meant the gunmen who shot him back into the mines if he rebelled or so much as murmured against his outrageous exploitation. No one was allowed in the Cabin Creek district without explaining the reason for being there to the gunmen who patrolled the roads, all of which belonged to the coal company. The miners finally struck — it was a strike of desperation.

Mother Jones was a leading organizer for the United Mine Workers Union and other working class causes for many decades. This article is reprinted with permission from *The Autobiography of Mother Jones*, edited by Mary Field Parton, pp. 148-168. Copyright © 1925; third edition, revised 1976 by Charles H. Kerr Publishing Co.; Chicago, IL.

The strike of Cabin Creek spread to Paint Creek, where the operators decided to throw their fate in with the operators of Cabin Creek. Immediately all civil and constitutional rights were suspended. The miners were told to quit their houses, and told at the point of a gun. They established a tent colony in Holly Grove and Mossey. But they were not safe here from the assaults of the gunmen, recruited in the big cities from the bums and criminals.

To protect their women and children, who were being shot with poisoned bullets, whose houses were entered and rough-housed, the miners armed themselves as did the early settlers against the attacks of wild Indians.

"Mother, it will be sure death for you to go into the Creeks," the brakeman told me. "Not an organizer dares go in there now. They have machine guns on the highway, and those gunmen don't care whom they kill."

The train stopped at Paint Creek Junction and I got off. There were a lot of gunmen, armed to the teeth, lolling about. Everything was still and no one would know of the bloody war that was raging in those silent hills, except for the sight of those guns and the strange, terrified look on everyone's face.

I stood for a moment looking up at the everlasting hills when suddenly a little boy ran screaming up to me, crying, "Oh Mother Jones! Mother Jones! Did you come to stay with us?" He was crying and rubbing his eyes with his dirty little fist.

"Yes, my lad, I've come to stay," said I.

A guard was listening.

"You have?" says he.

"I have!" says I.

The little fellow threw his arms around my knees and held me tight.

"Oh Mother, Mother," said he, "they drove my papa away and we don't know where he is, and they threw my mama and all the kids out of the house and they beat my mama and they beat me."

He started to cry again and I led him away up the creek. All the way he sobbed out his sorrows, sorrows no little child should ever know; told of brutalities no child should ever witness.

"See, Mother, I'm all sore where the gunmen hit me," and he pulled down his cotton shirt and showed me his shoulders which were black and blue.

"The gunmen did that?"

"Yes, and my mama's worse'n that!" Suddenly he began screaming, "The gunmen! The gunmen! Mother, when I'm a man I'm going to kill 20 gunmen for hurting my mama! I'm going to kill them dead — all dead!"

I went to the miners' camp in Holly Grove where all through the winter, through snow and ice and blizzard, men and women and little children had

MOTHER JONES

shuddered in canvas tents that America might be a better country to live in. I listened to their stories. I talked to Mrs. Sevilla whose unborn child had been kicked dead by gunmen while her husband was out looking for work. I talked with widows, whose husbands had been shot by the gunmen; with children whose frightened faces talked more effectively than their baby tongues. I learned how the scabs had been recruited in the cities, locked in boxcars, and delivered to the mines like so much pork.

"I think the strike is lost, Mother," said an old miner whose son had been killed.

"Lost! Not until your souls are lost!" said I.

I traveled up and down the Creek, holding meetings, rousing the tired spirits of the miners. I got 3,000 armed miners to march over the hills secretly to Charleston, where we read a declaration of war to Governor Glasscock who, scared as a rabbit, met us on the steps of the state house. We gave him just 24 hours to get rid of the gunmen, promising him that hell would break loose if he didn't. He did. He sent the state militia in, who at least were responsible to society and not to the operators alone.

One night in July, a young man, Frank Kenney, came to me. "Mother," he said, "I have been up to Charleston trying to get some one to go up to Cabin Creek, and I can't get anyone to go. The national officers say they don't want to get killed. Boswell told me you were over here in the Paint Creek and that perhaps you might come over into the Cabin Creek district."

"I'll come up," said I. "I've been thinking of invading that place for some time."

I knew all about Cabin Creek — old Russia. Labor organizer after organizer had been beaten into insensibility, thrown into the creek, tossed into some desolate ravine. The creek ran with the blood of brave men, of workers who had tried to escape their bondage.

"Where can we hold our meetings?" I asked.

"I don't know, Mother. The company owns every bit of dust for 20 square miles about. And the guards arrest you for trespassing."

"Is there an incorporated village anywhere near?"

"Eksdale," said he, "is free."

"Bill a meeting for me there Tuesday night. Get the railway men to circulate the bills."

Monday night, a fellow by the name of Ben Morris, a national board member came to me and said, "Mother, I understand you are going up to Cabin Creek tomorrow. Do you think that is wise?"

"It's not wise," said I, "but necessary."

"Well, if you go, I'll go," said he.

"No, I think it is better for me to go alone. You represent the National office. I don't. I'm not responsible to anyone. If anything happens and you are there, the operators might sue the Union for damages. I go as a private citizen. All they can do to me is put me in jail. I'm used to that."

He left me and went directly to the governor and told him to send a company of the militia up to Cabin Creek as I was going up there. Then he got the sheriff to give him a body guard and he sneaked up behind me. At any rate I did not see him or the militia on the train nor did I see them when I got off.

In Eksdale a sympathetic merchant let me stay in his house until the meeting began.

When I got off the train, two or three miners met me.

"Mother," they said, "did you know there is a detective along with you. He's behind you now . . . the fellow with the red necktie."

I looked around. I went up to him.

"Isn't your name Corcoran?" said I.

"Why, yes," said he, surprised.

"Aren't you the Corcoran who followed me up New River in the strike of 1902? You were working for the Chesapeake and Ohio Railroad and the coal company then."

"Why, yes," said he, "but you know people change!"

"Not sewer rats," said I. "A sewer rat never changes!"

That night we held a meeting. When I got up to speak I saw the militia that the national organizer had had the governor send. The board member was there. He had made arrangements with the local chairman to introduce him. He began speaking to the men about being good and patient and trusting to the justice of their cause.

I rose. "Stop that silly trash," said I. I motioned him to a chair. The men hollered, "Sit down! Sit down!"

He sat. Then I spoke.

"You men have come over the mountains," said I, "12, 16 miles. Your clothes are thin. Your shoes are out at the toes. Your wives and little ones are cold and hungry! You have been robbed and enslaved for years! And now Billy Sunday comes to you and tells you to be good and patient and trust to justice! What silly trash to tell to men whose goodness and patience has cried out to a deaf world."

I could see the tears in the eyes of those poor fellows. They looked up into my face as much as to say, "My God, Mother, have you brought us a ray of hope?"

Some one screamed, "Organize us, Mother!"

Then they all began shouting, "Organize us! Organize us!"

"March over to that dark church on the corner and I will give you the obligation," said I.

The men started marching. In the dark the spies could not identify them.

"You can't organize those men," said the board member, "because you haven't the ritual."

"The ritual, hell," said I. "I'll make one up!"

"They have to pay $15 for a charter," said he.

"I will get them their charter," said I. "Why these poor wretches haven't 15 cents for a sandwich. All you care about is your salary regardless of the destiny of these men."

On the steps of the darkened church, I organized those men. They raised their hands and took the obligation to the Union.

"Go home from this meeting," said I. "Say nothing about being a union man. Put on your overalls in the morning, take your dinner buckets and go to work in the mines, and get the other men out."

They went to work. Every man who had attended the meeting was discharged. That caused the strike, a

Engraving by Javier Iñiguez

long, bitter, cruel strike. Bullpens came. Flags came. The militia came. More hungry, more cold, more starving, more ragged than Washington's army that fought against tyranny were the miners of the Kanawha Mountains. And just as grim. Just as heroic. Men died in those hills that others might be free.

One day a group of men came down to Eksdale from Red Warrior Camp to ask me to come up there and speak to them. Thirty-six men came down in their shirt sleeves. They brought a mule and buggy for me to drive in with a little miner's lad for a driver. I was to drive in the creek bed as that was the only public road and I could be arrested for trespass if I took any other. The men took the shorter and easier way along the C. and O. tracks which paralleled the creek a little way above it.

Suddenly as we were bumping along I heard a wild scream. I looked up at the tracks along which the

130

miners were walking. I saw the men running, screaming as they went. I heard the whistle of bullets. I jumped out of the buggy and started to run up to the track. One of the boys screamed. "God! God! Mother, don't come. They'll kill . . ."

"Stand still," I called. "Stand where you are. I'm coming!"

When I climbed up onto the tracks I saw the boys huddled together, and around a little bend of the tracks, a machine gun and a group of gunmen.

"Oh, Mother, don't come," they cried. "Let them kill us; not you!"

"I'm coming and no one is going to get killed," said I.

I walked up to the gunmen and put my hand over the muzzle of the gun. Then I just looked at those gunmen, very quiet, and said nothing. I nodded my head for the miners to pass.

"Take your hands off that gun, you hellcat!" yelled a fellow called Mayfield, crouching like a tiger to spring at me.

I kept my hand on the muzzle of the gun. "Sir," said I, "my class goes into the mines. They bring out the metal that makes this gun. This is my gun! My class melt the minerals in furnaces and roll the steel. They dig the coal that feeds furnaces. My class is not fighting you, not you. They are fighting with bare fists and empty stomachs the men who rob them and deprive their children of childhood. It is the hard-earned pay of the working class that your pay comes from. They aren't fighting you."

Several of the gunmen dropped their eyes but one fellow, this Mayfield, said, "I don't care a damn! I'm going to kill every one of them, and you, too!"

I looked him full in the face. "Young man," said I, "I want to tell you that if you shoot one bullet out of this gun at those men, if you touch one of my white hairs, that creek will run with blood, and yours will be the first to crimson it. I do not want to hear the screams of these men, nor to see the tears, nor feel the heartache of wives and little children. These boys have no guns! Let them pass!"

"So our blood is going to crimson the creek, is it!" snarled this Mayfield.

I pointed to the high hills. "Up there in the mountain I have 500 miners. They are marching armed to the meeting I am going to address. If you start the shooting, they will finish the game."

Mayfield's lips quivered like a tiger's deprived of its flesh.

"Advance!" he said to the miners.

They came forward. I kept my hand on the gun. The miners were searched. There were no guns on them. They were allowed to pass.

I went down the side of the hill to my buggy. The mule was chewing grass and the little lad was making

a willow whistle. I drove on. That night I held my meeting.

But there weren't any 500 armed men in the mountains. Just a few jack rabbits, perhaps, but I had scared that gang of cold blooded, hired murderers and Red Warrior camp was organized.

The miners asked me to come up to Wineberg, a camp in the Creek district. Every road belonged to the coal company. Only the bed of the creek was a public road. At that time of the year — early Spring — the water in the creek was high.

I started for Wineberg accompanied by a newspaperman, named West, of the *Baltimore Sun*. We walked along the railroad track.

Again I met the gunmen with their revolvers and machine guns. Mayfield was there, too.

"You can't walk here!" he growled. "Private property!"

"You don't mean to say you are going to make that old lady walk that creek in that ice cold water, do you?" said the reporter.

"It's too damn good for her! She won't walk it!" he laughed.

"Won't I?" said I. I took off my shoes, rolled up my skirt and walked the creek.

At Wineberg the miners, standing in the creek and on its edges, met me. With our feet in water we held a meeting. Holding their shoes in their hands, their trousers rolled up, these men took the obligation to the union.

I was very tired. A miner stepped up to me and asked me to come to his cabin and have a dish of tea.

"Your house is on private property," yelled a gunman. "She cannot go."

"I pay rent," he protested.

"Private property, just the same. I'll arrest her for trespassing if she steps out of the creek."

The struggle went on with increasing bitterness. The militia disarmed both gunmen and miners but they were of course, on the side of the grand dukes of the region. They forbade all meetings. They suspended every civil right. They became despotic. They arrested scores of miners, tried them in military court, without jury, sentenced them to 10, 15 years in the Moundsville prison.

I decided to call the attention of the national government to conditions in West Virginia. I borrowed $100 and went out and billed meetings in Cincinnati, Columbus, Cleveland, and from these cities I came to Washington, D.C. I had already written to Congressman W.B. Wilson, to get up a protest meeting.

The meeting was held in the armory and it was packed: Senators, congressmen, secretaries, citizens. It is usual to have star orators at such meetings, who use parlor phrases. Congressman Wilson told the audience that he hoped they would not get out of patience with me, for I might use some language which Washington was not accustomed to hear.

I told the audience what things were happening in West Virginia, proceedings that were un-American. I told them about the suspension of civil liberty by the military. Of the wholesale arrests and military sentences.

"This is the seat of a great republican form of government. If such crimes against the citizens of the state of West Virginia go unrebuked by the government, I suggest that we take down the flag that stands for constitutional government, and run up a banner, saying, 'This is the flag of the money oligarchy of America!' "

The next day by 12 o'clock all the military prisoners but two were called down to the prison office and signed their own release.

From Washington I went to West Virginia to carry on my work. The day before I arrived, an operator named Quinn Morton, the sheriff of Kanawha County, Bonner Hill, deputies and guards drove an armored train with Gatling guns through Holly Grove, the tent colony of the miners, while they were sleeping. Into the quiet tents of the workers the guns were fired, killing and wounding the sleepers. A man by the name of Epstaw rose and picked up a couple of children and told them to run for their lives. His feet were shot off. Women were wounded. Children screamed with terror.

No one was arrested.

Three days later, a mine guard, Fred Bobbett, was killed in an altercation. Fifty strikers and their organizers were immediately arrested, and without warrant.

I went to Boomer where the organization is composed of foreigners, and I went to Long Acre, getting each local union to elect a delegate who should appeal to the governor to put a stop to the military despotism.

I met all these delegates in a church and told them how they were to address a governor. We took the train for Charleston. I thought it better for the delegates to interview the governor without me, so after cautioning them to keep cool, I went over to the hotel where they were to meet me after the interview.

As I was going along the street, a big elephant, called Dan Cunningham, grabbed me by the arm and said, "I want you!" He took me to the Roughner Hotel, and sent for a warrant for my arrest. Later I was put on the C. and O. train and taken down to Pratt and handed over to the military. They were not looking for me so they had no bullpen ready. So a Dr. Hansford and his wife took care of me and some organizers who were arrested with me. The next day I was put in solitary in a room, guarded by soldiers who paced day and night in front of my door. I could see no one. I will give the military of West Virginia credit for one thing: They are far less brutal and cold blooded than the military of Colorado.

After many weeks we were taken before the judge advocate. The court had sent two lawyers to my bullpen to defend me but I had refused to let them defend me in that military court. I refused to recognize the jurisdiction of the court, to recognize the suspension of the civil courts. My arrest and trial were unconstitutional. I told the judge advocate that this was my position. I refused to enter a plea.

I was tried for murder. Along with the others, I was sentenced to serve 20 years in the state penitentiary. I was not sent to prison immediately but held for five weeks in the military camp. I did not know what they were going to do with me. My guards were nice young men, respectful and courteous with the exception of a fellow called Lafferty, and another sewer rat whose name I have not taxed my mind with.

Then from California came aid. The great lion-hearted editor of the *San Francisco Bulletin*, Fremont Older, sent his wife across the continent to Washington. She had a talk with Senator Kearns. From Washington she came to see me. She got all the facts in regard to the situation from the beginning of the strike to my unconstitutional arrest and imprisonment. She wrote the story for *Collier's Magazine*. She reported conditions to Senator Kearns, who immediately demanded a thorough congressional inquiry.

Some one dropped a *Cincinnati Post* through my prison window. It contained a story of Wall Street's efforts to hush up the inquiry. "If Wall Street gets away with this," I thought, "and the strike is broken, it means industrial bondage for long years to come in the West Virginia mines."

I decided to send a telegram, via my underground railway, to Senator Kearns. There was a hole in the floor of my prison-cabin. A rug covered the hole. I lifted the rug and rang two beer bottles against one another. A soldier who was my friend came crawling under the house to see "what was up." He had slipped me little things before, and I had given him what little I had to give — an apple, a magazine. So I gave him the telegram and told him to take it three miles up the road to another office. He said he would. "It's fine stuff, Mother," he said.

That night when he was off duty he trudged three miles up the road with the telegram. He sent it.

The next day in Washington, the matter of a congressional inquiry in the West Virginia mines came up for discussion in the Senate.

Senator Goff from Clarksburg, who had stock in the coal mines of West Virginia, got up on the floor and said that West Virginia was a place of peace until the agitators came in. "And the grandmother of agitators in this country," he went on, "is that old Mother Jones! I learn from the governor that she is not in prison at all but is only detained in a very pleasant boarding house!"

Senator Kearns rose. "I have a telegram from this old woman of 84 in this very pleasant boarding house," said he. "I will read it."

To the astonishment of the senators and the press he then read my telegram. They had supposed the old woman's voice was in prison with her body.

"From out the military prison walls of Pratt, WV, where I have walked over my 84th milestone in history, I send you the groans and tears and heartaches of men, women and children as I have heard them in this state. From out these prison walls, I plead with you for the honor of the nation, to push that investigation, and the children yet unborn will rise and call you blessed."

Then the senate took action. A senatorial commission was appointed to investigate conditions.

One hour after this decision, Captain Sherwood of the militia, a real man in every sense of the word aside from the uniform, said to me, "Mother, the governor telephoned me to bring you to Charleston at once. You have only 25 minutes before the train comes."

"What does the governor want?" said I.

"He didn't say."

When I got to the governor's office, I had to wait some time because the governor and the mine owners were locked behind doors holding a secret conference as to how they should meet the senatorial investigation.

Governor Hatfield had succeeded Governor Glasscock, and he told me, when he finally admitted me, that he had been trying to settle the strike ever since he had been elected.

"I could have settled it in 24 hours," said I.

He shook his head mournfully.

"I would make the operators listen to the grievances of their workers. I would take the $650,000 spent for the militia during this strike and spend it on schools and playgrounds and libraries that West Virginia might have a more highly developed citizenry, physically and intellectually. You would then have fewer little children in the mines and factories; fewer later in jails and penitentiaries; fewer men and women submitting to conditions that are brutalizing and un-American."

The next day he attended the convention of the miners that was in session in Charleston. I saw him there and I said to him, "Governor, I am going out of town tomorrow."

"Where are you going?"

"I'm going to consult a brain specialist. My brain got out of balance while I was in the bullpen."

"Didn't you know I was a doctor?" he said.

"Your pills won't do me any good!" I said.

Shortly after the miner's convention, Governor Hatfield set aside all the military sentences, freeing all of the prisoners but eight. The operators recognized the union and many abuses were corrected.

The working men had much to thank Senator Kearns for. He was a great man, standing for justice and the square deal. Yet, to the shame of the workers of Indiana, when he came up for re-election they elected a man named Watson, a deadly foe of progress. I felt his defeat keenly; felt the ingratitude of the workers. It was through his influence that prison doors had opened, that unspeakable conditions were brought to light. I have felt that the disappointment of his defeat brought on his illness and ended the brave, heroic life of one of labor's few friends.

One day when I was in Washington, a man came to see me who said General Elliot had sent him to me. General Elliot was the military man who had charge of the prisoners sentenced to the penitentiary in the court martial during the strike. Never would I forget that scene on the station platform of Pratt when the men were being taken to Moundsville; the wives screaming frantically; the little children not allowed to kiss or caress their fathers. Neither the screams nor the sobs touched the stone heart of General Elliot.

And now General Elliot had sent a friend to me to ask me to give him a letter endorsing him for Congress.

"And did General Elliot send you?"

"Yes."

"Then tell the general that nothing would give me more pleasure than to give you a letter, but it would be a letter to go to hell and not to Congress!" ■

Solidarity on the Embarcadero

by Richard O. Boyer and Herbert M. Morais

San Francisco is a busy city of 600,000, its heart the waterfront, the chief source of its life. And yet the men who kept the city alive, who did its most important work, the longshoremen who loaded and unloaded the vessels that made the city prosperous with trade, the seamen who manned the ships, received in 1933 little more than $10 a week. To be precise, the average weekly wage of longshoremen was $10.45, while able seamen received $53 a month and ordinary seamen $36.

And yet even more important was the fact that the maritime workers were voiceless serfs in an industrial autocracy, powerless employees of a shipping industry which received millions on millions of dollars, according to the Black Senatorial Investigation, in subsidies from the Federal government. A few seamen belonged to a corrupt, sell-out organization, the International Seaman's Union, and still fewer to the militant Marine Workers Industrial Union (TUUL), but to all practical purposes they were unorganized. The longshoremen, since 1919, had been dragooned into a creature of the shipping industry known as the Blue Book Union, an employers' organization controlled by gangsters who forced the underpaid longshoremen to bribe them for jobs.

The shape-up, that is, a crowd of longshoremen packing around a foreman on the street, each one hoping that he would be chosen for work, was the common method of hiring. There was usually a three or four-day search or wait for work between jobs, but once gained a longshoreman might work 24 to 36 hours at a stretch on a single shift. Seamen,

Richard O. Boyer is an author and specialist in labor movement profiles: *The Dark Ship* a study of the Maritime Union and *John Brown: Profile of a Legend*. Dr. Herbert M. Morais (1905-1970) was a scholar, historian and teacher. This selection is reprinted with permission from *Labor's Untold Story*. Copyright © 1955; Third Edition 1970 by the United Electrical, Radio and Machine Workers of America (UE), New York, NY.

after they had once shipped out, too, had long periods of unemployment, worked on an average of between 14 and 16 hours a day.

In 1933, under the impetus of NIRA and Section 7 (A) as well as the spur of intolerable conditions, longshoremen in San Francisco and up and down the Pacific coast began flocking into the International Longshoremen's Association, AFL. Knowing something of Joseph P. Ryan, its president, they were determined on rank-and-file control. One of their leaders was a sharp-featured, sharp-witted longshoreman by the name of Harry Bridges. A tough and rugged character, his assets were an impregnable honesty and a stout belief in the ability and right of the rank-and-file to govern themselves.

Although Federal law made it mandatory that the shipping magnates negotiate in collective bargaining with any union that their employees chose, they unhesitatingly broke the law by refusing to so negotiate. Instead, in September, 1933, they discharged four rank-and-file leaders of the union. When the regional labor board ordered their reinstatement, the longshoremen surged in to the ILA with such unanimity that the Blue Book Union "became little more than an office with a telephone number."

After the employers had refused to negotiate or recognize the union over a period of months, 12,000 longshoremen went out on strike at 8 p.m. on May 9, 1934, in San Francisco, Seattle, Tacoma, Portland, San Pedro, San Diego, Stockton, Bellingham, Aberdeen, Grays Harbor, Astoria, and all other Pacific coast ports. The Marine Workers Industrial Union followed suit and by May 23, eight maritime unions and 35,000 workers were out on strike up and down the coast.

It was primarily unprecedented police brutality that turned the seamen's strike into a general strike of 127,000 San Francisco workers that in an instant transformed the city into a ghost town in which there was no movement. The police took their line from the Industrial Association, the combination of San Francisco's most powerful tycoons, organized in 1919 as a Law and Order Committee to break a waterfront strike and developing until it was the real ruler of San Francisco. The slightest utterance of its officials became newspaper headlines. The employer organization was almost decisive in the election of mayors, governors, congressional representatives. It maintained a powerful lobby in Washington. It was the Pacific coast's most powerful group, its members owning shipping companies, piers, warehouses, railroads, banks, utility companies, trust companies, land, insurance corporations, and public officials.

From 8 p.m. on May 9 officials of the Industrial Association and the San Francisco Chamber of Commerce said there was nothing to negotiate. There was only a communist insurrection to put down. Typical of the statements that filled the newspapers was that of J. M. Maillard, Jr., president of the Chamber of Commerce:

> The San Francisco waterfront strike is out of hand. It is not a conflict between employer and employee — between capital and labor — it is a conflict which is rapidly spreading between American principles and un-American radicalism . . . the welfare of business and industry and the entire public is at stake in the outcome of this crisis.

The port, officials of the employers' organizations declared, must be opened. The police must break and clear the mass picket lines from before the piers.

The longshoremen had drawn up a list of demands, pay of $1 an hour, a six-hour day, a 30-hour week, a union hiring hall, but officials of the Industrial Association declared there was no issue at stake but the suppression of a Red Revolt. Press, pulpit, and radio combined with tireless unanimity to whip up hysteria against workers striving to better their lives. Not unusual was the first-page story of the *Chronicle*, "Red Army Marching on City." The story read in part:

> The reports stated the communist army planned the destruction of railroad and highway facilities to paralyze transportation and later, communication, while San Francisco and the Bay Area were made a focal point in a red struggle for control of government.
>
> First warning communist forces were nearing the Northern California border was relayed from J. R. Given, Southern Pacific superintendent at Dunsmuir, to District State Highway Engineer Fred W.

Hazelwood who immediately reported to State Director of Public Works Earl Lee Kelly.

Bumbling Joseph P. Ryan, president of the International Longshoremen's Association but in league with the gangsters of New York, was rushed from New York to quiet the strikers. Long known as an ardent fighter against communism, he did his part as expected when unable to sell out the maritime workers. He said the strike was a communist plot and again the headlines shrieked. Then Edward F. McGrady, Assistant Secretary of Labor whose part in breaking the furriers' strike in New York may be recalled, was rushed from Washington and when he, too, could not succeed in forcing the longshoremen to give up their demand for a union hiring hall, he, too, said the strike was Red Revolution.

With the stage set and the police eager, the employers announced that they would smash the picket lines before the piers on the Embarcadero on July 3, 1934. At 1:27 p.m., with thousands of pickets massed before the piers, the steel rolling doors on Pier 38 went up and five trucks loaded with cargo, preceded by eight police radio patrol cars, moved. Mike Quin in his history of the strike tells what happened:

> A deafening roar went up from the pickets. Standing on the running board of a patrol car at the head of the caravan, Police Captain Thomas

M. Hoertkorn flourished a revolver and shouted, "The port is open!"

With single accord the great mass of pickets surged forward. The Embarcadero became a vast tangle of fighting men. Bricks flew and clubs battered skulls. The police opened fire with revolvers and riot guns. Clouds of tear gas swept the picket lines and sent the men choking in defeat. Mounted police were dragged from their saddles and beaten to the pavement.

The cobblestones of the Embarcadero were littered with fallen men; bright puddles of blood colored the gray expanse.

Squads of police who looked like Martian monsters in their special helmets and gas masks led the way, flinging gas bombs ahead of them.

The fighting continued for four hours before a vast gallery of San Franciscans, perhaps half of the city watching it from the hills which loom above the waterfront. Two airplanes, packed with the curious, circled low over the bloody battle area. The battle was fierce but it was only the prelude to Bloody Thursday. The next day, after the initial attack of the police, was July 4, and by common consent there was a one-day truce before the battle resumed on Thursday, July 5. Quin writes:

> There were no preliminaries this time. They just took up where they left off. . . . Teeming thousands covered the hillsides. Many high school and college boys, unknown to their parents, had put on old clothes and gone down to fight with the union men. Hundreds of working men started for work, then changed their minds and went down to the picket lines.

At 8 a.m. police went into action. One newspaper reported:

> Vomiting gas was used in many cases, instead of the comparatively innocuous tear gas, and scores of dreadfully nauseated strikers and civilians were incapacitated. There was no sham about the battles yesterday. Police ran into action with drawn revolvers. Scores of rounds of ammunition were fired, and riot guns were barking throughout the day.

But the strikers and their thousands of sympathizers fought on with their bare hands against bullets and bombs. Their only weapons were bricks and stones. Hundreds were badly wounded. Two, Nick Bordoise and Howard Sperry, were killed. Sperry was a longshoreman; Bordoise was a culinary worker, a member of the Cooks' Union and of the Communist Party. A reporter for the *Chronicle* in describing the bloodshed wrote: "Don't think of this as a riot. It was a hundred riots big and little. Don't think of it as one battle, but a dozen battles."

All day the battle raged and all day reinforcements from other unions poured into the riddled picket lines, workers declaring, "If they win this, there'll never be another union in Frisco!" The police, clubbing and injuring literally hundreds of passersby and bystanders, charged into the union headquarters of the longshoremen and wrecked it. At the close of the day, Governor Merriam ordered in the National Guard, 2,000 of them with full equipment, and Harry Bridges said, "We cannot stand up against police, machine guns, and National Guard bayonets."

The employers thought they had won. They had not. The strike was just beginning. "That night," writes Quin, "San Francisco vibrated to intense conversation. Every home or gathering place in town hummed with talk. Doorbells and telephones rang. Neighbors came in from next door. . . . Men had been shot down in cold blood. Authority had taken the shape of force and violence. Bedtime came and went but still the city talked. . . . A General Strike was being forged in the firesides of San Francisco."

The Painters' Union, Local 1158, sent out a call for a general strike and it had scarcely been issued when the Machinists Union, Local 68, took up the demand. But first labor had to bury its dead. More than 35,000 workers walked behind the coffins. There were no police about as the stern-faced workers marched through the heart of the city. One newspaperman wrote of the slain men: "In life they wouldn't have commanded a second glance on the streets of San Francisco, but in death they were borne the length of Market Street in a stupendous and reverent procession that astounded the city."

And Quin writes of the funeral:

> A union band struck up the slow cadence of the Beethoven funeral march. The great composer's music never applied more fittingly to human suffering. Slowly — barely creeping — the trucks moved out into Market Street. With slow, rhythmic steps the giant procession followed. Faces were hard and serious. Hats were held proudly across chests. Slow-pouring, like thick liquid, the great mass flowed onto Market Street.
>
> Streetcarmen stopped their cars along the line of march, and stood silently, holding their uniform caps across their chests, holding their heads high and firm.
>
> Not one smile in the endless blocks of marching men. Crowds on the sidewalk, for the most part, stood with heads erect and hats removed. Others watched the procession with fear and alarm. Here and there well dressed businessmen . . . stood amazed and impressed but with their hats still on their heads. Sharp voices shot out from the line of march. "Take your hats off!"
>
> The tone of voice was extraordinary. The reaction was immediate. With quick, nervous gestures the businessmen obeyed. Hours went by, but the marchers still poured onto Market Street.

Now locals were meeting all over the city, one after another voting for a general strike. In the debates it was admitted that communists were active in the struggle of the maritime workers. For that matter, it was said, they, or other Marxists, had been active in every big strike since the railroad strike of 1877. Trade unionist after trade unionist declared that for the San Francisco labor movement to fall for the employers' red scare was to agree to its own division, to less pay, longer hours. On July 10 the Alameda Labor Council went on record for a general strike. On July 12 the powerful locals of the teamsters' union in San Francisco and Oakland issued a call for union and solidarity, favoring the general strike.

William Green sent telegrams forbidding the strike, but by July 15 some 160 local AFL unions, with a membership of 127,000 workers, had voted general strike effective the following day.

The typographical workers and powerhouse employees stayed in but with these two exceptions members of every union walked out on the morning of July 16. Quin writes:

> The paralysis was effective beyond all expectation. To all intents and purposes industry was at a complete standstill. The great factories were empty and deserted. No streetcars were running. Virtually all stores were closed. The giant apparatus of commerce was a lifeless, helpless hulk.
>
> Labor had withdrawn its hand. The workers had drained out of the shops and plants like lifeblood, leaving only a silent framework embodying millions of dollars worth of invested capital. In the absence of labor, the giant machinery loomed as so much idle junk. . . .
>
> Everything was there, all intact as the workers had left it — instruments, equipment, tools, machinery, raw materials and the buildings themselves. When the men walked out they took only what belonged to them — their labor. And when they took that they might as well have taken everything, because all the elaborate apparatus they left behind was worthless and meaningless without their hands. The machinery was a mere extension of labor, created by and dependent upon labor.
>
> Labor held the life-blood and energy. The owners remained in possession of the corpse.
>
> Highways leading into the city bristled with picket lines. Nothing moved except by permission of the strike committee. Labor was in control. Employers, however, controlled an important factor. Through the "conservative wing" they held the balance of power within the General Strike Committee. But this "conservative wing" had to buck a strong progressive minority, and dared not move too obviously contrary to the will of the masses.

Three thousand additional troops were dispatched

to the strikebound city but that turned not a wheel. Mobs of vigilantes were sworn in as special police, armed with clubs and guns, but the workers were at home, with a new consiousness of their power and dignity. When they ceased working the world stopped. And all of the silk hats, dollars, and guns could not start it again without them.

The vigilantes swung into an orgy of lawlessness, wrecking union halls, raiding clubs of the foreign-born, beating their occupants, destroying progressive book stores, scattering all the volumes and pamphlets to the street. The police looked on as the vigilantes destroyed the offices of the *Western Worker*, a communist paper backing the strike. They watched as they wrecked the headquarters of the Communist Party, the Marine Workers' Industrial Union, the ILA soup kitchen, the Workers' Ex-Servicemen's League, the Mission Workers' Neighborhood House.

Then the police themselves moved into lawlessness as they arrested 500 old men, members of the unemployed, the helpless down-and-out, and charged that those hauled in were communist conspirators. "The Communist Party is through in San Francisco," announced Captain J.J. O'Meara, head of the police radical squad, before it was found that not one of the old men was a communist. They were finally released.

But the force and violence of police and vigilantes moved not a wheel. The city was like a tomb all of July 16. Nothing moved on July 17. San Francisco was a ghost on July 18. Yet on each of these days "the conservative wing" had succeeded in loosening the strike's grip. Restaurants were allowed to open on one day. It was extended to some trucking the next day. More exceptions were made the next. Rumors were spread that the strike was over. One of the biggest demonstrations in the history of American labor ended on July 19 when Deal, Vandeleur, and Kidwell, conservative AFL officials, refusing a rollcall vote, announced that the central labor body had ended the general strike by a standing vote of 191 to 174.

But the workers returned as if celebrating a victory. They put their hands to switch, throttle, wheel, and assembly line and death became life. The maritime workers, rejecting all attempts to divide the eight unions out on strike, remained on their picket line but with an increased strength. No police assaulted their lines now. National Guardsmen stayed their distance. Labor had demonstrated its power and the tycoons of the Industrial Association, fighting now among themselves, did not want another taste of labor's unity.

On July 30 the 35,000 maritime workers went back to work. Within a matter of weeks the longshoremen had gained, as a direct result of the strike, the six-

hour day, a 30-hour week, and time and a half for overtime. Wages were raised to a basis of 95 cents an hour, $1.40 for overtime. But above all they had won the basis for the union hiring hall, a method for democratic rotary hiring without which the union would have been powerless to protect its gains.

The seamen returned under conditions which granted recognition to the International Seamen's Union. But because the union was in the control of a reactionary clique subservient to the shipping interests, the seamen won little substantial gain. On the other hand, because the longshoremen's local was run by its rank and file, its members' gains were persistently extended.

Harry Bridges, the rank-and-file leader, was elected president of the San Francisco local of the International Longshoremen's Association and later he was elected to the presidency of the entire West Coast District. From then on he was a marked man. He had committed the unpardonable sin. He had raised wages. He had lowered hours. He had put more wages in pay envelopes. He had transformed employees into men with a voice in the decisions governing their own hire. If he had not done all these things himself, he at least had played an important part in accomplishing these worthy ends.

From the moment the Bridges leadership played a vital role in raising wages, Bridges was a communist in the eyes of the powerful Industrial Association of San Francisco. He could be neither bought nor frightened, bribed nor bullied, and with that established the employers marked him for destruction. Whether he was a communist or not made not a whit of difference. He had worked with communists and he was incorruptible.

On four separate occasions they have gathered together a choice selection of paid spies, perjurers, and criminals to testify as told or face prison. On four different occasions Federal authority or juries have found that Bridges is not a communist, has not been a communist, but has instead been persecuted as few men in history in an implacable plot to frame him. Even the Supreme Court of the United States so ruled. Despite this, powerful interests on the Pacific coast are now engaged in a fifth attempt to frame Harry Bridges.

But workingmen know that all the endless frame-up attempts against Bridges stem from his leadership of the San Francisco General Strike of 1934, a demonstration of iron-clad unity which inspired all American labor. It was an important factor in increased wages at points far from San Francisco. It was the prelude to even greater battles and greater victories.

■

Group Exercise

In preparation for this session, each group member should talk to at least one person who has a story to tell about a labor struggle in the past. This may be a parent or grandparent, some other relative, an older working class acquaintance or a veteran activist. Come prepared to share some of the highlights of the story.

After everyone has had an opportunity to present the results of her/his interview, see if you can determine any similarities that appear in these stories. Assign one person to write these down on a piece of newsprint. Discuss whether or not (or in what way) circumstances have changed regarding progressive labor union activity, especially as related to the items written down.

If this exercise proves successful, your group may wish to engage in an ''oral history'' project on the labor movement in your community.

For the second half of your group session, discuss one or several of the following questions:

1 What are some of the strengths and weaknesses of Left parties that you know about? What are some of the historical factors that have contributed to the development of these strengths and weaknesses?

2 What are some of the ways by which a labor union can be ''politicized'' in a progressive direction? Someone may wish to bring a report on such efforts as the Teamsters for a Democratic Union or Miners for Democracy.

3 What do you think should be the relationship between the general movement for a humane socialist society and the specific struggles for better working conditions and wages, women's liberation, black liberation struggles, gay liberation (and other oppressed groups), etc.? Can a genuine victory for women's liberation be achieved within capitalism? Does socialism ''guarantee'' a victory for women's liberation or the other liberation struggles?

4 How does ''red-baiting'' work? What is a proper response to it?

5 If you could devise the organizational pattern and membership requirements of a socialist political party, what would they be? Under what conditions would such a formation be possible? When is such a party likely to emerge?

Note: Before your group adjourns, take a moment to preview the Group Exercise at the end of Session 6, to assure adequate preparation for the next meeting.

Picheta

Christians and the Socialist Option

When we began our study of this volume, we examined our religious ideology in order to better address the question, *Which Side Are We On?* In Session 1, we considered the origin of ideas, and noted the pitfalls of succumbing to the dominant ideas promoted by and in the interest of the capitalist class.

The session immediately preceding included an overview of the history of the Left in the United States, noting several lessons to be learned from the successes and failures of people's struggles over the past decades.

This session strives to put elements of Sessions 1 and 5 together. The vignettes presented here reveal how Christian men and women have given expression to their ideology by struggling on the side of working people and the poor. In this effort, they are emulating Jesus of Nazareth who also lived in a "class" society, and had to make a choice of whom to champion.

To understand the liberating message of Jesus, a brief look at class structure and power relationships in early Palestine is of help. The *Sadducees* were the aristocracy — the big landowners, chief merchants and priests. The *Scribes* were the educated civil servants — teachers, lawyers, moralists and theologians of the Jewish community. The *Pharisees* were experts at oral interpretation of the Torah and had detailed knowledge of Mosaic law. The Scribes and Pharisees were part of the urban middle class.

Power in those days was concentrated in the Temple, which was both a center of religious and economic power. Juridical power in the form of the Sanhedrin was based in the Temple and represented the interests of the Sadducees, Scribes and Pharisees. Palestine was under Roman occupation. The success of Roman colonialism was dependent on an alliance between Rome and Palestine's upper classes.

And there were the *'am-ha-ares* — the common people, the masses. Among them were those who tilled the land, bore and raised the children, cared for the animals, fished the seas — the working people of the time. Of course, there were also the outcasts — beggars, the lame, the blind — those who did not have access even to basic necessities.

Against this background, it is easy to see how the outlook and practice of Jesus was in violent conflict with the social structure and mores of his time, and how his point of view quickly alienated him from the wealthy and ruling powers. His condemnation of the Sadducees, Scribes and Pharisees, his association with sinners, healing of the sick and lame, brought ideologies into sharp conflict.

When Jesus advocated identification with the poor and oppressed, he was really advocating the reorganization of the social order, symbolized by his proclamation that "the blind recover their sight, the lame walk, the lepers are made clean, the deaf hear, the dead are raised to life and the poor are hearing the good news." (Matt. 11:5)

This provides a framework for a rediscovery of the Gospel message in light of a new awareness of Jesus and his *praxis*. This rediscovery is enhanced by using the tools of Marxist analysis to discern the relationship between social classes.

In this session, we focus on Christians who believe that the message of Jesus leads to the conviction that to build a just society necessarily implies active and conscious participation in class struggle.

The first three articles concern Christians who were active in the 1920s, '30s, and '40s. Their witness is important as we begin to reclaim our radical Christian heritage.

We begin with a short history of how Claude and Joyce Williams organized the People's Institute of Applied Religion. Their strong biblical faith coupled with a Marxist analysis aided them in becoming effective union organizers, and their story gives us an insight into the merging of religion and activism.

Next, in the story of Winifred Chappell, we learn how firsthand experience of workers' struggles moved her to become radical in her Christian faith and radical in her politics. Chappell's commitment to socialism and feminism is expressed in both her writing and activity during the early years of the Methodist Federation for Social Action.

The third brief history describes the life and times of the Church League for Industrial Democracy (CLID), from its beginnings with Vida Scudder, a socialist and active Episcopal churchwoman, to its demise during the McCarthy era. CLID was organized to respond to the new developments of an "unchristian industrial economic system" and to create in-stead "a society that substitutes cooperation for mastery in industry and life." Its central concern was "the conflict between labor and capital."

In the final article, Dorothy Sölle calls us to "bring class struggle and cross together," and to take an active part against oppressive structures and systems. A central theme of her work is the conviction that the goal of Jesus' struggle is similar to that of all historical class struggles. Sölle challenges us to answer the question, *Which side are we on?* The role of Christians has never been, and cannot be, neutral. Those who claim neutrality choose to perpetuate a socioeconomic system which oppresses most of humanity. Sölle urges us to re-examine, in the tradition of the previously mentioned Christian activists, our own religious faith and commitment.   ■

People's Institute of Applied Religion

by Bill Troy with Claude Williams

"Is not this the carpenter, the son of Joseph?" Well, if he was a carpenter, he knew what it was to have horny hands and patched clothing. Because you couldn't do the kind of work he was, felling trees and dragging them to the house to make ox yokes and carts, without tearing your trousers. He was a carpenter. He knew what it was to work long hours with little pay. He was born and reared in a worker's home. He knew what it was to dwell in a shack, because carpenters even today don't build mansions for themselves but for other people!

That's the voice of the Rev. Claude Williams, speaking much as he did 35 years ago to groups of sharecroppers in the Arkansas Delta and shopworkers in the war defense plants of Detroit. Standing now in the close quarters of his Alabama trailer-home office, the preacher's voice rings as it did those many years ago, when conferences of workaday preachers and Sunday school teachers would meet for days in churches and union halls to consider the Biblical teaching: "The meek will inherit the earth when they become sassy enough to take it!"

Hanging on the wall before him is one of Claude's unique visual education charts. It is a large affair, three by four feet in dimension. At the top, it bears the legend, "The Galilean and the Common People." In circles and rectangles covering the chart is a suc-

Bill Troy is a campus minister at Southern Appalachian Community Colleges in Knoxville, TN. This article is the result of taped conversations and research in the papers of Claude and Joyce Williams at their home in Alabaster, AL. All quotations are by Claude Williams, unless otherwise noted. Joyce Williams had just died when this article first went to press in 1976. Claude died in Birmingham on June 29, 1979. They were co-workers and tireless fighters for justice and equality for 55 years. This article first appeared in Southern Exposure's "On Jordan's Stormy Banks," a study of religion in the South, Vol. 4, No. 3, pp. 46-53, available for $3 from P.O. Box 230, Chapel Hill, NC 27514. Reprinted with permission.

cession of modern, simple drawings, each depicting scenes from the life of the Son of Man.

Waving his homemade coat-hanger pointer at the chart, Claude refers to each drawing in turn as he recounts how Moses called the first strike down in Egypt, how Jeremiah spoke out fearlessly in the name of true religion against the rulers and priests of ancient Israel, and how the Son of Man was reared in this tradition by a poor family who belonged to a movement seeking to bring about the Kingdom of God in their own time and place.

This is the kind of talk that went on in the People's Institute of Applied Religion (PIAR), surely one of the most remarkable expressions of religion ever to appear in the South. The PIAR was created in 1940 as an independent means of training the grassroots religious leaders of the cotton belt in the principles of labor unionism. For its principal founders, Claude and Joyce Williams, it represented the unique melding of religious and political convictions that had grown in them over a long period.

EVOLUTION OF VIEWS

Claude and Joyce Williams came by their religion honestly. Both were born into fundamentalist homes, Joyce to a farming family in Missouri and Claude to tenant farmers in West Tennessee. They met and married in the early 1920s at Bethel College, a conservative Tennessee seminary of the Cumberland Presbyterian Church. But their religious views gradually began to change as they pastored their first Presbyterian charge near Nashville. Partly, as in the case of their increasing unease with racial segregation, the change was based on seeing the contradictions in their culture between Biblical teachings about justice and actual social practice. At the same time, avid reading led them to discover the refreshing vitality of modern religious social thought represented in Harry Emerson Fosdick's *The Modern Use of the Bible*.

The turning point came in 1927 when Claude enrolled in a series of summer seminars at Vanderbilt University taught by Dr. Alva W. Taylor, a Southerner, member of the Socialist Party and prominent exponent of the social gospel. He recalls that Taylor "had a way of removing the theological debris from the Son of Man under which he's been buried for all these centuries and making him appear human." Claude found it impossible, after this experience, to continue working in a conventional church ministry.

In 1930, the Williams moved to Paris, Arkansas, to serve a small Presbyterian mission church. Located in the center of the state's mining district, Paris offered more opportunities to practice their new religious ideas than they could have ever imagined. Their first real working acquaintance with political action came with their involvement in the miners' efforts to organize a union and join the United Mine Workers of America (UMWA). With characteristic energy, they opened the church, their home and their family life to this movement. They participated in strategy discussions, helped raise money, and Claude wrote many of the necessary documents and position papers. Their participation clearly grew out of their religion, and they learned that the warm response of the miners and their families was due, in part, to their interpretation that the union fight was completely consistent with Biblical teaching.

The Williams also began in Paris a program of study and learning that became a cornerstone of their long ministry. The Sunday evening "Philosopher's Club," held in their home, was a regular feature of church life. These meetings involved open and wide-ranging discussion of religion as well as the multitude of political and cultural ideas sweeping the country during these Depression years. They encouraged the young people to read, opening their own library for use at the church. Moreover, Claude was much in demand as a speaker throughout the coal fields. He traveled thousands of miles, addressing meetings of miners on behalf of the union, and from these contacts, "socio-Christian forums" grew in several west Arkansas towns. Through all these experiences, Claude was developing his own way of preaching/teaching, emphasizing exhortation and emotion, but likewise encouraging objective analysis and collective action.

Chiefly because of the Williams' work with the miners and the young people of Paris, the church elders eventually brought successful action within the presbytery to have Claude removed from the pulpit. In 1935, they were forced to move to nearby Fort Smith. They quickly became active with the organization of unemployed workers, and Claude was jailed for three months for participating in a demonstration. They moved again, this time to the relative safety of Little Rock, and were soon giving full time to workers' education and organizing with one of the most significant political movements to sweep the Depression South — the Southern Tenant Farmers Union (STFU).

By this time, having endured many difficult experiences and met a number of Marxist activists along the way, their political and religious views had become more radical. Likewise, their views about taking seriously the people's religion were taking concrete form.

They knew from their own backgrounds that working with poor people in the South, both black and white, meant working with people whose view of the world was strongly conditioned by religion. Everything that it means to be good, to live honorably, to find support through life's trials and hope in the future — these are the profound personal and social questions that poor Southerners have answered in religious ways for generations. The Bible is the book that points the way. For many, it was the only book they ever read. The church was the strongest institution in their lives; unlike most other things in life, it was theirs. It was a place where their own forms of community relationships took shape and where their own leaders found legitimacy. The Williams knew well the other-worldly and apolitical dynamics of this religion, but they also learned from experience how important it was to relate to church leaders if the union was to succeed.

As we spoke with the sharecroppers, we were obliged to meet in churches, both black and white. Most of the churches we met in, of course, were black churches. And it developed, especially with the black churches, that the pastor usually was present and chaired the meetings. Unless he said "Amen" with that certain inflection which got the people to saying "Amen" and rumbling their feet, we might as well go home.

The first big opportunity to test this view came in 1936 when a number of radical organizations in Little Rock, recognizing Claude's organizing ability, encouraged him to set up a school to train grassroots organizers for the STFU. In essential ways, the New Era School of Social Action and Prophetic Religion prefigured the People's Institute.

In December, 1936, we held this first school for the sharecroppers. Nine whites and 10 blacks. J. R. Butler (president of the STFU) got the students and I raised the funds. I wrote J. R. Butler from New York that we were gonna have the best school ever conducted in that land of ours "South of God, decency and democracy." Well, we did.

We went through every phase of union organizing. It was a 10 day school, night and day, solid. We didn't have any charts then, but we discussed the union problems. Then we'd assign someone to go down and organize the people in this county, or this neighborhood. Well, they'd have to study that and then make speeches as though these people were the local people. Then, after we'd done that, we had them go through organizing, setting up a local. Then we went into negotiation, getting a contract. The next to the last night, we had a group of Workers' Alliance people come into the meeting as planters with clubs to break it up. And it was so realistic. One very dynamic woman, whether it was spontaneous to the occasion or whether she just sensed, she jumped right out in the middle of the floor and began to sing: "We shall not, we shall not be moved. We shall not, we shall not be moved." . . . Well, they came around.

For the next three years, the Williams were deeply involved in STFU activity. Claude was one of the union's most skillful organizers and a member of the governing board. In 1938, when he became director of Arkansas' famous labor school, Commonwealth College, he made his work with the sharecroppers the field program of the institution. When sectarian conflict within the union's leadership led to his expulsion from the STFU board and his subsequent resignation from Commonwealth, it was natural that Claude would turn to what he did best. The People's Institute of Applied Religion became the vehicle which made use of the Williams' experience in religious workers' education.

REFINING THE APPROACH

By the time the PIAR came into being, the Williams had refined their approach into a more con-

scious and systematic religious form. The purpose was to work with the natural leadership of the South's poor, always in an interracial setting; to engage them on their own terms, in light of their own experience and their own religious world view; to translate their religious perspective into the need for collective struggle for economic justice; and to develop concrete leadership skills in union organizing. The work was always done on behalf of existing labor organizations.

The three to 10 day institute was the chief form of the PIAR's work. Roughly 50 people, equally divided between black and white, men and women, worked through morning, afternoon and evening in intense sessions. "These were people who had some tendency toward leadership," recalls Claude. "They were preachers or preacherettes or Sunday School superintendents or Sunday School teachers." Following the custom along rural churches, each participant often represented a number of communities; at one institute in Evansville, over 100 churches were represented.

The interracial nature of the institutes was a matter of principle and, in itself, constituted one of the most significant parts of the experience.

It was the first time some of them had ever been together in a meeting. Most, if not all of them, had never sat down to a meal together, and most of them thought they never would — especially the whites. The blacks never thought they'd have the opportunity. A black man got up and wept and talked when Winifred Chappell called him "brother." He never thought he'd ever live to see the day when a white woman said "brother" to him.

Even though they depended a great deal on spontaneity and inspiration, the meetings were carefully structured around the people's religious mindset and how it might be approached.

We were realistic, or we tried to be. We discovered that the fact that the people believed the Bible literally could be used to an advantage. For instance, if we read a passage from the book which related to some issue of which they were aware, although it contradicted what they had interpreted some other passage to mean, they had to also include this. Being so-called fundamentalists, accepting the Bible verbatim, had nothing whatever to do with the person's understanding of the issues that related to bread and meat, raiment, shelter, jobs and civil liberties. Therefore, our approach was not an attempt to supplant their present mindset, but to supplement it with a more horizontal frame of reference. And we found that supplementing and supplanting turned out to be one and the same thing.

We learned we had to contact these people at their consciousness of their need. We recognized that what the social scientist or the social worker saw as the need of the people and what the victim felt were two entirely different things.

145

WELLS WITHOUT WATER
(RUGGED INDIVIDUALISM)

SCRIPTURE: 2 PETER 2:1-22
TEXT: JER. 2:13

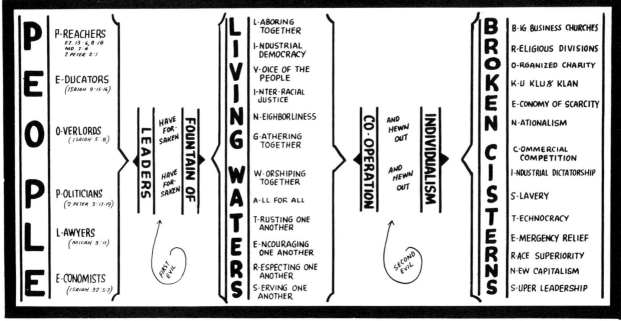

P-EOPLE		LEADERS HAVE FORSAKEN FOUNTAIN OF HAVE FORSAKEN	LIVING WATERS	CO-OPERATION AND HEWN OUT AND HEWN OUT INDIVIDUALISM	BROKEN CISTERNS
	P-REACHERS (EZ. 13:6, 8-18 MD. 7:4 2 PETER 2:1)		L-ABORING TOGETHER		B-IG BUSINESS CHURCHES
	E-DUCATORS (ISAIAH 9:15-16)		I-NDUSTRIAL DEMOCRACY		R-ELIGIOUS DIVISIONS
	O-VERLORDS (ISAIAH 5:8)		V-OICE OF THE PEOPLE		O-RGANIZED CHARITY
			I-NTER-RACIAL JUSTICE		K-U KLUX KLAN
			N-EIGHBORLINESS		E-CONOMY OF SCARCITY
			G-ATHERING TOGETHER		N-ATIONALISM
	P-OLITICIANS (2 PETER 2:17-19)		W-ORSHIPING TOGETHER		C-OMMERCIAL COMPETITION
	L-AWYERS (MICAH 3:11)		A-LL FOR ALL		I-NDUSTRIAL DICTATORSHIP
			T-RUSTING ONE ANOTHER		S-LAVERY
			E-NCOURAGING ONE ANOTHER		T-ECHNOCRACY
	E-CONOMISTS (ISAIAH 32:5-7)		R-ESPECTING ONE ANOTHER		E-MERGENCY RELIEF
			S-ERVING ONE ANOTHER		R-ACE SUPERIORITY
					N-EW CAPITALISM
					S-UPER LEADERSHIP

FIRST EVIL

SECOND EVIL

COPYRIGHT 1942 ..... **PEOPLE'S INSTITUTE** of **APPLIED RELIGION** -313 S.E. FIRST ST.- **EVANSVILLE • INDIANA**

Meetings always opened with a song, Scripture and prayer, a ritual still practiced in many grassroots political meetings throughout the South. Then:

> When we had them together at the opening session, we would say, "Now, we have come here to talk about our problems, the problems we meet every day of our lives. We want to start and let everyone tell us what the problems are that he or she meets, as it relates to food and clothes and shelter and health and freedom."
>
> Well, as long as this person would talk, we'd let him talk. If it took an entire day, we let everyone talk. Well, they were ready to talk, you know, after it got started, talking about the things that was close to them. With the result, after these meetings, they would sit down that evening to a meal together. And I never heard a murmur, they felt such a oneness.

Following these sharing sessions, either Claude or another workshop leader would begin with the first orientation chart. Claude realized that much of the written material distributed by political organizations was totally inappropriate for the sharecroppers. Those who could read were not prepared to wade through the typical political tract. They needed something visual, something more symbolic than literal, something that would suggest concepts based on the story people were already familiar with — the

Bible. So shortly before he left Commonwealth, Claude worked out four basic charts for orienting people to "the positive content" of the Gospel. A young artist at Commonwealth named Dan Genin made the drawings.

These charts were used throughout the history of the PIAR, and include "The Galilean and the Common People." Another, called "Religion and the Common People," recounts the origins of religion in superstition, the ways religion has been used by rulers to subject people, and the emergence of people's religion in the Old Testament. A third, entitled "Religion and Progress," illustrates how civil values like equality, freedom and justice support true democracy. A fourth chart, "Anti-Semitism, Racism and Democracy," counters the evils used during the Depression and World War II to create disunity among working people.

Over the years Claude introduced other charts, more diagrammatic than pictorial, but still employing the same simplicity. One, entitled "The New Earth," employs the equation FAITH + VICTORY − WORLD = RIGHTEOUSNESS (WORLD refers to "the present world system"). Another chart, called "Anti-Christs" deals with the forces of evil in the world, especially the Ku Klux Klan. Through these almost simplistic devices, Biblical concepts were translated into contemporary content and people were drawn into the learning process.

Usually, each session dealt with one chart, sometimes only sections of a chart, depending on what participants expressed as pressing needs and problems. The presentations were delivered in sermon fashion, full of the emotion and speaking style which people expected from somebody who had a deep conviction to impart. It was through the charts, more than anything else in the institutes, that the supplementing, supplanting process took place, for what people heard were the old familiar events from the Bible, buttressed by chapter and verse, but told in a way they never expected. They exclaimed, "We never heard it on this order!" and at the same time they said, "It makes sense to our minds."

The same spirit of involvement marked other sessions where participants used mimeographed worksheets to study particular problems such as peonage on the plantations, the poll tax and the lack of educational opportunities. Music also played an important part in the Institute's, as it did in the participants' churches. Not surprisingly, singing became part of the learning experience. In fact, out of the institutes (and the previous training schools in Arkansas) came some of today's best known freedom songs.

One time in this 10 day meeting in Memphis, about the third morning someone began to sing:
What is that I see yonder coming,
What is that I see yonder coming,
What is that I see yonder coming,
Get on board, get on board!
As she sung that through, the way she sung it, I could hear the drums of Africa! I said, my God, we've got to do something with that song. When she had finished, I got up. I referred to the songs we had sung in Arkansas. There's always one verse in the songs that's related to the people. Like (singing):
I'm going down to the river of Jordan
I'm going down to the river of Jordan one of
these days, hallelujah!
I'm going to walk on the freedom highway. . . .
I'm going to eat at the welcome table. . . .
Well, we changed the "I" to "we" and we sang:
We're going to walk on the people's high-
way. . . .
Well, when I sat back down there in Memphis, this woman got up and began in the same deliberate cadence:
What is that I see yonder coming,
What is that I see yonder coming,
What is that I see yonder coming,
CIO, CIO!
It is one great big union,
It is one great big union,
It is one great big union,
"It has freed many a thousand. . . .
Well, I went to New York and went to see Lee Hayes, Pete Seeger and Millard Lampell and the Almanack Singers. I repeated this and told them what happened. They took it to Paul Robeson. Paul Robeson said, "That's our song. We've got to use it. That's the basis of "The Union Train," been sung now around the world. And Miss Hattie Walls must be given credit for it. She's the one who first sang it.

The last hour of the institute was something like a praise meeting, full of singing and prayer and testimony about what the experience had meant to people.

"We thank you, for we are beginning to see the light."

"Where there's hate, there's separation; where there's separation, there's weakness. Let's stand together."

"Jesus meant for us to have economic freedom. Let's not expect God to fill our mouths when we open them."

"We want to thank you for the things we heard that we did not know. We thank Thee for unity. Break down every wall of partition. We pray for those in distress in body and mind. We realize Thy will can be done only in our bodies. . . ."

Then they went home to organize the union.

ATTRACTING SUPPORT

In its initial years, the Institute worked closely with the sharecropper movement and developing CIO activities in the South. A PIAR report for the Fall of 1941 describes a number of institutes held in the cotton belt places like the Missco, Arkansas, Federal farm; Longview, Texas; Hayti, Missouri; Osceola and Carson Lake, Arkansas. The meetings encountered increasing harassment and threats of violence from local planters, law enforcement officials and hired thugs.

At the Missco institute, 50 vigilantes appeared, and the leadership could not leave the project for fear of their lives. Because of the intimidation, several institutes were held on the periphery of the cotton belt where sharecroppers could be transported away from terror. In March, 1941, some 50 cotton belt church folks gathered in Evansville, Indiana, for an institute, and in late April another was conducted in St. Louis.

The work of arranging these institutes was carried out by the Williams and a band of colleagues who joined the Institute soon after its formation. Some were cotton field preachers who had remained with the STFU and remained active after the union joined the CIO's United Cannery, Agricultural, Packinghouse and Allied Workers of America (UCAPAWA). Chief among them was the Rev. Owen H. Whitfield, a black Missouri preacher, one of the strongest leaders to emerge from the sharecroppers movement. Whitfield was a co-director of PIAR, and he and his wife Zella participated in many institutes. Other friends from STFU days took state responsibilities, including the Rev. W. L. Blackstone in Missouri and Leon Turner in Arkansas. Claude's brother Dan, himself a preacher and sharecropper, was active in Missouri and helped arrange an institute in that state which was broken up by planters.

One of the Institute's most amazing recruits was the Rev. A. L. Campbell, a white preacher from Arkansas. Campbell worked on the 60,000-acre Lee Wilson plantation and attended the Evansville institute as a spy for the Ku Klux Klan. But the message he heard, particularly the frontal assault on Ku Kluxism, "converted" him, and thereafter he was one of the Institute's most single-minded and effective leaders.

Others helped. Don West, who had studied with Claude under Alva Taylor at Vanderbilt, took responsibility for Georgia. Harry and Grace Koger were also deeply involved. Harry, a former YMCA executive, was the regional organizer for UCAPAWA in Memphis. And Winifred Chappell, a co-worker with Dr. Harry F. Ward in the Methodist Federation for Social Action, was a co-founder and co-director of PIAR. She had been a prominent supporter of the textile strike in Gastonia, N.C., in 1929, and worked with Claude and Joyce in Paris, Little Rock, and later in Detroit. (See next article.)

These people formed a network throughout the South, continually traveling, speaking, organizing meetings, corresponding, leading and recruiting people for the union and the institutes. Each was trained in the institute methodology and the use of the charts; each brought to the task their own distinctive personalities and interpretations.

They were supported by a network of PIAR chapters and friends in northern urban centers, including many well-known progressives from labor and civil-rights organizations, along with professionals from religion, education, medicine and even a few businessmen. Claude, Winifred Chappell and others established and sustained these committees through frequent travel. The network provided the financial support necessary for the work in the South. For Claude and Joyce and the others working in the nation's poorest region, eating was always a catch-as-catch can proposition. Their ability to stay alive and to underwrite the Institute's activities depended in large measure on outside support. So, at certain times, did their legitimacy and their safety. More than once these groups came to the aid of people, including PIAR staff, who were in jail or under threat of terror.

In the summer of 1941, the PIAR conducted its most controversial, dangerous and significant meeting in the South. At the time, Memphis was one of the most brutal urban strongholds in America, total-

ly controlled by the violent and racist machine of Boss Ed Crump. When the CIO began to organize in Memphis, Don Henderson of UCAPAWA asked Claude and the Institute to hold a labor school, cautioning that he didn't want "any of that new wine in old bottles stuff." Claude and Joyce, the Kogers and Owen Whitfield, ignoring that instruction, used the charts in all classes, and Whitfield and Koger used them quietly in union meetings. Their work culminated in a 10-day institute that included packinghouse workers from Memphis and sharecroppers from as far away as Texas.

The conference was one of the most spirited and thorough ever conducted by the Institute, and it had more far-reaching effects. Memphis' considerable repressive establishment had been conducting a terror campaign against the CIO for months, and when word of the institute hit the newspapers, the forces of reaction struck swiftly. Harry Koger was jailed for questioning and a few days later Claude was taken to police headquarters and interrogated for two days. The "big union" had come to stay, however. Within months the CIO had dug a foothold into several Memphis industries and within a few years the Crump machine itself would fall. Encouraged to leave town for their own safety, Claude and Joyce once again moved the family and PIAR headquarters, this time to Evansville, Indiana.

During the war years, the Institute remained active throughout the cotton belt. The Williams did not stay in Evansville long, for in early 1942, Claude accepted the invitation of the Presbyterian churches in Detroit to establish a labor ministry there. Detroit was the center of national war production, and new migrants were streaming into the city from the South at an unprecedented rate. Racial tensions ran high, encouraged by an army of reactionary religious demagogues like Gerald L. K. Smith, Father Coughlin and J. Frank Norris. Aided financially by the lords of industry, these "apostles of hatred" preached a divisive message of racial purity and anti-unionism quite familiar to the Williams from their years in the South.

The program they established represented the continuation of the PIAR. With the cooperation of the new United Auto Workers, shop committees of working preachers were set up to use the charts and preach "realistic religion" in the plants at lunchtime. An interracial "Brotherhood Squadron" of speakers and singers appeared in churches. In 1943, Claude authored a scathing expose of the right-wing religious leaders; and Philip Adler, reporter for the *Detroit News*, wrote a series of favorable articles on Claude based on the report. Liberal church forces, along with other professional and civil-rights organizations, were enlisted to help combat the tremendous forces of reaction in the city, and the PIAR leadership played a crucial role in negotiations to end Detroit's second major war-time race riot in June, 1943.

As the war ended, the churches who sponsored the Williams' work bowed to the concerted counter-attack on Claude by Smith, Norris, Carl McIntyre, and the House Un-American Activities Committee. Charges of heresy were brought against a Presbyterian minister for the first time in over 100 years. (The inevitable guilty verdict came down in 1954.) The PIAR continued for several more years, but like all progressive forces during the McCarthy years, found the going rough. In a ceremony at St. Paul's Chapel in Brooklyn on July 20, 1948, the PIAR brought its formal history to a close, all members vowing to continue as volunteers of the Way of Righteousness. . . .

The work of the People's Institute of Applied Religion was based on the important notion that political movements need to meet people with an openness to the positive conviction and yearnings they express within their own frame of reference. The PIAR began by taking this approach to the religious rural poor of the South. In the interaction the Institute learned some important things about the people and their religion, and in its own unique way the Institute offered these lessons to the broader radical movement of the time.

From the whites, they learned that otherworldliness and fierce moralism are essentially a protest against, an escape from, conditions which starve and torment and rob people who have no effective way to resist. From black people, they learned that religion is all these things and more. It is also a way of looking at the world which embraces life's misery yet finds joy in the present and hope in the future, and which is willing to move politically when the realistic opportunity arises. The willingness of both groups to join an interracial movement for economic justice under the most threatening of conditions, and to do so within their religious faith, gave witness to the Institute's perceptiveness. It was these people, hundreds of poor black and white believers, who joined with the Williams and the PIAR to write a new chapter in the "Way of Righteousness." ∎

Rediscovering Winifred Chappell

by Miriam J. Crist

Winifred Chappell was an outstanding Christian socialist leader during the 1920s, '30s and '40s who gained prominence among left-wing church circles through her work with the Methodist Federation for Social Service (MFSS).

As a staff member of MFSS, she wrote extensively about the lives of working people, with particular focus on the struggles of women factory workers. If the decade of the 1920s has been mythologized as a time of prosperity and as the "flapper age," with women enjoying unprecedented new freedoms, Chappell's reports lifted up an entirely different picture. The women she wrote about were eking out a living by working nights in factories, standing beside their men on picket lines or coping with evictions from their company houses.

Since the rise of anti-communism in the 1950s, the history of people like Winifred Chappell has largely been ignored. Her contributions to the progressive church movement are part of that hidden history we need to rediscover. She stood up to repression and

The Rev. Miriam Crist is pastor of East Quogue and Flanders United Methodist Churches on Long Island, NY and is a national officer of the Methodist Federation for Social Action.

threats of physical violence, and found ways to express her faith and convictions in words and action.

FORMATIVE YEARS AND INFLUENCES

The life of this utterly fearless and devoted Christian woman had humble beginnings in Oakland Valley, Iowa, where she was born Nov. 24, 1879. Her father, the Rev. Ellis Samuel Chappell, was a Methodist preacher who moved with his family from parish to parish in the small towns of northern Iowa and South Dakota. Her mother, Mary Smorithit Chappell, was a woman who always placed people's welfare before material possessions, a trait which Winifred inherited.

Life in a Methodist parsonage was difficult; the Chappells had their share of poverty and hardship. When Ellis Chappell decided to enter Garrett Seminary in 1895, the family moved to the Chicago area. This enabled Winifred to attend Northwestern University, which she entered in 1899. Under the tutelage of George Albert Coe in the Philosophy Department, Chappell began to shape her ideas about life and religion. Coe felt the church, through its religious education, should adopt the methods of science to build the ideal society which would embody the values of Christianity — the Kingdom of God on earth, the divine-human democracy. He urged: "Abandon the doctrine and the practice of inequality of the sexes; abolish the sex caste in families." He saw private property as "an ancient wall of division within the family, a class distinction — a fundamental denial of human solidarity."

In 1906, pursuing her great desire to become a deaconess (one of the few church vocations then open to women), Chappell entered the Chicago Training School for Deaconesses, the progressive institution founded by Lucy Rider Meyer. After graduation, she stayed on at the school as a teacher and assistant principal. The Rock River Conference of the Methodist Episcopal Church consecrated her deaconess in 1908, and she held that status for life. In 1918, she authored a pamphlet for the Methodist Federation for Social Service addressed to church women, urging them to organize around the needs of women and children. She suggested that they learn about the Women's Trade Union League and support women's suffrage. She urged church women to be the "socialized church" that the General Conference (of the Methodist Episcopal Church) had so enthusiastically endorsed at the prompting of the Methodist Federation for Social Service.

After World War I, Chappell took a leave of absence to study at Columbia University for a masters degree in sociology. Her thesis, "Industrial Missions," provides the earliest evidence of her socialist thought, revealing her class analysis, opposition to U.S. imperialism, and knowledge and support of the international labor movement.

EARLY YEARS WITH THE FEDERATION

Chappell's work with the Methodist Federation for Social Service began in 1914 when she was elected to its Executive Committee. Grace Scribner, Chappell's predecessor, friend and classmate at the Chicago Training School was killed in 1922 by a hit-and-run driver in New York City. Grace willed all her books and her typewriter to Winifred. Chappell came to New York in the Fall of 1922 to assume Scribner's job at MFSS as Research Secretary with primary responsibility for preparation of the bi-monthly *Social Service Bulletin*. She took the job with the understanding that she and the Executive Secretary, Harry F. Ward, were to be partners. They held weekly conferences to consult about the *Bulletin* and the organization itself. Thus, while many of the articles in the *Bulletin* are not signed, we can assume that most of them were actually researched and written by Chappell.

Although Dr. Ward, who spent nearly every weekend speaking at a group meeting or church service, overshadowed all aspects of Federation life, Chappell soon carved out a special place for herself. She was continually in demand for summer institutes and conferences for the Epworth League and the YWCA. Her addresses were so well received that pastors invited her to occupy their pulpits on Sundays. As she became better known, she made repeated field trips (when she could get away from the office), often arranged by one of her former students. She also served on numerous committees and councils, such as the Federal Council of Churches and the YWCA Industrial Committee.

While Chappell's interests ranged over the whole spectrum of social, political and economic ills, she was particularly drawn to the concerns of working women in industry and was deeply involved in the Passaic, NJ, textile strike in 1926. Out of her research came articles for the *Social Service Bulletin* and an issue of the *Christian Century* devoted entirely to the Passaic struggle.

In this strike, where 16,000 workers were protesting a 10 per cent cut when wages were already pitifully low, the solidarity between men and women was very strong. Demands for a living wage for all workers came out of their desperate living conditions. Families of four, five, six or eight children lived on an income far below that which the Department of Labor recommended. Men's wages averaged $15 to $22 a week; women's $12 to $15. The Department of Labor said $50 a week was necessary for a family of five.

Such low wages forced many women to do night work in the mills, often nine and a half hours amid the noise and shriek of the looms. Most of these women were married, had young children, and worked at night so they could care for their children by day while their husbands worked in the same mills. During the day they tried to catch a few hours sleep while two or three young children played in the same room.

As Winifred researched the strike, she observed the women's participation in the meetings and on the picket lines:

> But what of the women? Mothers of children, some of them leading kiddies by the hand or even trundling baby carriages in the picket line; middle-aged women . . . elderly women. . . . They are the European peasant type . . . and their faces attract one's attention in the strike meetings, more than the

faces of the girls who flutter in and out of the strike headquarters, flirting with the staff.

The women listen intently at the union meetings as a speaker asks, "Did they consult you when the bosses wanted to cut your wages? No, they put up a sign saying that wages would be reduced." The women nod vigorously.

"And who earned the money for the Frostmann's (the mill owners) to travel abroad? You! You were working in the mills . . . and getting far less than enough to feed your children."[1]

Winifred observes that their class consciousness grows:

One cannot pity these women. One can only feel admiration for their undaunted spirits. "Go back to work? Me no scab!" they cry. "Solidarity forever" is their new battle-cry.[2]

Winifred, whose analysis and research were thorough and intensive, kept up on all aspects of the strike. She soon established herself as an astute and penetrating analyst of the intense labor struggles of the '20s. When conflicts erupted, she would go to the scene and deliver first-hand reports. Most notable were her articles on the Appalachian coal strikes and the New Bedford textile strike of 1928.

Chappell was clearly sympathetic with the left-wing union leadership of these strikes. She gave her support to many of the programs of the Communist Party at that time, although there is no evidence that she was ever a party member.

THE DEPRESSION YEARS

During the 1930s, the Methodist Federation and Chappell, herself, remained a voice of critical dissent. Chappell recognized that the developing depression was making new demands on people and the Federation would not escape. All along, she had been a sympathizer of Russia's experiment, and many of her articles carried references to its organization and plans. But now, the economic crisis in the United States demanded sharper political analysis.

Regarding the distinction between socialists and communists, she wrote:

Socialists hope to get control of the present state machinery and use it for the common good. Communists believe that the state in origin and history is an instrument of the exploiters and that state power must be seized by workers' soviets. These will represent a new machinery of government which will be used to serve instead of to exploit the masses. . . . But members of communist persuasion will need to be prepared to reconcile faiths and programs that on the surface appear irreconcilable.

Here is something to test ourselves by. . . . Will we be for or against the downtrodden ones? . . . When the test came in Russia, the church was on the wrong side.[3]

In keeping with the declaration of the General Conference (of the Methodist Episcopal Church) in 1932, that the "present industrial order is un-Christian, unethical and anti-social . . . and that the basic assumptions of our social order are un-Christian," the *Bulletin* ran a series of issues on fascism, socialism and communism.

These issues on political theories may have been costly to the Federation. The membership, already decimated by the Depression, was somewhat divided by the frank presentation of these political views and their implicit critique of the capitalist economic system.

Even so, Chappell had no qualms in aligning herself with other intellectuals, journalists, artists and teachers in declaring that she was voting for the Communist Party candidate, William Z. Foster, in the 1932 presidential election. She joined forces with such people as Lincoln Steffans, Sherwood Anderson, Theodore Dreiser and Edmund Wilson, who justified their action as "the only effective way to protest against the chaos, the appalling wastefulness and the indescribable misery inherent in the present economic system." This was her directive to the Federation constituency:

Let's keep moving leftward, for the beneficiaries of capitalism are not going easily to surrender their property or the prerogatives it brings. . . . Church folk have now to face up to the class struggle, just what it means, and what they are going to do about it. . . . Violence? There's no inclination to violence on the part of the disinherited in this country. *They're too meek.* It's the other side that resorts to force.[4]

For the next several years the Federation was devoted to a critical evaluation of the New Deal.

Another of Chappell's interests during this period was the pioneering work of the Rev. Claude Williams, who was organizing southern sharecroppers and tenant farmers. She had visited him in Arkansas at least twice in the early 1930s. Williams had concluded that the mainline churches were never going to educate workers and their leaders, so special schools were needed to undertake this task. Chappell was named to the National Committee of the New Era Schools of Social Action and Prophetic Religion and was enlisted as a visiting lecturer. The schools traveled around the country offering courses such as International Relations, Political Science, Labor History, Dramatics, and the Human Relations of Race, Class and Sex.

1933 through 1935 were critical years for the Federation. They were years of financial distress and dissatisfaction from within as well as attacks from without. One source of dissatisfaction within stemmed from the tension between education and direct action. This came to a head when a Chicago group of

Federation members formed the Christian Social Action Conference and then proposed that it merge with the Federation, possibly moving the Federation office to Chicago. As their name indicated, they were more interested in action, while the Federation had devoted much of its energy to analysis.

Chappell felt personally under attack and wrote in a memo to Harry Ward:

> I'm sure the Chicago men are dissatisfied because I don't *do* enough . . . God knows I'm dissatisfied too! How much more I could do with a little money to turn round with, I don't know. . . . If I ward off suggestions of things to do, it's because for me, as I am and in my restricted circumstances, they are simply not practical. On the other hand, when something comes up that I know I can do, I grab it.[5]

It was clear she envisioned herself a "propagandist of ideas," a role in which she excelled and she would have been happy, if funds were available, to let the office move and just be responsible for the *Bulletin*. The merger never materialized, nor did the move to Chicago, but the financial crisis continued. Chappell voluntarily went on a part-time basis with less pay and a chance to do some freelance writing and teaching.

But 1935 proved critical in other ways. In that year William Randolph Hearst syndicated a series of articles by the Rev. George Donald Pierce, declaring that the "Reds" were using the clergy in a drive to destroy the United States. "Rid the Methodist Episcopal Church of 'Red' Incubus" was the title of a series in which he attacked the social movement in the churches, collective bargaining, minimum wage laws, old age pensions, social security legislation, etc. He hoped that the General Conference would "deal with the McConnell-Ward-Chappell radical aggregation without gloves."[6] A Conference of Methodist Laymen was organized to oppose social Christianity in the church. This red-baiting had its reverberations within MFSS, with accusations that the Federation office was not employing an explicit enough "Christian emphasis" in its program and that the political positions of Ward and Chappell were questionable, particularly regarding the use of violence.

A special leadership conference was called in Pittsburgh to deal with this unrest. Chappell and Ward made statements only after it was unanimously agreed that their political views and affiliations were personal matters and that Methodists might be Republicans or Communists, as their consciences dictated.

The leftward direction of the Federation was implicitly affirmed by the conclusion that a planned economy (in effect, a socialist economy) ought to replace the profit system (that is, the capitalist economy). It was decided that there should be study and action. It was the duty of the pulpit and educational forces to pronounce judgment on the capitalist system as the enemy of society and religion.

At the 1936 General Conference, the controversy still raged, with several organizations of reactionary Methodist laymen aiming to quiet the Methodist radicals. But the Federation was not defeated. They confronted the "red-baiting" with an issue of the *Bulletin*, and increased their budget. They also hired a new field secretary, Charles C. Webber, a labor activist. Quoting Bishop McConnell, Chappell wrote, "We believe in a militant organization and we do not care a hoot about what the great church bodies think about us."

Then, seemingly without warning, the *Social Questions Bulletin* (as it had been renamed) carried a notice in June 1936 that the Federation was temporarily releasing Winifred Chappell for "a much needed rest."

She never returned to the Federation staff, despite a 1937 MFSS national resolution expressing "best wishes for complete recovery of health and a speedy return to the place in our organization that she filled so effectively." One wonders at such a complete and sudden break with all that had been her life for so many years. Was her illness real? Had the internal and external pressures taken too much of a toll? Or did she need an excuse to move in a new direction?

RENEWED COMMITMENT

While Chappell dropped out of Federation circles, she did not sever her leftist connections. Unknown to her Federation friends and colleagues, she went south to join her good friend, Claude Williams, who was now heading Commonwealth College in Mena, Ark., a college noted for its training of labor union leaders. Under Williams' leadership, however, Commonwealth was attacked by the same kind of red-baiting the Federation experienced. Chappell stayed at the college through upheavals in staff and legal harassment, and she became Dean of the faculty in 1938.

After Commonwealth College closed, Chappell joined Williams' "People's Institute of Applied Religion." She traveled for the Institute teaching such courses as "Religion and Racism," "True Religion and Prejudice" and "True Religion and Brotherhood [sic]." Chappell continued affiliation with the People's Institute even after her retirement in 1946. She also stayed active with the Federation. In 1942, on the occasion of its 35th anniversary, she participated in a symposium on "Putting Into Action the Federation's Wartime Program for the Maintenance and Extension of Democracy." When she returned to Chicago in 1947, she became a member of the Chicago chapter and remained active until her death in 1951.

In October of that year, the *Social Questions Bulletin*, which Chappell had co-edited for 14 years, ran this death notice:

> Miss Winifred Chappell died suddenly on July 21 in Chicago. Miss Chappell, with a rich Methodist deaconess background, was Office Secretary of the MFSA for many years and Assistant to the Editor of the *Bulletin*. In recent years, she had been a very active member and officer of Chicago's MFSA Chapter. To all who knew her, "Winnie" was an inspiring example of one who dedicated her entire life to bringing in the kingdom of brotherhood, abundance and peace for all God's children everywhere. She was utterly fearless and devoted, and will be sadly missed.[6]

This notice hardly did her justice. She was never the "office secretary," but indeed one of the executive secretaries; and she was not an "assistant to the editor" of the *Bulletin*, but one of the editors. One wonders how her invaluable contributions to the Federation and other left-wing movements in the church could have been so easily dismissed. Perhaps she was "unknown" to historians because she was a woman!

Chappell experienced sexism throughout her life. As a deaconess, she may have had a foot in the door of the male-dominated church, but her role was perceived by the male clergy as a helping one, a serving role, which she found difficult to transcend. At the Chicago Training School where she was hailed as a "brilliant teacher," she had excelled in a "woman's sphere"; but when she went to New York she held executive positions. Furthermore, she pursued

activities in labor unions and strikes. She developed an economic analysis — a critique of capitalism and the New Deal. All of this was man's territory.

Her socialist commitment to the working people and the poor brought her into conflict with the dominant feminist ideas of the times. Chappell, of course, did support suffrage, but in some ways her loyalties to the poor and exploited overrode her loyalty to radical feminism.

She is an inspiration to and continues to draw admiration from a later generation of Christian leftists who are often still fighting on the same battleground. Winifred knew which side she was on and she did not swerve from her commitment — not once. ∎

1. W. Chappell, "Women of Passaic", *Christian Century*, May 6, 1926, p. 582.
2. *Christian Century*, Aug. 5, 1926, p. 990.
3. W. Chappell, "Classifications", *Social Service Bulletin*, May 15, 1932, p. 1.
4. *Social Service Bulletin*, Sept. 15, 1932, p. 4.
5. Memo from Winifred Chappell to Harry F. Ward.
6. *Social Questions Bulletin*, May, 1936, "The Red Baiters and the Methodists", p. 1.

The Church League for Industrial Democracy

by Gordon Greathouse

BEGINNINGS

The Church League for Industrial Democracy (CLID) came into being shortly after a group met in May, 1919, in New York City under the leadership of Vida Scudder — a prominent Episcopal churchwoman who had been active in the Socialist Party as well.

A writer and somewhat of a mystic, Vida Scudder was deeply concerned over the claims of the social gospel, and possessed an unusual organizing ability. As a professor at Wellesley College, she had a wide network of friendships and was alert to the fact that a specifically socialist organization could no longer gain a wide following in the middle class.

Vida Scudder felt that church social action organizations had to be based in the middle class to be realistic and her greatest fear in the years following the first World War was that the middle class would support anti-left repression. Thus, when the group met in New York City, she effectively argued for forming an organization with broad middle class support by uniting liberals and socialists who would work for civil liberties and industrial reform without explicitly favoring socialism.

CLID's watchword was "industrial democracy," which meant that democratic principles should be extended to the workplace. CLID held that, unlike the U.S. government which is supposed to be of, by, and for *the people*, the industrial system is of, by and for *its owners*. Thus, CLID chose to respond to the new developments of an "un-Christian industrial and economic system" in order to create a more Christian society that "substitutes fraternal cooperation for mastery in industry and life."

By selecting the phrase "industrial democracy" CLID members also accepted the viewpoint that the

Gordon Greathouse is a Methodist minister. Former director of Church Research and Information Projects (CRIPS) New York City, he is now working in Brazil.

conflict between labor and capital was the central issue of social concern. Although not blind to racism and sexism, they felt that these could not be overcome until the competitive economic system was transformed. For them, once the possibility that some can advance by dividing and exploiting others was eliminated, racism and sexism would fade away.

Throughout the summer of 1919, meetings were held in several eastern cities in order to form a

Vida Scudder

national organization. In October, when the Episcopal General Convention met in Detroit, CLID emerged as a visible movement by holding public forums in the evening at which prominent labor leaders and social activists spoke. These activities continued throughout CLID's history. At some Conventions, they were expanded to having social activists give sermons in local churches. The purpose of these forums was to raise delegates' consciousness about social issues, and sometimes they were regarded as more interesting than the Convention itself.

ACTIVITIES OF THE 1920s

During the 1920s, CLID focused its activities in three areas: (1) civil liberties, (2) church education, and (3) corporate responsibility. In its first year of activity, CLID took up the fight against government and church repression of Episcopal teachers and ministers who "incurred persecution through advocacy of social change." The defense of civil liberties continued to be an important concern of CLID members, and one of its Presidents, Bishop Edward L. Parsons of California, was later a national Vice President of the American Civil Liberties Union.

Educating church members about labor issues was always a central purpose of CLID. From its first meeting, many voiced the concern that seminary curricula acquaint students with social and industrial problems in order that they could "know, preach and practice the social gospel." Thus, efforts were continually made to have CLID organizers speak to seminary communities. By 1921, two-thirds of the Episcopal Theological School and Berkeley Divinity School faculties had become members. In 1926, a

"Students in Industry Project" was set up in which seminarians took industrial jobs during the summer and met together on weekends with social gospel leaders, businessmen, and labor organizers to discuss how their experiences related to their faith and to church programs. This project continued into the 1930s in a modified form.

In an effort to educate church membership, CLID speakers led discussion groups at summer church conferences and spoke to university and church meetings. Joint conferences were held with the Fellowship of Reconciliation and the Fellowship for a Christian Social Order in several cities. Its field representatives worked closely with Y.M.C.A. groups and often were invited into pulpits in order to inform local churches about social problems.

In 1924, the Rev. William Spofford, a former Secretary of the Church Socialist League, became Executive Secretary of CLID. At this point its activities were greatly expanded, especially in the Midwest. His contact with all types of political and labor groups, along with his ability to interpret economic issues to church audiences, made him an invaluable leader. Under his direction, CLID membership passed the 1,000 mark and *The Clipsheet*, a quarterly publication, was started to keep members informed about League activities. At the same time, William Spofford was the Managing Editor of *The Witness* magazine which often carried news and advertisements about CLID and provided a current social analysis for a broader audience. Spofford was also very active in developing and promoting employer conferences, student workshops, and church-labor leader meetings.

The third area of CLID's activities during the 1920s was corporate responsibility. During this decade, the middle class by and large had a satisfactory standard of living. Those with social consciousness wanted to be assured that their life style was not the result of exploiting the working class. Thus, many church members read Vida Scudder's pamphlet *Christians and Investments* and tried to invest in "responsible" corporations.

During this period, hope still lingered that if corporate and labor leaders could just understand each other, industrial disputes could be avoided. Thus, a couple of conferences were called to get both sides together, but this idea was soon dropped.

Most members of CLID were sympathetic with labor, feeling that justice was on its side, particularly in the railroad, textile, and coal industries. One of the first attempts to assist labor was by providing food money for striking coal miners so they would not be starved into submission. This action brought the praise of seven Anglican bishops whose letter of appreciation arrived in time to be read at the 1922 General Convention.

In later years, CLID leaders played fact-finding and mediating roles in such labor disputes as the Patterson Silkworkers Strike (1925) and the Passaic Textile Strike (1926). For a period in the early '20s, they took out ads in major newspapers setting forth their position about industrial disputes. These and other activities won them the respect of many labor leaders and their members were frequently invited to labor meetings. A number of union newspapers praised the League for its concern about social justice and for its support of labor.

These efforts did not occur without resistance. From the very beginning, publications such as the *Manufacturers Record* of Baltimore carried articles criticizing the League. In 1925, opponents of CLID submitted a memorial to the House of Bishops to condemn the League as well as the Fellowship of Reconciliation and the Civil Liberties Union. When this failed, they brought a resolution against "Politics in the Church" to the 1928 General Convention, but it also failed.

The stock market crash in 1929 created an entirely new atmosphere. During the "Roaring '20s" many members of the middle class naively believed that prosperity would remain forever and its benefits would gradually pervade society. The working class was not so easily deluded since the 1920s for them were "The Lean Years." Nevertheless, the Great Depression once again made capitalism the central issue, and capitalist defense of its privilege through fascism became a chief danger.

1930s AND THE GREAT DEPRESSION

The Depression also gave rise to three important people's movements: The Congress of Industrial Organizations, the Southern Tenant Farmers Union, and the United Front against Fascism. Each of these movements joined together liberals and radicals in the struggle for economic justice and democratic rights. In later years, participation in these coalitions became the focus for bitter criticism and persecution, but at the time, they were the avenues for meaningful activity for socially-concerned Christians.

During these years, CLID's activities were greatly expanded and its membership grew. Its struggle for economic justice and democratic rights throughout the previous decade were now regarded with pride by Episcopalians. Soon it had a dozen chapters in the East, Midwest and West and more than 3,000 members spread across the country. Its activities now took on a new form and intensity.

Throughout the '30s, an important part of CLID's program continued to be educational activities. The summer intern jobs were expanded and drew together students from nearly a dozen seminaries. As seminary students took various types of jobs in Cincinnati, they were able to come together and share their reflections on how religious values might be applied to the workplace. In 1931, a School for Social Ethics, a mini-university, was started at Wellesley College where prominent church leaders taught summer courses throughout the '30s.

In addition, CLID continued to play an important role at Episcopal Summer Conferences as well as at General Conventions. Some chapters developed public seminars while others participated in Conferences for Seminary Students. Literature and study programs were developed for all members who were interested and at some points CLID cooperated with organizations such as the People's Institute of Applied Religion in leadership training programs. In all these and other activities, their primary concern was helping Christians live out their faith by engaging in activities for social justice.

By the beginning of the 1930s, CLID had dropped its discussion about corporate responsibility. As unemployment grew and working conditions deteriorated, its activity in investigating labor conditions and supporting strikers took on a new importance. In 1931, CLID joined with other groups to provide relief funds for striking textile workers in Danville, Virginia and in the following year they sent 21 members of the clergy to investigate working conditions in the Kentucky coal fields.

By the second half of the 1930s resistance to the Depression had reached a higher level. Industrial and tenant farmer unions were rapidly gaining strength and the United Front had a broad base of support.

CLID, too, was developing with and responding to these advances. Strike volunteers were organized to join picket lines and teams were sent across the country to preach the social gospel.

Throughout this period, CLID took an anti-capitalist position and presented a positive view of socialism. Nevertheless, its primary concern was to develop support around particular issues rather than raise consciousness about how these were caused by capitalism or how socialism might eliminate the problem. Few, if any, of CLID's leaders were members of the Socialist or Communist parties, but they had no qualms about cooperating with anyone who was honestly working for social justice. The issue was support for a particular cause rather than party affiliation. This was a cause of much persecution during the McCarthy Era, with its sweeping denunciation of "fellow travelers."

Many of CLID's activities in the second half of the 1930s were done in cooperation with other organizations in the United Christian Council for Democracy (UCCD). UCCD was a federation of left Christian groups which came together in 1936 under the leadership of Reinhold Niebuhr. While each organization maintained its own orientation, all rejected the "profit-seeking economy and the capitalistic way of life." CLID was a member of UCCD together with the Fellowship of Socialist Christians led by Reinhold Niebuhr, the Methodist Federation for Social Service led by Harry F. Ward, the Rauschenbusch Fellowship for Baptists, the Reformed Council for Social Reconstruction, as well as other groups of Presbyterians, Congregationalists, and Evangelicals. In the years immediately after World War II, CLID held annual meetings with these other organizations in order to share perspectives. While the Council was never more than a federation, it did make important contributions in civil liberties and labor relations by bringing progressive Christians together.

CONTINUED LABOR SUPPORT, STRUGGLES AGAINST RACISM & FASCISM

During this period, CLID was active in three areas. CLID's primary focus continued to be support for labor struggles. In this period that meant assisting sharecroppers in southern states to organize themselves into the Southern Tenant Farmers Union (STFU). STFU developed under the leadership of the Socialist Party and CLID helped by raising funds and sending field workers. In 1936, for example, funds were sent to help Arkansas sharecroppers who had lost their land, and a field worker was sent to the Delta Cooperative Farm in Mississippi.

Supporting labor struggles also meant aiding the development of industrial unions through the CIO. CLID understood the need for organizing the unor-

ganized as well as joining workers together in industrial rather than trade unions. Thus, CIO organizers were frequently asked to speak to church groups and were regarded as a leading force in the working class.

A second area of CLID's activities in the second half of the 1930s was the struggle against foreign and domestic fascism. Fascism arose in Italy in the early 1920s, and it gained strength in Europe and the United States as capitalists backed it to protect their interests and stifle domestic protest. CLID realized that unless people were organized to stop it, fascism would continue to grow and eliminate democracy. Thus, they saw the Spanish Civil War as a crucial conflict between fascism and democracy, and supported the loyalist cause. They sent funds for orphans through the friends of Spanish Democracy and tried to educate congregations through articles in church publications and pamphlets.

A third area CLID became involved in during this period was the struggle against racism. Although their activities in this area were greatly expanded in the post-war years, during this period they saw reactionaries using racism to divide and weaken the labor movement. Thus, they issued a number of pamphlets to raise members' awareness, and endorsed programs to eliminate racial discrimination in government and to combat lynching.

As CLID became more active in all these fields, it again became the focus of attacks by conservatives. At the 1937 General Convention, Merwin K. Hart led the Church Layman's Association in an attack on CLID for being a Marxist organization. With support from Bishop Manning, they were able to get a resolution passed in the House of Deputies to bar CLID from future Conventions. This resolution was overwhelmingly defeated by the House of Bishops but the fight arose again at the 1940 Convention with the same result. Similar attacks were mounted in Congress — in 1938 by the Dies Committee and again in the 1950s by Senator Joseph McCarthy's redbaiting.

In the 1940s, CLID expanded its activities to include support for relief projects in China and the Soviet Union. With the end of World War II, a new and broader program was drawn up that included on the domestic front a call for full employment and a guaranteed annual income along with opposition to the closed shop, the poll-tax, and legislation that deprived women of equal rights. On the international front, they called for support of the Dumbarton Oaks Conference and "people's movements in liberated countries," and opposed any relations with Franco's regime in Spain.

ELSA, EXPANSION AND REPRESSION

In order to reflect this broader program, the name was changed to the Episcopal League for Social Ac-

William Spofford

tion (ELSA) in 1946. This expanded emphasis, however, was built on a weak foundation. In the postwar years, the term "industrial democracy" lost its power to draw people together in common cause. As industry boomed with European reconstruction and the production of long-awaited consumer products, most members of the middle class lost interest in industrial issues. At the same time, William Spofford, who had led CLID for the last 20 years, was no longer able to continue his activities as both Managing Editor of *The Witness* and Executive Secretary of CLID. Thus, for the next two years his son (now Bishop) William Spofford, Jr. carried on these activities with ELSA. He in turn was succeeded by three other Executive Secretaries.

In the early 1950s ELSA succumbed to the repressive atmosphere of the McCarthy period. As church radicals were attacked within the church and without, many shied away from organizations such as ELSA. In addition, without a unifying issue such as

industrial democracy, many joined other organizations to further their social concerns. Finally, without a unifying leader it was no longer possible to maintain an active organization, and ELSA slipped into oblivion. Thus, in effect, ended the three decades of the turbulent life of CLID.

EVALUATION OF STRENGTHS AND WEAKNESSES

CLID's strength was that it reflected the strategies for social justice appropriate to its time. With the achievements of organized labor in the 1930s and the 1940s, a significant part of CLID's goals were achieved. One of its most valuable assets was its strong grass-roots support. Without that constituency, CLID could never have resisted repeated attacks on its program, nor had the funds to continue. A second major asset was its strong working relationship to all types of political and labor organizations. CLID never could have contributed significantly to industrial struggles had the leaders of these organizations lacked confidence in CLID's commitment to social justice.

One of its main weaknesses, however, was its single-issue orientation. CLID seldom showed an awareness of the systemic causes of the crises it was trying to overcome.

Without the rallying point of a common task, the progressive movement in the Episcopal Church went a number of different directions, such as civil rights (The Episcopal Society for Cultural and Racial Unity), pacifism and peace work (The Episcopal Peace Fellowship), anti-imperialist politics (*The Churchman* magazine), anti-sexism (Women's Ordination Now) and gay liberation (Integrity).

Whether a movement in the Episcopal Church will soon emerge which will bring together these different concerns and commitments, grounded in a cogent analysis of the present-day systems and structures of injustice, is yet to be seen. That possibility is dependent in large measure on whether the church is willing to build upon and learn from its own history.

However, we must be careful not to canonize our history. Throughout the last 200 years we see the same forces to be resisted — sexism, racism and imperialism — but their structures and forms have changed through time. Our analysis and strategies must change as well. By recovering the vitality of our tradition, we can work and dream in our own time.

■

On Being Christian and Socialist

by Dorothy Sölle

CLASS STRUGGLE

Why use this ugly concept *class struggle*? What has it to do with the Christian faith? If we can agree that the concept of sin may be spelled out under the conditions of an industrialized society as structural alienation from nature, from ourselves, from our being part of the human family and from our fellows, then we must go on to ask, in whose interest are these forms of production and distribution? Who profits from the alienation of the majority domestically and from the exploitation of the majority of the world population?

We are living in a polarized, divided society. There are extreme inequalities in the share of total social production, inequalities which make pale the one between a king and a beggar in the Middle Ages. There are material and political privileges which

Dorothy Sölle is a German socialist feminist theologian. She teaches at Union Theological Seminary in New York City.

separate the owners of the means of production from the dependent majority. The inequality of wealth, income and power constitutes class division, and a society which is determined by class privileges necessarily produces class struggle.

Its primary, permanent and unavoidable form is the class struggle "from above." Our day-to-day life is filled with the imposition of class struggle from above which is aimed at maintaining privileges. There are, of course, hard and soft methods used. The hard ones are economic pressure, cut-backs, closing down of whole plants and moving them to places where labor is cheaper. The soft ones are veiling the struggle, manipulation of the opponents and the propagation of the bourgeois ideology that tells us there is no struggle because "we are all in the same boat." But if you carefully look around and ask yourself why this young journalist lost her job or why the contract of this teacher was not renewed, to name only middle class examples, you will find that it is class struggle from above which very often takes on racist and sexist forms. Privileges cannot be maintained without domination and coercion.

When the Supreme Court, in December 1976, decided that pregnancy or childbirth is not a temporary disability for which a company has to provide income replacement payments, this is class struggle in the form of sexist discrimination. It concerns mainly lower-income families or single women who, ironically are encouraged by this legal decision to elect abortion. It is class struggle imposed from above because the court serves the privileged interests of the companies.

On the other side, there is class struggle initiated from below, what we have come to see as the only form of struggle but which is actually secondary and periodic. Class struggle from above happens quite naturally in the upper and parts of the middle classes; they quickly sense where their privileges are threatened and defend them. The lower and some parts of the middle classes, however, have to make a conscious decision on this question. Naturally they tend more towards political apathy and fatalism and say, "There's nothing you can do about it." The songs of the working class are filled with moving calls to make this decision. *"Which side are you on, which side are you on?"* is their repeated question.[1]

There are hard and soft forms of class struggle from below as well, but the most important means of the struggle developed by the working class is a nonviolent one, namely, the strike. Thus, class struggle, far from being an ideological invention, is a fact. The question is not whether it exists or happens in this country; only the question, "which side are you on?" makes sense. Neutrality is not possible, because it is life itself, not only more income, but the quality of life, which is at stake. Neutralization, however, is one of the most important educational goals of bourgeois institutions, most often labeled as objectivity or non-partisanship. Specifically, middle class persons are attracted by this position which is seemingly beyond the struggle. Middle class persons are not decided or firm in their point of view. They don't really know where to go, or perhaps, with whom to go. Their interests are not clearly defined as between the ruling class and the working class. Therefore, they fluctuate and waver between both possibilities. On the one hand they are informed and enlightened enough to see what the oppression of the people really means and even how it affects themselves. On the other hand they are afraid of social change which would reduce some of their privileges.

Historically, this irresolute wavering of middle class people has had terrible consequences. Let me recall two examples. In the early '30s in Germany, many liberal-oriented people went over to the Nazis. The fear of communism was the best catalyst to make them fascists, and Hitler won the election of 1933

with the middle classes and the support of the Christian Democrats. We can interpret the Chilean experience in the same way. It was not only the power of U.S. dollars to pay the striking Chilean truck drivers, it was also the middle-class decision for fascism that built up the political prisoners' camps.

The teaching of history is bitter, but it should not discourage us. The ambivalence of the middle class means openness, too. To speak personally, I cannot abstract from my life and conditions, from my being a woman, being white, having had a good education which provided some time for me to read Kant, Kierkegaard, etc. The positive result of this bourgeois education is that it gave me some distance — I am not totally defined by my most elementary needs and interests. I have to make decisions. The danger of this middle class situation is that it binds me in this endless wavering. Kierkegaard criticized this as the infinite reflection, which hinders a person from making a decision and taking a stand. Intellectual, religious neutrality that fears the decision for or against faith is not so far from intellectual political neutrality. Indeed, both are aspects of the same attitude. There is a high degree of reflection, hesitation and skepticism involved, to which a more refined education often leads. Avoidance of *praxis*, hesitance to join a common struggle, even the refusal to sign a political statement or open letter due to "stylistic reasons," reluctance to act at all are characteristic of this reflective middle class position.

People do not like the rather primitive question, "Which side are you on?" But if we try to avoid the question, we have already made our decision. This is true for faith as well as for class struggle. In other words, the openness of middle class people, their freedom to listen to both sides only remains as a strength when neutrality is broken.

With the last remarks we are close to a theological reflection. As we know, the Gospel does not allow neutrality. There is one story in the New Testament which has become more and more important to me. I think it's a terrible story about our class and its vacillating situation. It is the story of the rich young man who came to Jesus asking him, "What must I do to win eternal life?" He had kept all the commandments since he was a boy. Then, as it is related in Mark's Gospel, Jesus looked straight at him, his heart warmed to him, and he said, "One thing you lack; go sell everything you have and give it to the poor and come and follow me. At these words, his face fell and he went away with a heavy heart; for he was a man of great wealth." (Mark 10:17-22)

Let us take this story as one about our middle class situation between the oppressor and the oppressed. It is no less depressing than the story about middle classes in Germany in the '30s or the story about middle classes in Chile before 1972. But the biblical story is not told to us to make us even more hopeless and powerless than we are. It is told to us in the hope that we can find our counter-story.

The facts of class division and class struggle do not determine our thinking totally, and Marxism is misunderstood when it is taken as another brand of determinism. Being members of a social class defines our short-run interests but, by no means, the totality of our interests. There are free spaces and possibilities for individuals, as well as for whole strata of society, to make a decision about which side they are on.

The Gospel tells us about Jesus' struggle. One may hesitate to label as "class struggle" his efforts against the domestic ruling class of the Sadducees and the imperialist oppression by the Romans; but there is no doubt about the side he was on: It was the side of the poor, the religiously uneducated and therefore the despised women, the outcasts, publicans and tax collectors. He recruited friends among fishermen in the rural proletariat. There is no question that the goal of his struggle was the same as that of all historical class struggles: To overcome a society which is divided into classes and to build a new one, in which brotherhood and sisterhood will be possible. He fought against alienation as we do, and this is the common base on which we may understand how he helps us. To bring class struggle and the cross together means to ask Jesus to help us, as we do him, in joining his old and not yet ended struggle.

For people to begin the day with the Bible and the newspaper, to pray together because they have struggled together (and *vice versa*) is a new experience, say of the last 10 years, for Christians in base communities in Latin America and resistance groups in the First World. We cannot put our lives any longer in two boxes, a pious one and a revolutionary one; we have one life only and we will give it as a whole to the common cause.

"Anyone who wishes to be a follower of mine must leave self behind; that person must take up the cross and come with me. Whoever cares for his or her own safety is lost; but if anyone be lost for my sake and for the Gospel, that person is safe. What does anyone gain by winning the whole world at the cost of true self? What can a person give to buy that self back?" (Mk. 8, 35f.) Jesus calls people to take up their cross and follow him. It is a call to take up sides and to join the struggle. This is, to be sure, an interpretation which contradicts the current ones, which usually relate the taking up of one's cross to personal life and its fate. The cross is then seen as the individual's specific misfortune, for example, a life-long disease, an unhappy marriage, an unpleasant job. The call to take up these crosses means: "Accept

these facts of your life, endure what cannot be changed; hold out and bear it." I don't find too much biblical ground for this common exegesis. It does not deal with the wholeness of a social-political situation; it does not talk to men and women in the midst of their active life, but with borderline cases only, and it changes the decisive act of *taking up* one's cross into the more passive one of *accepting* what is actually already placed upon one's back. But did Jesus really call us only to endure, or did he not call us to struggle? Is "surrender to your fate" the same as "take up your cross and follow me?"

The cross of Jesus was by no means a fate for him only to accept and endure. It was definitely of his free will to leave his father's house. It was his decision to move from Galilee where his base was evidently stronger, and finally he ran freely into his own catastrophe, which we call the cross, as Che Guevara also did when he left Cuba and went to Bolivia and as thousands of organized workers did who could have had a more peaceful and restful life as well.

However, bourgeois theology is not capable of providing more than an individualistic framework of Christian existence. What liberation movements need is a revolutionary appropriation of the cross in the depth of their struggle.

I now want to present three dimensions of cross and class struggle. To take up one's cross means:
- to break neutrality
- to make visible the invisible, and
- to share a vision.

To entitle these dimensions with nouns, I would say: Class struggle is decision, compassion and vision.

"BELOVED, LET US NOW LAY OUR BURDENS AND CONCERNS UPON THE ETERNAL POWERLESSNESS OF EXISTENTIAL DESPAIR"

DECISION

The first step, indeed is to break neutrality. To use the language of the Exodus symbol, let us say: Neutrality comes out of Egypt. It is Pharaoh who teaches us to be neutral, not one-sided, and to look always at the other side of the coin, to listen to the experts, to respect the technological givens. Of course, Pharaoh is not totally wrong, but his perspective is taken from the given culture of injustice and his goal is to soften the injustice without changing the system. The perspective of Christ, however, is extremely one-sided, because the side in which he is interested is the side of the victims in a given situation. To see with the eyes of the victimized is the way Christ looked at the world. It is exactly what led him to the cross. "Take up your cross and follow me" means: Join the struggle. Break neutrality. Leave the wavering position in between the old and the new world. What was Jesus' struggle all about? Why could he not stay peacefully at home in Nazareth? Why did he not fulfill the role expectations of his time: Observance of the law, piety towards the dead, faithfulness towards one's family and worship of a God who takes care of the rest?

Jesus must have felt this kind of living as a kind of death; as being cut off from transcending what is given. It was exactly the death against which he organized resistance. Living like the prodigal son in a foreign country, tending the swine of another man, working for a pittance — Jesus called this type of life death. "He, my son, was dead," as the father in the parable said. Jesus' struggle was organized resistance against death. As Christopher Blumhardt, a German pastor and social democrat of the 19th Century said: "Where has Christ been present? Among the lowly. That is why they called him riff-raff, sinner. That was really what he was since he was a socialist. He took 12 proletarians and made them his disciples. Who then can accuse me of denying my Christian faith because I have chosen solidarity with proletarians and because I myself desire to be a proletarian? . . . Before God, there are no differences among people . . . It is life lived in the spirit of Christ that has brought me to socialism."

In my attempt to relate some present experiences of the struggle to earlier forms, I came upon one of the most remarkable women in the American labor movement, Mother Jones. She was born in 1830 and lived for a full 100 years. She spent 50 of those years fighting fiercely on behalf of her "children," as she used to say, the coal miners and the rest of the working class. She lost her own four children and her husband during a yellow fever epidemic in 1867, and a few years later she became active in the Knights of Labor. Her autobiography is a fascinating document of American working-class history and, by the way,

is written in a manner that comes close to the oral tradition of literature we know from the first three Gospels. They are mostly short, clear-cut scenes of class contestation, often pointedly retold, ending up in a biting remark of Mother Jones who very soon had won recognition as a fiery speaker and absolutely fearless agitator.

Since she belonged to the working class, it was not necessary for her to learn how to break neutrality. The temptation was rather to become an accomplice of the ruling forces through the open and subtle forms of bribery. Let me quote one scene from her story which happened during a steel strike in 1919 when she was in jail:

> While in my cell, a group of worthy citizens, including town officials and some preachers, came to see me.
>
> "Mother Jones," they said, "why don't you use your great gifts and your knowledge of men for something better and higher than agitating?"
>
> "There was a man once," said I, "who had great gifts and a knowledge of people and he agitated against a powerful government that sought to make folks serfs, to grind them down. He founded this nation that we might be free. He was a gentleman agitator!"
>
> "Are you referring to George Washington?" said one of the group.
>
> "I am so," said I. "And there was a man once who had the gift of a tender heart and he agitated against powerful men, against invested wealth, for the freedom of blacks. He agitated against slavery!"
>
> "Are you speaking of Abraham Lincoln?" said a little man who was peeking at me over another fellow's shoulder.
>
> "I am that," said I.
>
> "And there was a man once who walked among the poor and the despised and the lowly, and he agitated against the powers of Rome; he agitated for the Kingdom of God!"
>
> "Are you speaking of Jesus Christ?" said a preacher.
>
> "I am," said I. "The agitator you nailed to a cross some centuries ago. I did not know that his name was known in the region of steel!"
>
> They all said nothing and left.[2]

To break neutrality means to denounce and unmask the enemy. Jesus uses the word "hate" for this unmasking of the enemy, who may be representative of the given order of family, as father and mother, brother and sister. Class struggle does not necessarily take on the form of personal hatred, but the unmasking of those who profit from the status quo creates borderlines. The same is the case when one allies oneself publicly with the oppressed, as Jesus did, when he ate and drank with prostitutes.

COMPASSION

Mother Jones tells a story which may remind some of you of similar experiences. During a steel strike meeting in 1919, a man tried to pass out leaflets about the blockage against Russia and the hunger it caused. The organizer of the strike tried to hinder him.

> "What is the matter with these leaflets?" I asked the organizer.
> "Nothing, Mother, only if we allow them to be distributed the story will go out that the strike is engineered from Moscow. We can't mix issues. I'm afraid to let these dodgers circulate."
> "Women and children blockaded and starving! Men, women and children dying for lack of hospital necessities! This strike will not be won by turning a deaf ear to suffering wherever it occurs. There's only one thing to be afraid of . . . of not being human!"[3]

The humaneness of the struggle comes out of a comprehensive compassion. To see the victim in a given situation means to render visible the invisible. People become invisible, persons become non-persons with the help of economic, societal and political structures, which are exploitative and veiling at the same time. Jesus' struggle was specifically led against a societal and religious order which had placed itself above people as an alienating power. Men's and women's true interests, what Jesus calls their life, did not count any longer. The order was manifest in the law. The law told the people to keep the Sabbath and not to heal the sick on the Sabbath, except in extreme cases of danger to life. Jesus broke the law and healed on the Sabbath the man with the withered arm, who obviously could have waited for the next day. (Mk. 3, 1-6) Thus he relativized the validity of the ruling order. The spell of a solidified order was broken.

The same happened through Jesus' relativization of natural bonds and his critique of family and piety. What is the burial of a father over against the struggle for the Kingdom of God? A new community replaced the old family relations which so often are used to let the invisible who are outside of the clan remain invisible. Jesus distanced himself from the family asking: "Who is my mother? Who are my brothers?" and he counted in his family the ones who joined the struggle. "Whoever does the will of God, is my brother." (Mk. 3,35) The old order was manifest in the rules of family and profession, laws and religion. The most important order, the religious one, was based on religious knowledge and excluded the majority of the population, especially women. Jesus worked together with these unlearned masses. We may describe his work in terms of a new language for the poor. He listened to them; he learned their often unheard cry; he helped them to develop their language and he spoke out for them.

The history of the struggle of the working class has the same quality of rendering visible what was before invisible and forgotten. In 1923, the jails were full of strikers who had protested working conditions. Many of them had been in jail for months. Their wives and little children were in dire want. Mother Jones went to see the Governor in Charleston. He received her courteously.

> "Governor," I said, "listen — do you hear anything?"
> He listened for a moment. "No, Mother Jones, I do not."
> "I do," said I. "I hear women and little boys and girls sobbing at night. Their fathers are in jail. The wives and children are crying for food."
> "I will investigate," said he.[4]

To render audible the unheard, to make visible the invisible is actually what theology is all about: To render visible the invisible God. As it is written in the first letter of John: "Our theme is the word of life. This life was made visible, we have seen it and bear our testimony. We here declare to you the eternal life which dwelt with the Father and was made visible to us," and later, "Though God has never been seen by anyone, God dwells in us, if we love one another; love is brought to perfection within us." (John 1:2 and 4:12) To render visible the invisible is to participate in the ongoing process of revelation as it happens in the struggle.

In the beginning of this century, for children to labor for 12 hours a day was considered normal. Mother Jones organized a march of these mill children and they went all together to the East Coast. In Princeton, opposite the campus of the university, they held a meeting.

> I called upon the mayor of Princeton and asked for permission to speak opposite the campus of the University. I said I wanted to speak on higher education. The mayor gave me permission. A great crowd gathered, professors and students and the people; and I told them that the rich robbed these little children of any education of the lowest order that they might send their sons and daughters to places of higher education. That they used the hands and feet of little children that they might buy automobiles for their wives and police dogs for the daughters to talk French to. I said the mill owners take babies almost from the cradle. And I showed these professors children in our army who could scarcely read or write because they were working 10 hours a day in the silk mills of Pennsylvania.
> "Here's a text book on economics," I said, pointing to a little chap, James Ashworth, who was 10 years old and who was stooped over like an old man from carrying bundles of yarn that weighed 75 pounds.
> "He gets $3 a week and his sister who is 14 gets $6. They work in a carpet factory 10 hours a day

while the children of the rich are getting their higher education."[5]

VISION

The third dimension of cross and class struggle is the shared vision. It is not enough personally to have a vision of a more human life; there are millions of individual dreams of the better land where we could be free. But they remain in the same sentimental mood of powerlessness which we earlier characterized as a lack of faith. The powerless dream is a part of the general disorder. It pays a certain compensation to the dreamer for the missing life, but life itself goes on under the principle: Smash or be smashed.

The biblical vision of the kingdom of God needs to be shared in the struggle. We need to remember the victories already won and to recall the experiences of those before us, because no one is to be left out. "The strike will not be won by turning a deaf ear to suffering wherever it occurs," as Mother Jones said. It is a universal vision which binds together those who call it the Kingdom of God and those who speak of the classless society. I wouldn't simply identify both these visions. The kingdom means more than overcoming class society and its struggles. It means no less than a society free of domination. And neither the kingdom nor the classless society will drop from heaven like snow. Both visions are clearly distinguished from mere individual dreams and illusions through our own participation in the struggle for them. It would not be possible to struggle together and take up the cross together without the shared vision, which gives us our strength.

This strength is built on the unity with the whole, of which the small struggling group, the cell, is only a part. Jesus claimed one-ness with God. We should stop hearing these words in an exclusively christological sense. They are talking about the deep strength given to everybody in the struggle, the experience of wholeness and at-one-ness, of God being reunified with humanity and its hopes. It is not so important whether we use a theistic language, a God-talk to express this feeling or a non-theistic, a humanistic one. What is more important is that we become able to transcend the limits of our individual strength which is so quickly eaten up and to transcend the limits of our short life time. This transcendence means that we need more hope than we actually have and more love than we presently take and give.

The advantage I see in a religious language is its capacity to express and to communicate our struggle for transcendence.

Jesus died with the cry: "My God, my God, why hast Thou forsaken me?" To join the struggle means to join this cry. If there would be any Christian faith within the culture of injustice, we would hear the cry, like Mother Jones heard the cry coming out from the wives and children of the prisoners. If there would be love, there would be a cry for love's power that we call God.

And yet, Jesus' cry begins with the words, "My God, my God." Jesus didn't give up the vision. Our struggle, too, lives out of the vision, otherwise we could not bear the cross. In this sense, resurrection is already present in the cross.

RESURRECTION & LIBERATION

Last year I went to a conference of the Christians for Socialism in Italy. One evening, I got into an argument with two participants, both priests. I felt offended by some of their remarks which seemed to me uncritical, anti-liberal and anti-Protestant. Finally I asked them: "What exactly do you have against Protestantism?" They kept silent for a while, and then the older one, who came from a small village in southern Italy, said: "You feel the same way we do about the trouble of being a Christian in the industrialized world. There is a certain incompatibility of Christianity and the modern world. We may easily agree about this. The problem, however, is with the solution you Protestants are offering. You've changed religion to make it compatible."

Instead of changing religion until it fits the modern world, what these priests want is to change the world until it fits the biblical view of human beings. Are they not right? I went back to review the years of my theological studies and readings. What essentially was done in Protestant faculties and churches was to adjust religion to the modern world. This world itself was seen as a given, so the task for the theologian was to modernize and shift the outdated religion. It never came to us as students of theology to think the other way around; to change society until it fits better to the promise of the Gospel and its vision of life. In this sense, we did not talk about alienation as a destructive social structure, as sin, but we talked about humanity's rebellion against God. We shortened and reduced the biblical concreteness and accuracy about social economic realities. We did not take seriously the biblical talk about the rich and the poor. We spiritualized these notions or forgot them. The working people became invisible in theological circles; we did not know anything about their condition. We related sin to the rebellious personality, and we were not taught to think in collective categories. We cut off the concept of sin from our national history as Germans in the 20th Century, and we separated it neatly from our economy. We experienced alienation, but we ontologized it into an everlasting fate — a "given" with human existence. Thus, we avoided calling it "sin" and facing it in our society.

We related the cross to the endurance of the suffering, lonely person. We cut it off from the struggle. Mother Jones says: "I learned in the early part of my career that labor must bear the cross for others' sins, must be the vicarious sufferer for the wrongs that others do." But we were caught in the academic theology, and we didn't even see the crosses around us. Finally, we thought about resurrection only as a life after death instead of believing in it here and now.

The emphasis was on seeing one's relatives again in the hereafter, on coming home after a long and troublesome journey, on resting in the evening after a hard work day. The old imagery was of the City of God with its golden gates. To walk freely and to speak of justice publicly was forgotten. The change of imagery reveals something about the reduction of a hope which once spoke inclusively and wholistically about this world in terms of the world to come and now came to speak merely of an after-hope, which desires nothing but rest and peace.

The bourgeois culture thus changed religion in-

stead of changing the world. We Protestants reduced the symbols of our religion and shrank them down to our selves, to our personalities. We used the religious notions and symbols for one purpose: To serve the highest value of the bourgeois culture, namely individualism. The starting point of modern economic activity is the individual entrepreneur, and capitalism has managed to eliminate almost any form of cooperative working and possession. Mainstream religion had to bless this process. Thus, religion became a tool in the hands of the bourgeois class and functioned only to console the saddened, to enrich the personal life, to give meaning to the individual. Sin became my personal failure, the cross was my unique suffering, and resurrection my individual immortality.

In order to understand what the forgotten resurrection means, let us listen once more to the teaching of the American working class. I am referring to a famous song about the labor organizer and song writer Joe Hill. In January 1914, Hill was arrested in Salt Lake City on an alleged murder charge. Despite vigorous protests from politicians all over the world and public meetings in this country, he was finally executed on November 1919. The night before he was shot, a speaker at a protest meeting cried, "Joe Hill will never die." Twenty years later this song was written.

> I dreamed I saw Joe Hill last night
> Alive as you and me.
> Says I, "But Joe, you're 10 years dead."
> "I never died," says he.
> "I never died," says he.
>
> "In Salt Lake, Joe, by God," says I,
> Him standing by my bed,
> "They framed you on a murder charge."
> Says Joe, "But I ain't dead."
> Says Joe, "But I ain't dead."
>
> "The copper bosses killed you, Joe,
> They shot you, Joe," says I.
> "Takes more than guns to kill a man,"
> Says Joe, "I didn't die."
> Says Joe, "I didn't die."
>
> And standing there as big as life
> And smiling with his eyes,
> Joe say, "What they forgot to kill
> Went on to organize
> Went on to organize."[6]

■

1. The song "Which Side Are You On?" was written by Florence Reece in Harlan County, KY, in 1931.
2. *The Autobiography of Mother Jones*, 1925, Third Edition, Chicago, 1976, p. 218f.
3. Mother Jones, *op.cit.*, p. 223f.
4. Mother Jones, *op.cit.*, p. 233f.
5. Mother Jones, *op.cit.*, p. 76f.
6. Edith Fowke and Joe Glazer, *Songs of Work and Protest*, 1973, p. 20.

Group Exercise

1 Most of us have little knowledge of left Christian history. In this session we attempt to reclaim some of our radical heritage. To research and rediscover the lives of Christian socialists who have struggled before us is not only an important task but also an extremely interesting one. The history which surrounds the lives of these men and women is both fascinating and informative; many lessons can be learned. Ask group participants to work in teams of three or four to identify someone from their local or national church who had been politically active during previous decades. Information can be obtained from numerous sources: Church and public libraries, discussions with church elders, priests, ministers and deacons. Ask each team to collect as many historical records as are available (photos, newspaper clippings, old church bulletins). Spend an hour and a half together sharing your findings.

2 Dorothy Sölle describes three dimensions of cross and class struggle. In light of the lessons learned from the life and times of people within your religious community who have struggled before you, how now can you break your own neutrality, make visible the invisible, and unite your group to share a common vision?

How Do We Organize?

We have come a long way in our study through the use of this guide. After an examination of political and religious ideologies (Session 1), we concluded that ideas are never neutral, but rather, are rooted in some concrete social context. Every worldview represents the interests of a particular class of people.

Looking at the world around us, we studied capitalism and how it functions in the context of its present crisis (Sessions 2 and 3). We have seen that capitalist organization and solutions benefit and serve the interests only of the capitalist class, definitely a minority.

In the quest for an alternative form of organization that serves the majority of people who work and suffer the full burden of the present capitalist crisis, we began to study socialism. We also briefly surveyed a number of other popular ideologies that claim to offer solutions; and we found them deficient (Session 4).

After taking a quick look at the history of the U.S. movement to socialism (Session 5), we addressed our own need to situate ourselves as Christians in the class struggle (Session 6). We urged that this be done in a personal, institutional and systematic way in an effort to reclaim our history — to take the side of the working class and the poor and make a commitment to socialism.

We now focus our activity on two fronts. As Christians committed to socialism we have the responsibility to struggle both within the institutional churches and within society for a completely reconstructed social order.

In this final session of *Which Side Are We On?* we address the difficult problem of organization with the question, what means, what type of political instrument will guarantee the rule of the working class majority?

To present a blueprint or model for a future socialist society would be idealistic and utopian. And to suggest particular local action priorities or recommend a specific organizational vehicle would be foolhardy and beyond the scope of this guide. Entire volumes have been written on the question of organization (see bibliography). Instead, we must develop a method for evaluating our political action and commit ourselves to further study. This session was written to aid that process.

The theory and practice of the revolutionary tradition over the past century teaches that socialist goals require revolutionary struggle. As socialists, we advocate revolution — not reform — of the present system. Liberals and social democrats claim they want the same good things we do: Jobs, housing, education, health care, etc. But they believe a desirable society can be obtained through a series of gradual reforms within the present system. Frequently, their vision of the "good life" is restricted to "things" like wages, housing and social services. Liberals and social democrats are primarily concerned with the distribution of social wealth, failing to understand that the capitalist system cannot grant even their limited demands.

We also want these things but even more importantly we want working men and women to exercise their full powers of imagination and creativity to build a society that satisfies all their needs. We emphasize the need for working people to control, plan and organize their own labor. Therefore, we emphasize control over the means of production. Focusing on the problem of distribution alone leads to a "socialism" of the social workers. We reject the prospect of our own labor being subject to the control of another class, be it either the capitalist class or a class of professional social managers. The working class must organize society according to its own interests.

But we also recognize that struggle for reform is necessary when those reforms advance revolutionary goals. We are opposed to ultra-left arguments that revolutionaries should never compromise, never take office, never work in unions, churches or other community organizations because such activity only strengthens capitalist institutions and leads to co-optation.

Revolutionaries should clearly distinguish between reforms and "reformism." It is possible to forge practical links between specific reforms and overall revolutionary goals. Because revolution is not an event but an historical process, all our activity must constantly be evaluated and given priority according to certain criteria:

- Do our struggles for reforms within church and society build class consciousness and advance the unity of the working class as a whole?
- Do our struggles for reform strengthen the economic defense and political self-organization of working class people?
- Do these same struggles contribute to bringing the goals and principles of socialism into the working class movement?

(See: *Must We Choose Sides?* Session 6, "By What Standards Do We Judge Our Struggles?")

For a socialist revolution to succeed it is necessary for the working class and its allies to build organizations capable of taking power from the capitalists. Working class parties traditionally have played a major role in advancing the revolutionary process. Other types of organization have proven necessary but insufficient. Labor unions, for instance, are geared toward making economic gains within the capitalist system, not restructuring it. Community organizations most often are limited to single issue reforms. A revolutionary party is the kind of organization that can bring together the most politically conscious and capable members of the working class and others who see the need for socialist transformation of society (what Marxists call the "vanguard" of the proletariat). A party can provide leadership to help the working class develop its own organization, discipline, theory, the proper choice of tactics and the outlining of a main strategy, as well as a vision of the new society.

However, unlike previous historical periods

(see Session 5) the present one is characterized by the absence of a single leading organization for our movement. No one party organization has emerged to unite socialists throughout the land. Those who have written and who will read this volume come primarily from progressive, church-related community organizations. We do not yet have the theoretical foundation or practical experience to participate actively as leaders in the process of party formation. But, in the meantime, we must build upon our strengths. Many among us have the experience of struggling for social and economic justice and for human rights in our communities. In the past decade many have fought for full-employment and for decent low-income housing, for women's rights and the rights of gays, for health care and better education for ourselves and our children. The more experienced among us recall the lessons from the civil rights, student and anti-war movements of previous decades.

Reflecting on all of these struggles for

reforms, we realize that while some things have changed, the challenge that lies ahead is great. We must stop erosion of the hard-won gains of the past. In a period characterized by widespread feelings of powerlessness, cynicism and the obvious bankruptcy of our two-party system, to seek out new forms of political organization for our time becomes a necessary condition to assure working people victories. Although no leading party organization has emerged to unite socialists during this period, several revolutionary parties and pre-party formations have been organized during the last decade. We can seek them out, evaluate their positions, and form alliances with the organization that makes the most sense to us (see appendix).

Several short readings have been selected to provoke reflection and discussion. In the previous session we have seen that during earlier periods of U.S. history prophetic Christians banded together to articulate their biblically-based faith and gave witness to their commitment to socialism. Like the Society of Christian Socialists, the Church Socialist League and numerous other organizations that have struggled before them, Christians for Socialism today shows how the practice of Christian faith is consistent with active participation in the revolutionary struggles of our time. Our first reading outlines the history and general perspectives of the Christians for Socialism movement in the United States.

"Opposition to the Tax Revolt" is a brief account of how members of Detroit Christians for Socialism organized to defeat repressive tax legislation in Michigan. "The Transformation of St. Mark's Church" relates how ideology and theology, Bible study and social analysis can be integrated into a long-term study program that serves the needs of a local church. Both these readings provide creative insight for dealing with questions of organization and further study.

The next reading recounts the history and experiences of "City Life," a small socialist organization in Boston. Working on tenants' issues, City Life members have attempted during their first five years to integrate themselves into their community, broaden their base both in terms of class and race, and develop socialist politics appropriate to this period. It relates how one group is meeting some issues we all face: Reformism, the question of organization and the wide range of class, educational backgrounds and sexual orientation of its members. These same issues are common to most organizations in which many of us have taken part.

The excerpts from "New Testament Letters" and "Combat Liberalism" are complementary readings. They provide practical guidance for ideological struggle and have been reflected upon time and again by Christians and socialists around the world.

The Group Exercise which concludes this last session of *Which Side Are We On?* was designed with two purposes in mind: 1) to complete an evaluation of the readings presented in this book and 2) to begin a self-critical evaluation of our own activity that will become a guide for future work.   ■

Christians for Socialism:
U.S. HISTORY & PERSPECTIVES
by Kathleen Schultz

In Northern California, a Christians for Socialism (CFS) chapter worked to defeat an anti-gay state proposition, while in Detroit, members mobilized the religious community against three "tax revolt" resolutions. Cincinnati members work in neighborhoods against forced displacement of low-income people. In all 10 chapters, CFS is making new solidarity links with workers' struggles and members are raising children to resist the racist, sexist and pro-capitalist indoctrination of school, church and media. Across the country, members of Christians for Socialism are helping to shape a new society.

Christians for Socialism is a movement, not a party or church. Its members come from various denominations and religious backgrounds and have differing political preferences within socialism. As a movement, CFS does not take a defined position on many issues. However, it does work in the following tradition:

- CFS is committed to the Gospel and socialism.
- CFS works for an economic system designed to meet people's needs rather than to make profits for a few.
- CFS is committed to the working class — to support the interests of poor and working people, not the interests of the wealthy.
- CFS is committed to liberate the churches from the economic and cultural bonds of capitalism and authoritarianism.
- CFS is opposed to racism and sexism, and supports people of all sexual orientations.
- CFS is influenced in its analysis of the modern world by the writings of Marx, Lenin, Mao Zedong and other progressive thinkers of our time from the ranks of feminists, peoples of color and theologians of liberation.
- CFS works for a socialism rooted in authentic democratic traditions.

HISTORICAL ROOTS & NEW BEGINNINGS

Christians with socialist commitment are not new to U.S. history. A rich tradition exists, dating from the 1870s. The Society of Christian Socialists, founded in Boston in 1889 by Episcopal priest William D.P. Bliss, had active chapters in several U.S. cities. In rural Iowa, at what is now Grinnell College, George D. Herron, Congregational pastor and professor of Applied Christianity, was a vigorous advocate of public ownership of the means of production and a champion of Christian involvement in the socialist reconstruction of U.S. society. Herron's ideas, along with those of other like-minded people, were widely circulated in the Christian-socialist weekly, *The Kingdom*, which he began in 1894.

Widespread ignorance about these and other U.S. pioneers of Christian-socialist commitment (e.g., Claude and Joyce Williams, Vida Scudder, Winifred

Kathleen Schultz is National Executive Secretary of Christians for Socialism in the United States. She is also active in the Detroit Alliance for a Rational Economy (DARE), Latin America solidarity work, and an alternative group in the Immaculate Heart of Mary Congregation of women religious (IHM). This article has been adapted from a version which first appeared in *Radical Religion*, Vol. IV, Nos. 3-4.

Chappell) is testimony to the church's complicity in what William Appleman Williams has called America's "great evasion" of our Marxist and socialist heritage.

Today, the movement known as Christians for Socialism in the United States (CFS/U.S.), rooting itself theologically in the biblical tradition and ideologically in the Marxist critique both of capitalism and religion, is once again challenging U.S. churches to acknowledge their capitalist captivity.

In the United States, CFS had its beginning at a meeting in Washington, D.C. on May Day, 1974. A small group of Christians from various denominations came together to form a national socialist-Christian organization. These left Christians did not come together because of an intellectual preoccupation with Marxism or with "Christian-Marxist dialogue." Theirs was a history born of commitment to the Gospel. While many had participated in poverty and Civil Rights struggles in the '60s, nearly all had been active against the war in Vietnam. Those coming from Detroit had also engaged in urban community struggles and anti-racism work. Some New Yorkers represented publication collectives. Washington, D.C. area representatives had focused work on U.S. foreign policy.

Although some representatives had first-hand experience of U.S. imperialism, having lived for a time in a Third World country, most had been radicalized by their life and work experiences in this country. Because of their changing ideological perspectives, they also had begun to draw new meaning from the Gospel and Christian tradition. Together they formed ACTS 4:32 — American Christians Towards Socialism. This name had its recognized drawbacks — the national chauvinism apparent in the use of "American" as well as limitations of political perspective in the designation "Toward." On the positive side, the title, as an acronym, provided a rich biblical reference to the egalitarian practice of the early Christian community. It demonstrated a practical commitment to struggle for change.

Within a year, ACTS had organized five U.S. chapters, and was called on to participate in the first international encounter of Christians for Socialism in Quebec in 1975. It sent four delegates to this historic meeting of representatives from 16 nations. Through shared analyses and reflection, delegates worked to define CFS thought and action "as a point of reference for Christians in the international class struggle."

Three general characteristics serve as the basis for political, theological and organizational priorities adopted by CFS wherever it exists: CFS is present in revolutionary struggles; its members practice a Christian faith consistent with those struggles; and CFS activists define their tasks in relation to both their political and Christian commitments. These characteristics give coherence to Christians for Socialism around the world despite the use of varied organizational forms and names in different places.

The final document of the Quebec gathering spoke with great hope of "the growing number of Christians on five continents (who) are joining in the struggles for the liberation of the people," giving rise to a new practice of faith and new forms of life — both with a proletarian and a socialist character. "This is evidence of a new Christianity coming to be, one that is an alternative to a Christianity allied ideologically and structurally to the dominant system of exploitation." The opportunity to participate in such a growing worldwide movement is an advantage that was not available to previous generations of U.S. Christians. CFS in the United States continues to be strengthened by its association with the international movement.

EARLY GROWTH & CHAPTER HIGHLIGHTS

In the two year period following the 1975 international meeting, local ACTS chapters began to develop a distinct character based on diversity in regional politics, the situation of local churches, and the communal life of each group. Members began to study regularly, reflect upon their political activity and celebrate their faith within small groups. Specific political and ecclesial tasks were defined and adopted by individual members and chapters as a whole.

An *ACTS Bulletin* of that period detailed some of the chapters' diverse activities. Members of the Northern California chapter worked together to develop strategies for commitments to various social movements — farmworkers, women, the Latino community and gay liberation. In Chicago, union efforts of parochial teachers and steelworkers suggested the need to form a local church-labor coalition. In Iowa, a regular newsletter for a state-wide network of pastors and laity continued to disclose the liberating force of the Gospel in the regular texts of Sunday worship. Major anti-imperialist struggles and national lobbies on military and foreign policy occupied ACTS people in New York and Washington, D.C.

While much diversity was apparent, similar efforts were also tried. Several ACTS chapters initiated study programs. Others sponsored local hearings which examined the crisis conditions of the cities. ACTS members in left parties and other socialist organizations worked to strengthen their chapters' local organizing strategies. Many ACTS members participated vigorously in the social action networks of their denominations. Nationally, ACTS coordinated publication and distribution of political and theological analyses.

In mid-summer of 1977, representatives from six

chapters and four new groups in formation held a national conference to reflect on the experience of ACTS' first three years and to formulate tasks for the future. Some earlier insights deepened, especially on problems peculiar to the U.S. context: The absence of a broad-based socialist party, little popular consciousness of the history of socialist struggle, the lingering effects of McCarthyism, and a liberal tradition of "social Christianity" without a critique of capitalism.

New lines of analysis were developed relating the global capitalist crisis to domestic repression and international Trilateral policy. The continued use of religion in support of capitalist exploitation was explored. Evidence of right-wing activity in U.S. churches was examined. The effects of popular religious movements such as the Charismatics, the Unification Church, the growth of holiness churches and the serious membership decline of the mainline churches were also probed. All these considerations informed the strategy resolutions that members adopted to develop ACTS' distinctive tasks.

Since 1977, the number of ACTS chapters has increased to 10. The local chapter, where CFS' purpose is realized and fashioned in a most fundamental way, continues to be the primary organizational form. As one chapter reflects:

> The locally-based programs of ACTS chapters are concerned with concrete practice, reflection, communication and celebration of faith in Christ, taking the actual daily experience of members as the point of departure and return. In taking up such tasks, we adopt the most valid and serviceable instruments of social, economic, political and cultural analysis, and we embrace the demands of Jesus' practice, recognizing in him the foundation of a new humanity.

In the Fall of 1978, ACTS formally changed its name to Christians for Socialism in the United States, signaling a new stage of self-identity, determination and organizational capacity.

PERSPECTIVES

During this six-year history some major characteristics of CFS in the United States have taken shape. These were present in CFS since its beginning. Now "tested" by the first years of practice, they continue to be of central importance.

First, CFS has been and remains *consciously ideological* in its public practice, formal statements and member self-identification. CFS takes a class stand. It supports the interests of working people and the poor. With this emphasis, U.S. Christians have sharpened their role in revolutionary change and broadened their critique of the religious institutions which defend capitalism. This explicit orientation has helped Christians with a consistent social witness to

legitimate their use of Marxist methodology and political analysis. CFS also calls for doctrinal, liturgical and pastoral transformation of the churches. Such an identification gives CFS impetus for its work in the Christian churches and a clearer identity within the U.S. Left.

Second, CFS political and religious *ecumenism* encourages broad-based activity interrelating the progressive struggles of both battlegrounds. In the Christian sector, CFS represents Christians of "politicized" (progressive and liberation) consciousness inside and outside of the mainline Protestant denominations, the Roman Catholic Church, the Peace churches (Anabaptist, Mennonite), and more recently, the Evangelical churches.

In the political sector, a significant number of CFS members are engaged in Marxist-Leninist parties, socialist organizations, feminist-socialist caucuses, and anti-imperialist groups. Many CFS members are involved in the large and active body of political independents in the U.S. movement for socialism. As a part of their political work, most are active on the major issues of our times (e.g., sexual rights, food and land use, energy, anti-racism and anti-nuclear work, the corporate responsibility movement). In all these contexts, working class interests and demands are being advanced in significant ways. These ecclesial and political linkages help advance the growth of the U.S. Left as a whole. As socialist ideas are introduced and take root in religious organizations, people, who are at first unlikely to be attracted to secular organizations of the Left, become open to seeing them as allies.

Third, like other efforts that are *national in scope*, CFS in the United States contributes to overcoming sectarian barriers — political and religious. It also moves beyond a "localism" in vision. Within various denominational structures, CFS members develop strategies for a broad-based network of class-conscious Christians. This has given impetus to an emerging Left within the churches. Within political organizations, CFS supports principled debate of analysis and strategy while struggling to overcome sectarian narrowness.

Finally, CFS insists on local activity and base-building. This *praxis orientation* has meant chapter and member activity is characterized by a public witness. There are specific church involvements and political engagements at both local and national levels. This facilitates the development of class consciousness and socialist practice.

The advance of these CFS perspectives in the United States depends on its membership's continuing commitment to liberation, authenticity of witness, and ability to engage even larger numbers of Christians in this process. ∎

Opposition to the Tax Revolt
by David J. and Judith W. Snider
and Hugh C. White

In the summer of 1978, groups that had advocated tax cuts for years moved from a shadowy half-life to the center of Michigan's electoral politics. All at once, the spotlights were theirs. Most politicians endorsed the three tax resolutions that were on the ballot for the November election. They apparently thought the tax revolt forces represented unstoppable power. Opposing the tax resolutions were the Michigan Education Assn., the American Federation of Teachers, the AFL-CIO, New Detroit, the League of Women Voters, and the Michigan Council Against Parochiaid. A minority of elected officials also opposed the resolutions, including Congressman John Conyers, Jr., and in Detroit, Mayor Coleman Young and Council members Kenneth Cockrel, Erma Henderson, Clyde Cleveland, Maryann Mahaffey, William Rogell, David Eberhard, and Nicholas Hood.

In the early months of the public debate over the tax revolt resolutions, the primary church voices were those of Catholics and Protestants supporting the Voucher Resolution (Proposal 4) that would have provided millions of dollars for their schools. Early in the Fall, other religious groups began to discuss the issues, became critical of the tax revolt resolutions, and entered the public debates alongside those who were determined to defeat the resolutions. Members of the Detroit Chapter of Christians for Socialism (CFS) were at the heart of this effort. Our experience offers an example of a way that members of CFS can join with other religious persons and groups to exercise some power in the political arena.

One major result of our effort was a paid political advertisement that was placed in the *Detroit Free Press* five days before the election. The following excerpts from that statement, signed by 120 leaders

The authors are members of Detroit Christians for Socialism. This article is reprinted with permission from *Radical Religion*, Vol. IV, Nos. 3-4. Copyright © 1979 by the Community for Religious Research and Education, Berkeley, CA.

and members of Michigan's religious groups, show how we attempted to relate our liberation faith and biblically-based ethic to the three tax revolt resolutions.

> For those of us who are Jews or Christians, the issue in these proposals is how to be faithful to our God who sides with the poor. We are called to fight alongside oppressed groups who are demanding justice. This call — at the heart of Judaism and Christianity — is present in the following passage which Jesus read from the prophet Isaiah:
>
> *The Spirit of the Lord is upon me because (the Spirit) has anointed me to preach good news to the poor. (The Spirit) has sent me to proclaim release to the captives and recovering of sight to the blind, to set at liberty those who are oppressed, to proclaim the acceptable year of the Lord (Luke 4:18, 19)*
>
> The tax revolt expressed in Proposals E (Headlee) and J (Tisch) and measures such as Proposal H that try to ride its popularity announce bad news to the poor and new bondage to those who are oppressed. In the spirit of Isaiah and Jesus we proclaim our opposition to Proposals J (Tisch), E

(Headlee) and H (Voucher) and our support for the poor who struggle to be free.

The statement included this brief analysis of who would profit by the tax proposals:

> Only landlords and industries which own property would receive across-the-board benefits from J (Tisch). If E (Headlee) had been in effect in 1977 and 1978, only wealthy communities would have had tax cuts. E (Headlee) also provides the wealthy with constitutional protection against tax reform that would require them to pay a more equitable share of taxes for human needs.
>
> If J (Tisch) and E (Headlee) were passed, Michigan probably would follow California, where corporations and landlords received $4 billion of the $7 billion tax cut. Proposal H would provide millions of dollars to parochial schools and to private schools for the wealthy. But all taxpayers would pay.

Our religious leaders' statement also included this analysis of who would lose:

> The people who would be hurt most would be those with the least money and political power, those with the greatest need of good, dependable public services. Average-income persons would also be hurt by cuts in basic public services. Groups would be thrown into competition for shrinking pieces of the United States' economic pie.

When the Nov. 7 ballots were counted, we were relieved that two of the three proposals were defeated. The Voucher Proposal (H), which would have granted generous benefits to schools attended by wealthy students and probably would have created additional racial segregation, was defeated. The Tisch Proposal (J), which would have cut most property taxes by about 43 per cent, also was defeated. But Headlee (E) passed. It limits state taxes to the present level of about 9.5 cents of every dollar of personal income, and it restricts property tax increases to the national rate of inflation.

In this project to defeat unjust tax proposals, members of Detroit CFS learned some things that are useful to us — and perhaps to others — as we explore

'I guess I was living ahead of my times. I revolted against taxes three years ago'

ways to exercise power in future political struggles. The following account describes some of our strengths and weaknesses in this project.

For our Sept. 17 meeting, the Detroit CFS Executive Committee scheduled the chapter plenary time to focus on the tax proposals. Zolton Ferency, a longtime socialist who had just been defeated in his effort to become the Democratic nominee for governor, spoke on the issues. When we had heard Ferency, we agreed that the issues were critical, and we were alarmed at the power of their proponents. We wanted religious communities to oppose them and some of us were already involved in other groups that were against the resolutions. However, at this point, the chapter took no time as a group to explore ways we might mobilize more religious people and groups to oppose the resolutions. When we recall that Headlee (E) won by only 82,357 votes — 51.7 per cent — out of 2.37 million votes, it is obvious in hindsight that we should have begun our process earlier.

In mid-October an aide to Congressman John Conyers, Jr. urged the preparation of a religious leaders' statement opposing the Michigan tax proposals. Suddenly we realized that we had a way to mobilize religious communities.

Congressman Conyers had been impressed with the political significance of a religious leaders' statement on unemployment that was prepared two years earlier by the Michigan Interfaith Full Employment Committee and was endorsed by more than 15 Michigan bishops and other religious leaders. We like to use this call to specific action on a new issue to remind ourselves that often we have more power and experience in political struggles than we remember and use. One of the best ways we can move from frustrated powerlessness to powerful action for justice is to inventory our group's experiences of specific social action methods.

Although the Detroit CFS as an entire chapter did not endorse the religious leaders' statement, CFS members drafted the statement that soon was signed by 120 religious leaders, including 10 bishops or persons who exercise similar denominational roles. We lost the Catholic bishops because our statement opposed the Voucher proposal which was strongly promoted by all the Catholic dioceses of Michigan through the Michigan Catholic Conference, as well as the two tax cut proposals. A substantial number of Catholic sisters, nevertheless, signed our statement. This was an important sign of differences within the Catholic community about the social role of the parochial system and, more specifically, the Catholic institutional role of attempting to ride the tax revolt wave to a victory for parochial aid.

We received useful critiques from Jewish signers who pointed out that the statement should have had a specifically Old Testament biblical passage along with the New Testament passage. Further, we missed the signatures of numerous rabbis because we did not think to ask for assistance in getting them.

Three dimensions of the statement quoted above provided the basis of our agreement and tell much about who we are. First, there is a biblical perspective on faith and ethics that many of us have understood anew by listening to the liberation theologies of blacks, Latin Americans, and women in the United States. A second dimension of the statement is its explicit commitment to the poor and oppressed, and the third dimension is its opposition to the politics and economics of the powerful who oppress. Commitment to the liberation of the oppressed and opposition to those who oppress are ways we express our biblical faith. Because the group of Detroit CFS members who drafted the statement shared these three perspectives, we worked together easily.

We are encouraged to realize that many religious persons who may not share our commitment to socialism are ready to take a public stand against proposed policies which would increase oppression — even though religious leaders knew that their positions on these issues would be controversial. Bishop Coleman McGehee of the Episcopal Diocese of Michigan played a significant role in the project; encouraging us to develop the statement, enlisting his staff to critique and strengthen it, and by supporting it financially. His position also encouraged other religious leaders to sign the statement which was distributed through the Christian Communication Council of Metropolitan Detroit Churches.

The religious groups' statement opposing the tax revolt resolutions was useful in several settings in addition to our paid *Detroit Free Press* advertisement. Members of the Episcopal Diocese of Michigan passed a shortened version of the statement at its 145th Convention meeting 10 days before the election day vote. This action acquainted over 600 convention delegates with the analysis, and a Jackson newspaper carried the Convention's action to several thousand more readers outside Detroit. A Kalamazoo newspaper reprinted the entire ad and the President of the Michigan Education Assn. praised it and read the analysis to members meeting in Convention before the election. A specially-planned news conference with denominational heads and other signers put the statement in the *Detroit News*. We were encouraged that it was in fact news when members and leaders of Michigan's religious groups spoke out against the tax revolt resolutions.

We learned again in this project that some persons with substantial power in religious organizations are eager to work with others in an *ad hoc* coalition for specific social justice goals. They committed substantial money and staff time. On the other side of the ledger, however, is the fact that volunteers kept this effort alive at the points at which normal organizational procedures would have let it die. The combination of paid and volunteer staff in this project provided the means to mobilize the religious community that was worth the headaches. We look forward to initiating such action in relation to future issues being fought in the public policy arena.

Tax revolt forces came to center stage of Michigan politics in the summer of 1978. By November, 1978, the tax revolt contests in over a dozen states took center stage of national politics. Now, the spotlights go readily to the proposals from the same interests for a Constitutional Convention to require a balanced budget or for a Constitutional Amendment that would set limits on Federal spending analagous to those Proposal E (Headlee) sets on Michigan spending.

If CFS and other religious and secular groups are to exercise power for justice on tax-related issues, we must develop long-term projects that enable us to capture the political spotlights and focus them on our analysis of the issues. We suggest four strategies that will enable us to act with power for justice: (1) monitor who benefits and who loses from already-enacted tax revolt measures; (2) monitor and publicize the activities and goals of corporations, exposing the "free ride" that banks and corporations take at the expense of individual tax payers;[1] (3) relate the economic pressures people feel from growing taxes and inflation to changes within the international economy and the growing concentration of corporate power that leads to more inflation; (4) develop and support reform proposals that bring justice instead of the injustice of tax revolt measures.[2]

Our experience in October and November, 1978, suggests that a significant number of people in established religious organizations and roles will participate in efforts to carry out one or more of these strategies. Our challenge is to develop ways to implement do-able strategies on the state and local level with as much power as we exercised last Fall. ■

1. "In 1960, 51 per cent of 'net income' of corporations went for Federal income taxes; in 1974, the percentage dropped to only a little more than half that level, to 28.1 per cent" (From *Statistical Abstract 1977*, pp. 258, 563; quoted in S.M. Miller, "The Recapitalization of Capitalism," *Social Policy*, November/December, 1978, p. 8) As corporations pay less of the tax load, middle-income persons pay more. Annual "corporate tax payments (not including social security contributions)" dropped from 25.2 per cent of Federal revenues in 1958 to less than 15 per cent in 1973. "Income is being reallocated by the tax system in such a way as to subsidize corporations at the expense of other taxpayers." (Richard J. Barnet and Ronald E. Mueller, *Global Reach: The Power of the Multinational Corporations*, Simon and Schuster, 1974, pp. 273, 274.) This shift of tax burden is one result of the rapid growth of political action committees that have lobbied effectively to reduce corporate taxes.

2. A longer version of this essay develops these strategies in greater detail. It is available from the authors (17214 Wildemere, Detroit, Michigan 48221).

The Transformation of St. Mark's Church:

A PROFILE OF RADICAL CHRISTIAN EDUCATION

by George D. McClain

The power of the liberating Gospel of Jesus Christ is manifest in a remarkable way in a small Iowa working class congregation on the Mississippi River. Over the last decade, the people of St. Mark's United Methodist Church of Camanche have marched against the war in Vietnam and organized local support for Native Americans in the Wounded Knee confrontation. Perhaps most significantly, they have closely identified with workers' struggle, giving public support to a local wildcat strike, picketing stores selling Farah slacks, aiding rank and file organizing efforts, and helping form an unemployed and workers' rights organization. The pastor, Gil Dawes, recently was asked to address the Iowa state convention of the United Auto Workers; and the 1979 state convention of Iowa's Communist Party was held at St. Mark's Church.

Camanche is part of an industrialized region of some 40,000 people centered in Clinton, Iowa. Fifty years ago, this was the scene of socialist organizing; the area at one time had its own socialist newspaper. Over the years, however, the FBI, the American Protective Assn., the KKK, and the McCarthy era have succeeded in eradicating all memory of those days. Presently, the area is dominated by an all-pervasive reactionary mentality.

The one exception to the prevailing conservatism is St. Mark's Church. What has made the difference? On the one hand, there are some dedicated open-minded Christians at St. Mark's, the majority of whom are from working class families. On the other hand, Gil Dawes, who had been radicalized while serving as a United Methodist missionary in Argentina, was appointed their pastor.

But these ingredients could be found elsewhere.

What appears to be unique is that at St. Mark's a remarkable adult education process has been taking place which has replaced the congregation's fundamentalist worldview with a radically Christian one and exposed the usually unexamined but implicit connections between some traditional theologies and capitalism.

This congregation has faithfully and courageously followed the familiar admonition to teach, preach, and act with the Bible in the one hand and the newspaper in the other, to examine the concrete realities of today's world.

In the Bible, the people of St. Mark's Church perceive a genuinely revolutionary tradition that began in a slave revolt within Imperial Egypt, later sparked a colonial insurrection against the Roman Empire, and during the Middle Ages led to the class war known as the Peasants' Rebellion. Jesus Christ is known as one who came to liberate humankind from both material and spiritual oppression.

At the same time, St. Mark's Church is committed to understand and to participate in God's ongoing activity today. This means, for example, that the congregation conscientiously seeks to discern how God is at work within an industrialized region dominated by plastics manufacturers (Dupont), grain handlers and processors (Bunge and Clinton Corn), and other agribusiness interests (Ralston Purina). It means ascertaining God's liberating will in a community where the majority of the workers have unskilled or semi-skilled jobs paying $3.00 to $3.50 per hour, when shift work leads to considerable family tension and community instability, and where most workers are either unorganized or in company unions.

Through this process, the people at St. Mark's have come to understand that not only theology but *ideology* needs to be explicitly incorporated into the church's education program. Ideology is always present in church education in a covert, masked form.

The Rev. George D. McClain is Executive Secretary of the Methodist Federation for Social Action and editor of the MFSA bi-monthly publication, *Social Questions Bulletin.*

Rachel Burger

Only by dealing with ideology openly can various ideologies be tested in the light of the Gospel to determine which is most nearly in harmony with Christian faith and God's work today.

Each Wednesday night at St. Mark's an adult study group meets for two hours, with an average attendance of about 12 over the last eight years. These people form the inner core of a total membership of about 200 persons. Since they are active in all aspects of the church life, their study serves to inform the program and organization of the church as a whole.

The two-hour time period is divided between an hour of Bible study and an hour of news analysis.

The Bible study is based on the Scripture passages to be discussed in the coming Sunday morning sermon. The verses are read aloud; background material is presented, and the discussion which follows focuses on the past and present significance of the readings selected. This process has been very helpful in clarifying and sometimes redirecting the sermon to be presented on Sunday. It is also the process by which an alternate theology is shaped.

To give an example, the discussion of the text, "The Spirit of the Lord . . . has anointed me to preach good news to the poor" (Luke 4:18), went along these lines:

Rachel Burger

Rachel Burger

Rachel Burger

To preach good news to the poor is to say by word and deed that God will not leave them in the condition of poverty anymore. It means that God identifies with them in their poverty to such an extent that what we do to them, we do to God. This being the case, no palliatives of charity will do, but only the justice of the Kingdom of God, in which the "last" are to take first place in our considerations and planning, and the "first" are to take last place. This is genuine good news to the poor, and because it is, one can see very clearly why the faithful preaching of the Gospel is simultaneously bad news to the rich. The Gospel spells the end of a world where the rich and poor coexist. When the Gospel is preached, the poor have ears to hear and eyes to see, but the rich young rulers turn away sorrowfully.

In the second hour of study, the significance of that week's events is weighed. As the group analyzes the news of the day, they continually examine various ideologies at work and measure over and over again their capacity to make sense of what is happening. Various articles and books have been used to add depth and consistency to informational analysis. Sources include *Introduction to Socialism* by Huberman and Sweezy; *World Hunger: Ten Myths* by Lappe and Collins; *Peoples and Systems*, a study of the United States, the Peoples' Republic of China, Tanzania, and Cuba; and *The Enemy* by Felix Greene.

The first hour shapes theological understanding; the second hour shapes an ideological alternative. Relating the two in the same session week after week makes clear that they are, of necessity, interrelated. This form of teaching helps to overcome the Greek dualism in the prevailing Christian outlook which separates mind from matter, spirit from flesh, and soul from body. It returns, instead, to a holistic view more characteristic of the Hebrews and of Jesus himself, a genuinely incarnational understanding of life.

The criterion used for separating the insignificant from the significant is the ideological framework which the study group has come to believe to be the most faithful to the Gospel — namely, a Marxian one. They are aware of the irony that a Marxist method of social analysis enables them to discover their authentic roots as a Christian community.

On Sunday morning, the Scripture passages studied the previous Wednesday are read aloud with the minister coming down from the pulpit and standing between the front pews. Members of the congregation are urged to read along in the Bibles in each pew. The sermon based on the passage is then preached, without notes, from the same place, ending with an invitation to ask questions or make comments relative to the Scripture or the sermon. This leads to a five or 10 minute exchange in which members of the congregation engage in a dialogue.

Following worship, the discussion is continued during a coffee hour, for which at least half of the adults usually stay, so a large percentage of the congregation participates in at least two hours of reflection together each week. No attempt is made to limit the discussion to Scripture or the sermon. It is assumed that these will naturally lead participants to include an ever widening number of everyday concerns — both personal and social.

By the time the coffee hour has concluded, those who began the process in the study group on Wednesday night will have dealt with the same theological and ideological matters three times. This repetition has been a valuable means of rooting a distinctive understanding which can be built upon week after week.

It is this kind of biblically and ideologically-based adult Christian education which has led many in the congregation to march against the war in Vietnam, leaflet and picket with workers involved in labor disputes and contribute to liberation struggles around the world.

The people of St. Mark's have also felt it necessary to link up in organizational efforts beyond their congregation. Many, for instance, have been active in forming state chapters of the Methodist Federation for Social Action and Christians for Socialism. They have found that organizing beyond the local level helps avoid an isolated, provincial point of view.

This process of adult education has required much courage in the face of risks and losses. Perhaps hardest to bear have been the attempts of some to force the minister to leave. Also painful has been the departure of some members. Recently, for instance, some who have stuck with the church through this long period of transformation have left because the Communist Party of Iowa held its convention at the church. Initially, the church went through a period of serious membership loss and even now faces financial uncertainty.

On the other hand, the church's social witness has drawn to its membership many persons who were discouraged by the middle-of-the-road stance of most churches, some so discouraged that they had ceased attending church. And, above all, the church has been the agent for the transformation of people's lives, from a self-centered to a genuinely Christ-centered, world-centered existence.

What has happened at St. Mark's is significant for the history of the churches in our day. The achievement of St. Mark's in recovering and embodying the liberating Gospel stands as a sign that not just individuals, but entire congregations can throw off the capitalist shrouds that usually cover over the Gospel and be reborn to participate in the power of Christ to transform death-bearing social and political struggles into ones which promote the fullness of human life.

■

"City Life":
LESSONS OF THE FIRST FIVE YEARS
by Kathy McAfee

The 1970s have been rough for the working class movement in the United States and rough, of course, for the Left. But for the members of City Life, a community-based socialist organization in Boston, that movement is still very much alive. It helps to shape our lives and gives us plenty of hard work to do. It provides us with a sense of history and community, a network of personal support, and the vision of a future worth fighting for.

Until December, 1978, when we changed our name, City Life was known as the Tenants Action Group (TAG). TAG was formed in 1973 in Jamaica Plain, a racially-mixed, mostly working-class section of the city, and most of our work is still centered here. This work is carried out primarily through the three City Life organizing committees: Tenants, Workplace and Education. The organization also puts out a newspaper in English and Spanish called *CommUnity News/Noticias de la Comunidad*. We have a variety of other activities, including social and cultural events and study groups that we offer to

Kathy McAfee is a leading member of the City Life organization in Boston. She was one of the founding members of the Tenants Action Group. This article is excerpted from a longer one which was first published in *Radical America*, Vol. 13, No. 1. Copyright © 1979. Reprinted with permission.

potential new members.

TAG began as a group of five and has grown into an organization of about 35 people. This includes a "core" membership (13 at the present time) committed to a fairly high level of group discipline and to taking responsibility for the over-all direction of the organization. Outside is a larger group of people who belong to one of the organizing committees and regularly attend meetings but who have not (yet) joined the core group.

Our goal is to build an organization with solid roots in our workplaces and neighborhoods. We want it to be a group in which working class people can grow and develop as socialists and as leaders in the struggle. And with City Life as a base, we want to help build a class-conscious working class movement that can resist the deterioration of living conditions in the city, and begin to pose socialism as the only plausible alternative to the "urban crisis." . . .

Since it has been our practical experience, and not just our theory that has brought us to this position, a short history and description of our group may help to explain it.

BEYOND SPECULATION

The five original members of TAG settled in Jamaica Plain in 1972 with the intention of organizing in a working class community. All of us had come to some form of Marxism, or at least a class perspective, as a result of our experiences in the '60s. We were searching for a way to go beyond leftist speculations about how the working class "should" or "could" be reached. We wanted to find ways for ourselves and our neighbors to develop consciousness and power as working class people.

Since the Vietnam war was at its height, our first project was the production of an anti-war newsletter, the Jamaica Plain *Weekly War Bulletin*, which we handed out every Saturday at supermarkets and laundromats. The response was generally sympathetic, and as we met more local people through the *Bulletin*, we looked for ways to organize more directly around the material conditions of people's lives.

Housing seemed the obvious answer. Even a glance at the situation — acute shortage of apartments, worsening conditions, higher rents, replacement of homeowners by speculators, urban renewal and "gentrification" at the expense of working class residents — made it clear that the system of housing for profit was a disaster for all but the profiteers. We were also influenced by the half dozen or so tenant organizations in the Boston area, some founded by ex-student leftists, which were mobilizing to defend rent control legislation, block evictions, and promote rent strikes.

When we formed the Tenants Action Group, we saw our goal as building tenant unions that would be capable of fighting for better housing conditions, mainly through direct action (rent strikes, etc.) and that would be willing to support each other. We assumed that as the tenant unions grew, they would somehow come together to form a larger mass organization. We also thought that in the process of helping people to stop evictions and rent increases, we would be able to persuade many of them that housing was only one example of the failure of capitalism to meet our needs, and that only socialism could provide the basis for better housing and a better way of life. We also expected that some of the more highly conscious tenants would become members of TAG.

At that time, we put more emphasis on direct tenant action and on forming tenant unions than on building TAG as an organization. We thought that without the experience of successful struggle, few people would become convinced of the possibility of working class power, and that, conversely, working class power had to be built through action and organization at the base. We felt certain — and we still believe — that no revolutionary movement can succeed *in the name* of the working class, and that any genuinely working class movement has to be based in some type of grass-roots "struggle organiza-

tions." We saw tenant unions as one possible form of such organizations. (Worker's councils or worker-controlled unions might be other forms.)

Beyond this, our politics were vaguely defined. TAG had no written goals or principles, even for our own members, and no formal program for study. Every issue of the *CommUnity News* carried articles criticizing "the profit system" with specific examples from housing, health, sports, etc., and we tried to raise the question of socialism with the tenants with whom we worked. But action, and not education, remained our first priority.

Between 1973 and 1976 our efforts yielded some respectable results: Several tenant unions formed, many rent increases defeated, repairs won, and evictions stopped. There were three cases in which our group, along with other local activists, helped to organize human blockades to prevent the eviction of an old woman, the demolition of a house, and the violent harassment of several Puerto Rican families by white neighbors. Less dramatic but just as important was the increased awareness in the community of tenants' rights, and of the anti-working class policies of the city and Federal government and the local banks.

RE-EVALUATION

However, most of the tenant unions failed to survive during periods between crises, much less come together spontaneously in a militant working class movement. This, along with the failure of TAG to grow beyond a cadre of 10, led us to review our strategy in part. We began to realize that in our attempt to avoid a top-down, overly-centralized organization, we were neglecting to provide the kind of structure and leadership that were absolutely crucial to enabling local working-class people — and ourselves, for that matter — to develop as militants and as socialists.

While many people from the community were interested in TAG, few had become full members. Looking back, it is easy to see why. TAG's structure was amorphous, with the criteria for joining and the responsibilities of membership only vaguely defined. Since we had no system for teaching what we knew about organizing, only a highly confident and motivated person could really participate. And, such people had to make a near-total commitment, since there was no way for someone to get involved a little at a time.

We had no program for political education or group study, and we were putting little effort into collective, critical analysis of the work we were doing. As a result, our goals in organizing were often undefined. We had a hard time recognizing when we had succeeded or failed, much less learning from our mistakes and passing that knowledge on to new members.

We were also failing to provide potential new members with enough of the things that inspired and sustained *us* as revolutionaries: i.e., a sense of socialism as a historical and international movement; personal support, comradeship and honest criticism; in other words, an alternative culture and community.

From the beginning, we had been open about being socialists, and this was a decision we did not regret. Far from being "scared off," many of the people we met were impressed or at least intrigued by our commitment and political ideas. But we realized that we could not expect new people to join our group and make a commitment to socialism unless we could offer a clearer picture of (1) what socialism is and what it could mean in the United States, (2) how we can get there from here, and (3) the specific ways that a new person can get involved, learn, and contribute.

BUILDING AN ORGANIZATIONAL STRUCTURE

It was the recognition of these needs that led us, in early 1976, to restructure the group, giving more attention to building TAG as an organization. The structure we set up then is the one we have today. The first step in restructuring was to set up a system of separate core group meetings for internal organization, and committee meetings for planning our external organizing. There were several reasons. For one thing, there was more internal business to be dealt with: Finances, relations with other groups, child care, cultural events, recruitment of new members, personal tensions, etc. Also, we had begun to branch into other areas of organizing besides housing and we needed separate committees for each area.

A third reason for setting up this kind of structure was to make a distinction between core group members, who belong to a committee and also attend internal meetings, and committee members who work on a committee without taking responsibility for the organization as a whole. One advantage of making this distinction is that organizational policy is set by those who have the most experience with and commitment to the group. Another advantage is that when we meet someone who is interested in the group or in a particular issue, but who is not yet a socialist, or who is not used to working collectively, who is uncomfortable with big meetings and political lingo, that person can be asked to join a committee. That way, the new person has a chance to get involved gradually, developing skills and confidence, while the rest of the organization gets to know that person.

The organizing committees are semi-autonomous in that they recruit their own committee members and plan their own week-to-week work. But major decisions that affect the whole organization, such as holding a demonstration or joining a coalition, must be worked out with the rest of the group. The work of each committee is also reviewed and evaluated yearly by the whole organization.

At the same time that we set up the committee structure, we also adopted specific requirements for core membership, including a commitment from each member to take some degree of leadership responsibility in his or her committee and a share of the organization's bureaucratic work. Potential new core members are required to go through an orientation process that involves a six-month study series and at least three months of work on one of the committees. We also established criteria for who we want to bring into the core membership, giving priority to people who are working class both in background and in current occupation.

Another part of the new structure set up in 1976 was an elected leadership body of four people which coordinates the work and growth of the organization. The most important way that it does this is by planning and chairing the monthly core meetings at which we make all major policy decisions. (We expect that as City Life grows, frequent core meetings may become unworkable, but we want to keep the principle of strong leadership, plus democratic decision-making, intact.) Another aspect of our new structure is a yearly autumn retreat at which we sum

up the past year's work and plan for the new year.

THE IMPORTANCE OF STUDY

At the 1977 retreat we made a decision to give a more central place to collective study. We adopted a study plan which we have been following for the past year and are scheduled to complete in 1979. The plan included 10 topics, all problems that we felt we needed to work on in order to clarify our direction as an organization. We set aside two to eight sessions for each topic and established sub-committees to prepare each one, so that every member would have the experience of planning, leading, and summarizing the discussions. The topics were:

> What do we mean by socialism?;
> Leninism and forms of revolutionary organization;
> Review of basic Marxist economics;
> Racism and nationalism in the United States;
> Methods of constructive criticism;
> The urban fiscal crisis and the tax revolt;
> Classes in the United States today;
> Sexism and the family;
> The dialectical method in study and practice;
> The role of reforms in a revolutionary movement.

There were several reasons why we decided to make collective study a priority. In the first place, it was clear from the way that differences were starting to crop up that we needed to clarify our organizing strategy. We needed a better sense of what we could hope to accomplish in this period, a clearer basis for deciding which projects to get involved in and how to evaluate the results. We needed a more definite idea of the type of organization we were trying to build and its relation to our broader revolutionary goals, including written summaries of our principles that could be made available to prospective new members. We needed a method for incorporating the results of experience into our theory, for revising our goals, and for working out political differences. Otherwise, we were likely to grow in different directions and splits would be inevitable.

A second motivation for group study was to fill in the gaps between members with different kinds of intellectual and political backgrounds. At first, some of us doubted that such an ambitious study plan would work in a group that, by this time, included both former graduate students and working class people who had never been to college. Would it be irrelevant or too hard for some, and boring for others? But the study turned out to be challenging for every one of us, tapping the diverse insights and experiences of different members and sharpening our collective powers of analysis.

The study has had an equalizing effect within the group, not because our heads are now stuffed with equal amounts of information, but because it has increased the ability of each of us to analyze readings, apply them to our experience, and make political judgements based on what we *do* know. We feel the purpose of study is to learn to think for ourselves, not just absorb a line. . . .

Without a doubt, our collective study — both the process of studying together and the context of what we've learned — has been the most important factor in consolidating our group and developing our organizing program in the past year. However, when the current study plan has been completed and as new people join, we plan to adopt a more decentralized and less intense program of collective study.

LIFE IN "CITY LIFE"

City Life's current structure, with its requirements for organizing and study, puts a lot of demands on individual members. As a minimum, each core member is expected to attend committee meetings (usually once a week) and participate in the committee's organizing work, to attend monthly core meetings and bi-weekly study sessions, to help prepare and lead one or more sections of the study, work on two issues of the *CommUnity News* each year, and pitch in with miscellaneous work, such as painting the office, attending a coalition meeting, or setting up a film showing. Right now we don't see any way to avoid this heavy a work load, but we try to be supportive by pairing up for tasks, helping each other with study and child care, and other means of sharing our emotional and material resources. We try to be flexible about work requirements at times of personal crises and transition.

There are times for each of us when we do feel overburdened. We also recognize that many working class people have responsibilities to work and parenting that make it almost impossible for them to function as core members of a group this demanding. Our hope is that as we grow larger we will be able to have a broader division of labor and reduce our work requirements somewhat. Meanwhile we encourage people in this situation to work with us as committee members and to participate in other activities as much as they are able.

In spite of these problems, it is clear to all of us that the tighter structure set up in 1976 has resulted in more growth and development in the group than the previous un-structure. It has made it possible for working class people who had no previous experience with the Left to function as full members of the group, including as core members. While it has not eliminated all the problems and tensions that arise from the differences in our class backgrounds, it has given us a context for dealing with them. Also, several of our working class members, on their own initiative, have been meeting occasionally during the

past year as a "new people's caucus" to discuss these and other problems. One of the suggestions that came out of the caucus was a "buddy system." Each new member can choose a "buddy" from among the old members, whose responsibility it is to give the newer person support in raising issues and to fill them in on political debates, the group's history, etc.

Of the five original members of our group, four were women, and women still make up the majority of our membership. A sizeable minority of our members are gay. Although it hasn't been our policy to give priority to recruiting female and gay members, we are glad it worked out this way. The influence of feminism and gay liberation has helped us in defining our goals, understanding what motivates people to change, and becoming more sensitive to each other and the people we work with as whole people. To us, questions of how people raise kids, share housework, give and accept criticism, and lend emotional support are as important as their understanding of imperialism or the state. We can't expect to build class consciousness without confronting racism, sexism, and individualism. We include discussion of these issues in the meetings at which we evaluate our individual and collective work, and a lot of personal struggle about them goes on outside of meetings.

A great deal of our day-to-day work is with black people: Tenants, parents, and workers. Although the core of our membership is all white at this stage, our goal is to become, or to become part of, a multiracial organization. Becoming a bi-lingual organization presents an additional challenge. We now publish seven of the 16 pages of our newspaper in Spanish. A group of Latin Americans (most of whom are from Puerto Rico) takes a large part of the responsibility for the Spanish section, including planning, layout and writing some original articles in Spanish every issue. But, although we sometimes have meetings with tenants in Spanish, all of our internal organizational meetings are still in English. We hope to reach the point where we can have Spanish-speaking organizing committees or subcommittees and offer study groups in Spanish.

OUR PROGRAM FOR ORGANIZING: THE CONTEXT

Our experience, as well as our study, has shown us that both the material conditions and the quality of working class life are under attack now in Boston. Of course, this is true throughout the country, but we've focused our analysis on Boston because we think the forms of resistance must be geared to the particular nature of the attacks. In this city, a number of factors, including the impact of world-wide recession, the decline of the industrial Northeast, the fiscal crisis of state and local governments, and the nature of Boston as a center of finance, administration and research/education have combined to trap the city's working class in a double squeeze.

Economic growth (both real and paper) in the real estate, finance, insurance, and health industries have required the transformation of the central city, inflation of rents and property value, the destruction of working class housing, and the displacement of poor and minority residents. At the same time, the replacement of moderate-wage manufacturing jobs with low-wage service and clerical jobs, combined with stiffened employer resistance to unionization, have kept average real wages from rising. In short, there's less housing; what there is costs more, and we have less money to pay for it.

Meanwhile, the fiscal crisis (precipitated by recession, rising taxes, and blackmail by the banks) has resulted in government service cutbacks, speed-up of city and state workers, and a policy of urban "triage." What this means for working class communities is that hardly a dollar of public funds is spent unless it helps someone to make a profit (usually through urban "renewal" and gentrification), while areas that are not currently profitable are left to rot. Anything that gets in the way of this process, such as the Rent Control program won through tenant struggles in the late '60s, is being eliminated. Neighborhoods are further disrupted as ethnic and racial groups are played off against each other, while traditional community institutions like neighborhood schools, churches, and political machines have grown steadily weaker. (These institutions, although racist and hardly progressive, at one time gave some working class communities the means for bargaining for concessions from the city's ruling class.)

The desegregation of Boston public schools needs to be understood in this light. Although the process was begun in response to demands for equality by black people, members of the state's corporate bourgeoisie have used the school restructuring program linked to busing as a means of regaining partial control of the school system from the more openly racist locally-based politicians. Although the desegregation plan has weakened local patronage machines, it has also aided the streamlining of the school system in the interests of the corporations and the further removal of education from the control of working class parents. And the closing of many older schools in black and mixed working class neighborhoods as part of the plan has further weakened the ability of these communities to resist deterioration and displacement.

TOWARD CLASS-CONSCIOUS STRUGGLE

It is in this context that City Life has begun to formulate our plan for fighting back. The thrust of our current organizing program can be summed up by the slogan *Save Boston for Boston's Working Class*. This theme developed from two directions simultaneously: From our analysis of what's happening economically and politically to Boston, and our own needs as working class people — tenants, parents and workers — striving to survive here. For us, the battle has three main fronts, corresponding to our three organizing committees:

(1) The fight to save working class housing and stop the destruction of minority and working class neighborhoods.

(2) The fight against racism and for working class Parent Power in the public schools.

(3) The fight for a decent standard of living for people who live and work here, through organization of lower-wage workers, and linking workers and the community in struggles for better services.

We are convinced that as conditions worsen, growing numbers of people will become involved. We see our role as helping to build the struggles, while trying to convey to people that it is not just a particular neighborhood, or school, or ethnic group, or category of workers that is getting screwed, but the working class of the city. At the same time, we

need to convince people that if the city is to be saved, it is only us working class people who can do the saving. In other words, our job is to help turn existing, fragmented struggles into a united, class-conscious movement.

The following description of our three committees may give a better picture of how we are organized:

Tenants Committee: Although we sometimes go door-knocking in buildings owned by targetted slumlords, most of the tenants we work with are people who get in touch with us for help. We get as many as 100 calls a month from people who hear about us from friends, the *CommUnity News*, or radio ads. We give advice to everyone, but we put the most energy into helping people who are working class and who are willing to work collectively with neighbors. As we work with people, we try to persuade them that each major rent increase, eviction, or demolition of a sound house is a blow to the whole working class community, and that homeowners, as well as tenants, have an interest in defending working-class housing. We try to get white people to recognize the effects of racist housing policies and to understand their own interests, as working class people, in supporting black and Latin struggles.

When we give aid to a tenant, we usually ask the person to reciprocate by doing something for the group (like answer phones) or for another tenant (like help someone contact a housing inspector). This helps to counteract the idea that we are some kind of social service agency. If the new person shows some initiative and interest in the group, we encourage him or her to come to a tenants committee meeting. The next step would be to talk to the person about City Life and invite him or her to actually join the committee.

We haven't given up on tenant unions; in fact, a few of the groups we helped organize still exist. But we found that functioning tenant unions are hard to sustain, especially when there is a high turnover of residents in the building or development. We have also found that often the hardest thing to ask a new person to do as a first step is to organize his or her own neighbors. But by joining the committee, new people can get support in their own situations, experience in working collectively, exposure to socialism and the idea of building a working class movement, and the skills and confidence they need to go back and organize in their own buildings or neighborhoods.

Most of the other Boston area tenant groups from the early '70s have fallen apart (as TAG probably would have had we remained a single-issue organization), and thus the tenants movement has ceased to exist. But we think there is the potential to rebuild city-wide resistance to gentrification and neighborhood deterioration on a *class* basis and so we are trying to strengthen our ties with working class people and groups in other parts of the city. We also spend some time discussing ruling class plans for housing and the city and trying to formulate a socialist alternative.

Education Committee: This committee is made up of parents of kids in Boston public schools. The impulse for starting it arose from the need to deal

with our children's problems as well as from a desire to organize other parents. So far, the committee's work has centered around the Racial-Ethnic Parents Councils, parents advisory groups set up in each school as part of the desegregation plan. By giving parents a foot in school doors, the REPCs have aided the growth of a city-wide parents movement, responding to worsening conditions and struggling over a variety of issues ranging from transportation and classroom size to racist administrators. Often immediate problems, such as the lack of basic supplies, are so pressing that it is hard to get to the more fundamental issues.

The City Life Education Committee members play an active role in these struggles and in doing so, relate them to the broader issues of race and class. They also try to increase the participation, class consciousness and power of working class parents within the movement, such as by forming support groups of parent activists, and by challenging the notion that the education "experts" know what is best for our kids. Another way the committee tries to

reach new parents and get its view across is by writing a regular column in the *CommUnity News*. We use the column to expose the racist, sexist, and anti-working class bias in school structures and curricula, and to give a sense of what education *could* be like if working class people were in control of it.

The Workplace Committee: The membership of this committee reflects the economic base of Boston. Some members work in manufacturing, transporta-

tion or printing, but as many have clerical or service jobs in industries such as health and education. This is City Life's newest committee, and we are still too small to concentrate people in any one industry or to carry out a city-wide strategy. Most of the committee members, however, are rooted in organizing at their own workplaces, and the committee functions as their support group. The committee has also mobilized support for a variety of local workers' struggles and is beginning to set up events and study groups to which members can invite the people they get to know at work.

But primarily, at this stage, the job of this committee is to formulate a City Life strategy for our workplace organizing in Boston. Among the questions the committee has been discussing are: What is the role of socialists in union organizing drives and union shops? What are the peculiarities of organizing in service industries? What are the boundaries of, and divisions within the United States and the local working class? How can we promote struggles that build the *positive* side of class consciousness, i.e., workers' desires to take pride in and have control over our own work?

WHY TALK ABOUT SOCIALISM?

Our organizing has deepened our conviction that a class-conscious movement has to have socialism as its explicit goal. The question of socialism cannot be put off because we have reached the stage at which only a socialist program can point the way out of the trap the cities are in. Short of eliminating profit as the basis of the housing industry, there is no way to break the cycles of disinvestment and decay, and of inflated housing costs, gentrification, and displacement. Likewise, only the socialization of investment will be able to reverse the loss of jobs and end the fiscal crisis. And nothing less can provide the material basis for the elimination of racism.

Changed political and economic conditions make this clearer today than it was in the 1960s. Then it was possible to struggle in the name of justice for civil rights, "participation," and gains in housing and welfare for the poorest sectors of the working class. The economy was still expanding at a rate that allowed the poor to be given a piece of the pie without much being taken off the plate of anyone else. What most of these poor people's struggles, no matter how militant, boiled down to was a demand for the state to "give us more." But at that time, to an extent, they could succeed. Today this is no longer the case. The idea that if we could only revive the mass disruptions and other tactics of the '60s, we could stop the erosion of the gains made back then ignores economic reality.

In the 1960s — previous to global recession, the energy squeeze, and the balance of payments crisis — the growing rate of inflation, egged on by staggering public debt, could still be tolerated. But today, inflation is becoming a threat to capitalist growth and, among other things, public spending has to be held down. An increasing proportion of public funds must be spent to subsidize profitmaking, directly or indirectly. The alternative (within the limits of capitalism, of course) would mean reduced incentives to invest and economic contraction.

In other words, today there is much less flexibility in the system. Even when those in power might prefer, for political reasons, to grant concessions such as urban reconstruction, welfare programs, or environmental controls, they find it hard to do so without cutting into someone's profit and undermining the economy in one way or another. Thus, when something is given with one hand, it is taken away with the other (wage gains are eaten away by inflation, tax cuts to homeowners are compensated for by other, equally regressive, forms of tax exploitation or by service cutbacks, and so on). Now that the U.S. empire has passed its peak, there will be few ways that working class people in this country will be able to win *more*, in material terms, except at the expense of other sectors of the working class. Under these circumstances, there is little chance of reform movements within a capitalist frame of reference winning any substantial improvements in working class living standards.

This is one reason why our strategy differs from that of the current populist reform groups. It is our view that these groups will be able to win few, if any, economic gains, and that such gains will either be illusory or, at worst, will actually increase the gap between the more advantaged sectors of the working class (whites, longer-term residents, homeowners) and the lower-income, less-established sectors.

In every area of our organizing we are confronted with the ways in which working class people are in conflict with each other. The deepest divisions are along lines of race, but there are other ways that groups are pitted against each other: Tenants vs. homeowners; one neighborhood vs. another; the steadily employed vs. the marginally employed and welfare recipients; citizens vs. undocumented residents; public school parents vs. taxpayers with no kids in the school system; city vs. suburban residents; and of course women vs. men and homosexuals vs. heterosexuals. If a movement broad enough to have real power is to be built, many more of these people will have to be persuaded of the common class interests that transcend particular divisions. The context for building class consciousness is struggles that unite people around interests that they have in common.

However, a movement that is limited to individual economic gains, and whose goals are defined solely in terms of "economic justice" will not be able to develop this class consciousness and class unity. There can be no economic reform program — within the framework of capitalism — that addresses the needs of us all. A movement based primarily on the promise of direct material benefits without a change in the system will either set its followers up for cynicism when the demands cannot be won, or will be dashed on the rocks of racism and interest-group politics when it becomes clear that some people's needs must be sacrificed for the benefit of others.

Does this mean we should stop fighting for economic reforms? Definitely not. But it does mean that our goal in waging these struggles must be to challenge the basic assumptions of capitalism, the constraints that stand in the way of *all* of us having fulfilling and materially secure lives. One side of this challenge involves exposing the fundamental irrationality and exploitation — not just the "corruption" and "injustice" — of the present system. The other

speech or pamphlet alone will convince people that the missing dimension, sense of community and collective purpose, can be regained and is worth fighting for. But the actual experience of collective struggle *can* convince and transform people, just as it did many of us in the '60s.

Another essential ingredient for socialism is working class leadership and the confidence among working people that we can take over and run things better. To us in City Life, socialism means that the working class is in power at all levels of society. But the power to govern is not something we can just "take"; it has to be created through struggle, mass participation and over a long period of time. This is why we say the means are as important as the ends. In any particular battle, the extent to which people are mobilized, take collective risks, break through old patterns of individualism, sexism, and racism, gain a sense of their potential power, and strengthen the skills and accountability of leadership is as important as whether the particular demand is won or lost.

This is a point on which we disagree with both the populists and with the traditionalist Marxist-Leninist groups, and where we think the two approaches have a lot in common. Both the populist and the current party-building groups, from what we have seen, tend to rely on hierarchical forms of organization and on methods of struggle which do little to increase the confidence, decision-making ability, and leadership potential of rank and file members.

City Life does not claim to have all the answers. While we have a lot of confidence in the politics that have been laid out here, there is clearly a lot more that we need to learn. With the support of the rest of the group, I decided to stick my neck out and publish this article in the hope that other people and organizations will respond with descriptions of their own organizing experience and their conclusions from that experience, whether they tend to support or call into question the lessons we have drawn. ∎

aspect involves the development of an alternative, a socialist program that must be conveyed to people in convincingly concrete terms.

A socialist program for the United States isn't something we can develop simply by sitting down and writing it. Although we could sketch some of the broad outlines now, to a great extent such a program will only begin to appear plausible, winnable, or even desirable to people as the struggle develops and as people are changed in the process. For one thing, a workable socialism will require the redefinition of many of our needs away from individualized consumption and in the direction of more collective forms. Under socialism, less alienating and individualized forms of housing, transportation, and recreation could provide the basis for some of the non-material benefits — like security, increased social contact, a feeling of community — that people now perceive as missing from their lives. But no

Combat Liberalism
by Mao Zedong, 1937

We stand for active ideological struggle because it is the weapon for ensuring unity within the party and the revolutionary organizations in the interests of our fight. Every communist and revolutionary should take up this weapon.

But liberalism rejects ideological struggle and stands for unprincipled peace, thus giving rise to a decadent, philistine attitude and bringing about political degeneration in certain units and individuals in the party and the revolutionary organizations.

Liberalism manifests itself in various ways.

To let things slide for the sake of peace and friendship when a person has clearly gone wrong and refrain from principled argument because he or she is an old acquaintance, a neighbor, a schoolmate, a close friend, a loved one, an old colleague or old subordinate. Or to touch on the matter lightly instead of going into it thoroughly, so as to keep on good terms. The result is that both the organization and the individual are harmed. This is one type of liberalism.

To indulge in irresponsible criticism in private instead of actively putting forward one's suggestions to the organization. To say nothing to people to their faces but to gossip behind their backs, or to say nothing at a meeting but to gossip afterwards. To show no regard at all for the principles of collective life but to follow one's own inclination. This is the second type.

To let things drift if they do not affect one personally; to say as little as possible while knowing perfectly well what is wrong; to be worldly wise and play safe and seek only to avoid blame. This is the third type.

Not to obey orders but to give pride of place to one's own opinions. To demand special consideration from the organization but to reject its discipline. This is a fourth type.

To indulge in personal attacks, pick quarrels, vent personal spite or seek revenge instead of entering into an argument and struggling against incorrect views for the sake of unity or progress or getting the work done properly. This is a fifth type.

To hear incorrect views without rebutting them and even to hear counter-revolutionary remarks without reporting them, but instead to take them calmly as if nothing had happened. This is a sixth type.

To be among the masses and fail to conduct propaganda and agitation or speak at meetings or conduct investigations and inquiries among them, and instead to be indifferent to them and show no concern for their well-being, forgetting that one is a communist and behaving as if one were an ordinary non-communist. This is a seventh type.

To see someone harming the interests of the masses and yet not feel indignant, or dissuade or stop or reason with that person, but to allow that person to continue. This is an eighth type.

To work half-heartedly without a definite plan or direction; to work perfunctorily and muddle along. This is a ninth type.

To regard oneself as having rendered great service to the revolution, to pride oneself on being a veteran, to disdain minor assignments while being quite un-

equal to major tasks, to be slipshod in work and slack in study. This is a tenth type.

To be aware of one's own mistakes and yet make no attempt to correct them, taking a liberal attitude towards oneself. This is an eleventh type.

We could name more. But these eleven are the principle types.

They are all manifestations of liberalism.

Liberalism is extremely harmful in a revolutionary collective. It is a corrosive which eats away unity, undermines cohesion, causes apathy and creates dissension. It robs the revolutionary ranks of compact organization and strict discipline, prevents policies from being carried through and alienates the party organizations from the masses which the party leads. It is an extremely bad tendency.

Liberalism stems from petty-bourgeois selfishness; it places personal interests first and the interests of the revolution second, and this gives rise to ideological, political and organizational liberalism.

People who are liberals look upon the principles of Marxism as abstract dogma. They approve of Marxism, but are not prepared to practice it or to practice it in full; they are not prepared to replace their liberalism by Marxism. These people have their Marxism, but they have their liberalism as well — they talk Marxism, but practice liberalism; they apply Marxism to others but liberalism to themselves. They keep both kinds of goods in stock and find a use for each. This is how the minds of certain people work.

Liberalism is a manifestation of opportunism and conflicts fundamentally with Marxism. It is negative and objectively has the effect of helping the enemy; that is why the enemy welcomes its preservation in our midst. Such being its nature, there should be no place for it in the ranks of the revolution.

We must use Marxism, which is positive in spirit, to overcome liberalism, which is negative. A communist should have largeness of mind and should be staunch and active, looking upon the interests of the revolution as one's own life and subordinating personal interests to those of the revolution; always and everywhere a communist should adhere to principle and wage a tireless struggle against all incorrect ideas and actions, so as to consolidate the collective life of the party and strengthen the ties between the party and the masses; a communist should be more concerned about the party and the masses than about any individual, and more concerned about others than about self. Only thus can one be considered a communist.

All loyal, honest, active and upright communists must unite to oppose the liberal tendencies shown by certain people among us, and set them on the right path. This is one of the tasks of our ideological front.

■

New Testament Letters

by St. Paul and Other Writers of the early Christian Church

You must give up your old way of life; you must put aside your old self, which gets corrupted by following illusory desires. Your mind must be renewed by a spiritual revolution so that you can put on the new self that has been created in God's way, in the goodness and holiness of the truth.

So from now on, there must be no more lies: You must speak the truth to one another, since we are all parts of one another. Let your words be for the improvement of others, as the occasion offers, and do good to your listeners.

—*Ephesians* 4:22-25 & 29

Be at peace among yourselves. And this is what we ask you to do: Warn the idlers, give courage to those who are apprehensive, care for the weak and be patient with everyone. Make sure that people do not try to take revenge; you must all think of what is best for each other and for the community.

—*1 Thessalonians* 5:14-16

And in fact you have there a great many people who need to be disciplined, who talk nonsense and try to make others believe it. They have got to be silenced. People of this kind ruin whole families, by teaching things they ought not to, and doing it with the vile motive of making money. . . . So you will have to be severe in correcting them, and make them sound in the faith so that they stop doing what they are told to do by people who are no longer interested in the truth.

—*Titus* 1: 10-14

If a person disputes what you teach, then after a first warning, have no more to do with that person: You will know that any person of that sort has already lapsed and is self-condemned as a sinner.

—*Titus* 3:10-11

Never be a dictator over any group that is put in your charge, but be an example that the whole community can follow.

—*1 Peter* 5:13

If our life in Christ means anything to you, if love can persuade all . . . then be united in your convictions and united in your love, with a common purpose and a common mind. That is the one thing which would make me completely happy. There must be no competition among you, no conceit, but everybody is to be self-effacing. Always consider the other person to be better than yourself, so that nobody thinks of his or her own interest first but everybody thinks of other people's interests instead.

—*Philippians* 2: 1-5

Group Exercise

Spend your first half hour together sharing insights and discussing your own questions arising from reflections on the readings for this session.

Take an hour and a half to evaluate how organizations deal with the problem of reformism. First, critically examine the Christians for Socialism and City Life readings. Then, apply the questions below to the work of organizations in your church or community in which members of your study group have been involved:

1 Describe the theology (if applicable), ideology and analytical tools these organizations use for evaluating their own actions and the world around them. Are they able to judge the trends and needs of the times?

2 How does the activity of these organizations add or detract from building class consciousness and strengthening the self-organization of working people?

3 Do these organizations introduce socialist ideas to the working class movement or do their struggles for specific reforms only improve the capitalist system? If the latter, what happens to the reforms sought and those who fight for them?

Please use the last half hour collectively writing a letter to the editors of this volume. We have spent much time in selection and preparation of these materials. Our future efforts in Christian education can benefit by knowing what you experience to be the major strengths and weaknesses of this study guide. Thank you for taking this task seriously. Please mail your critique to the address on the back cover.

This study guide provides merely the first steps toward the development of a social analysis and the firm biblical and theoretical base we all need to deepen our Christian commitment and continue the struggle for socialism throughout the 1980s. After more closely examining the appendix that follows, communicate with one or another of the resource groups listed, and get together again in a few weeks to plan a program for further action.

Appendix

BIBLIOGRAPHY

Session 1

Christians and Marxists. Jose Miguez Bonino. Grand Rapids, MI: William B. Eerdmans Press, 1976.

Communication and Class Struggle. Armand Mattelart and Seth Siegelaub. New York, NY: International General, 1979.

Disciplines in Transformation: A Guide to Theology and the Behavioral Sciences. William W. Everett and T.J. Bachmeyer. Washington, D.C.: University Press of America, 1979.

Doing Theology in a New Key. Robert McAfee Brown. Philadelphia, PA: Westminster Press, 1978.

Doing Theology in a Revolutionary Situation. Jose Miguez Bonino. Philadelphia, PA: Fortress Press, 1975.

History and the Theology of Liberation. Enrique Dussel. Maryknoll, NY: Orbis Books, 1976.

Ideology in Social Science. Robin Blackburn, ed. New York, NY: Pantheon Books, 1972.

Is Liberation Theology for North America? The Response of First World Churches. New York, NY: Theology in the Americas, 1978.

Liberation of Theology. Juan Luis Segundo, S.J. Maryknoll, NY: Orbis Books, 1976.

Marx and the Bible. Jose Miranda. Maryknoll, NY: Orbis Books, 1975.

Session 2

Capital. A Critique of Political Economy. Karl Marx. Volume 1 introduced by Ernest Mandel. Translated by Ben Fowkes. Middlesex, England: Penguin Books in association with *New Left Review*, 1976.

Capitalist System. Second Edition. Richard C. Edwards, Michael Reich, and Thomas E. Weisskopf, eds. Englewood Cliffs, NJ: Prentice-Hall, 1978.

Contribution to the Critique of Political Economy. Karl Marx. New York, NY: International Publishers, 1970.

Economic Report of the President. Washington, D.C.: U.S. Government Printing Office, January, 1980.

Imperialism, the Highest Stage of Capitalism. V.I. Lenin. Beijing, China: Foreign Languages Press, 1970.

Political Economy. John Eaton. New York, NY: International Publishers, 1973.

Political Economy: A Beginner's Course. A. Leontiev. San Francisco, CA: Proletarian Publishers, n.d.

Stagflation: A Radical Theory of Unemployment and Inflation. Howard Sherman. New York, NY: Harper and Row, 1976.

U.S. Capitalism in Crisis. Economics Education Project. New York, NY: Union for Radical Political Economics, 1978.

Wage, Labor and Capital. Karl Marx. New York, NY: International Publishers, 1933.

Wages, Price and Profit. Karl Marx. Beijing, China: Foreign Languages Press, 1970.

What's Happening to Our Jobs? Second Edition. *Why Do We Spend So Much Money?* Somerville, MA: Popular Economics Press Pamphlets, 1973.

Session 3

Between Labor and Capital: The Professional Managerial Class. Edited by Pat Walker. Boston, MA: South End Press, 1979.

Classes in Contemporary Capitalism. Nicos Poulantzas. London, England: Verso, 1974.

Classes in the United States: Workers Against Capitalism. Charles Loren. Davis, CA: Cardinal Publishers, 1977.

Class, Crisis and the State. Erik Olin Wright. London, England: New Left Books, 1978.

Hidden Injuries of Class. Richard Sennett and Jonathan Cobb. New York, NY: Vintage Books, 1973.

Imperial Brain Trust. Laurence H. Shoup and William Minter. New York, NY: Monthly Review Press, 1977.

Labor and Monopoly Capital. Harry Braverman. New York, NY: Monthly Review Press, 1974.

State in Capitalist Society. Ralph Miliband. New York, NY: Basic Books Publishers, 1969.

Twisted Dream: Capitalist Development in the U.S. Since 1776. Douglas Dowd. Cambridge, MA: Winthrop Publications, 1977.

Worlds of Pain: Life in the Working Class Family. Lillian Breslow Rubin. New York, NY: Basic Books Publishers, 1976.

Session 4

"Capitalist and Maoist Economic Development" in *Review of Radical Political Economics,* Vol. 4, No. 2, pp. 26-38. New York, NY: Union for Radical Political Economics, 1970.

"Conference Report: Socialism in the Present-Day World" in *Socialist Revolution* #35, Vol. 7, No. 5, pp. 69-87. David Plotke. Oakland, CA: New Fronts Publishing Co., 1977.

"Contradictions of Socialist Construction." *Synthesis,* Vol. 3, No. 1. San Francisco, CA: Synthesis Publications, 1979.

"Critique of the Gotha Program" in *Marx-Engels Reader.* Robert Tucker, ed. New York, NY: W.W. Norton and Co., 1972.

Formation of the Economic Thought of Karl Marx. Ernest Mandel. New York, NY: Monthly Review Press, 1971.

Marx-Engels Reader. Robert Tucker, ed. New York, NY: W.W. Norton and Co., 1972.

People and Systems Packet (on the United States, China, Cuba, Tanzania) with Leaders Guide. New York: Friendship Press, 1975.

Socialism in the Soviet Union. Jonathan Arthur. Chicago, IL: Workers Press, 1977.

Toward Socialism in America. Harold Freeman. Cambridge, MA: Schenkman Publishing Co., 1979.

Transformation of Political Culture in Cuba. Richard Fagen. Palo Alto, CA: Stanford University Press, 1969.

Session 5

American Socialist Movement: 1897-1912. Ira Kipnis. New York, NY: Monthly Review Press, 1952, 1972.

American Socialism and Black Americans: From the Age of Jackson to World War II. Philip S. Foner. Westport, CT: Greenwood Press, 1977.

American Trade Unionism: Principles and Organization, Strategy and Tactics. William Z. Foster. New York, NY: International Publishers, 1947.

Autobiography of Big Bill Haywood, originally published as *Bill Haywood's Book.* William D. Haywood. New York, NY: International Publishers, 1929.

Autobiography of Mother Jones. Mary Harris Jones. Chicago, IL: Charles H. Kerr Publishing Co., 1926, 1976.

Communistic Societies of the United States. Charles Nordhoff. New York, NY: Dover, 1966.

Eugene V. Debs: The Making of an American Radical. Ray Ginger. New York, NY: Collier Books, 1949, 1962.

History of the Communist Party of the United States. William Z. Foster. Westport, CT: Greenwood Press, 1952, 1968.

History of the Labor Movement in the United States (4 Vols.) Philip S. Foner. New York, NY: International Publishers, 1947, 1955, 1964, 1965.

Labor Radical: From the Wobblies to the CIO, A Personal History. Len De Caux. Boston, MA: Beacon Press, 1970.

Labor's Untold Story. Richard O. Boyer and Herbert M. Morais. New York, NY: United Electrical, Radio & Machine Workers of America, 1955, 1970.

Radicalism in America. Sidney Lens. New York, NY: Thomas Y. Crowell, 1969.

Rebel Girl. Elizabeth Gurley Flynn. New York, NY: International Publishers, 1955.

Them and Us. James J. Matles and James Higgins. Boston, MA: Beacon Press, 1974.

Tom Watson: Agrarian Rebel. C. Vann Woodward. New York, NY: Oxford University Press, 1938, 1963.

We, the People: The Drama of America. Leo Huberman. New York, NY: Monthly Review Press, 1932, 1947, 1960.

Session 6

Christianity and Socialism. Washington Gladden. New York, NY: Eaton and Mains, 1905.

"Christianity and Socialism in America, 1900-1920." Robert Handy. *Church History,* XXI (March, 1952), pp. 39-54.

"Christian Socialism in America," John Spargo. *The American Journal of Sociology,* XV (July, 1909), pp. 16-20.

Christianizing the Social Order. Walter Rauschenbusch. New York, NY: Macmillan Company, 1912.

Early Days of Christian Socialism in America. James Dombrowski. New York, NY: Octagon Books, 1936, 1966.

Forging of American Socialism: Origins of the

Modern Movement. Howard H. Quint. Columbia, SC: University of South Carolina Press, 1953.

"Friend or Foe?" Social Christianity's Response to Socialism Prior to the Great Depression. Robert Craig. *Radical Religion*, Vol. 1, No. 1 (Winter, 1973), pp. 45-65.

"George D. Herron and the Social Gospel in American Protestantism." Robert Handy. Unpublished Ph.D. dissertation. Chicago, IL: University of Chicago, 1949.

"History of Christian Socialism in America." Paul F. Laubenstein. Unpublished S.T.M. thesis. New York, NY: Union Theological Seminary, 1925.

"Introduction to the Life and Thought of Harry F. Ward." Robert Craig. *Union Seminary Quarterly Review*, XXIV (Summer, 1969), pp. 331-356.

Session 7

"Christians for Socialism USA" and "The Methodist Federation for Social Action." *Radical Religion*, Vol. IV, Nos. 3-4 (1979) and Vol. V, No. 1 (1980).

Communist Manifesto. Karl Marx and Friedrich Engels. Beijing, China: Foreign Languages Press, 1970. (Many other editions available.)

"From Capitalism to Socialism." *The Capitalist System,* Chapter 14, pp. 517 ff. Richard C. Edwards, Michael Reich, Thomas Weisskopf, eds. Englewood Cliffs, NJ: Prentice-Hall, 1978.

On Organization. V.I. Lenin. Articles from the Collected Works. San Francisco, CA: Proletarian Publishers, n.d.

On the Transition to Socialism. Paul Sweezy and Charles Bettleheim. New York, NY: Monthly Review Press, 1971. See also *Monthly Review* Nov., 1974; Jan., 1975; Mar., 1976; and May, 1977

for continuation of this discussion.

Reform or Revolution. Rosa Luxembourg. New York, NY: Pathfinder Press, 1973.

Socialism and Revolution. Andre Gorz. Garden City, NY: Anchor Press/Doubleday and Co., 1973.

Socialist Alternatives for America: A Bibliography. Jim Campen, ed. New York, NY: Union for Radical Political Economics, 1974.

"What Is To Be Done?" and "State and Revolution." V.I. Lenin. *Essential Works of Lenin.* New York: Bantam Books, 1966.

"Where Do We Go From Here?" *U.S. Capitalism in Crisis*, Part V, pp. 331 ff. New York, NY: Union for Radical Political Economics, 1978.

FILMS

An excellent directory, a few valuable periodicals and three select film distributors:

REEL CHANGE: A Guide to Social Issue Films, a listing of the top 16mm political films available for U.S. distribution. Informative and evaluative descriptions of more than 500 titles, subject indexed and cross-referenced. Includes annotated resource section and a directory of over 300 distributors. Available from the Film Fund, P.O. Box 909, San Francisco, CA 94101. $6.95 paperback plus $1.25 shipping and handling.

Chamba Notes, a quarterly newsletter that focuses on developments in African and black American filmmaking. Published by the Chamba Organization, P.O. Box U, Brooklyn, NY 11202. $5/year.

Cineaste, a quarterly magazine on the art and politics of cinema. Essays deal with cinema in its social, political and economic context. 419 Park Ave. South, 19th Floor, New York, NY 10016. $6/year.

Jump Cut, a bi-monthly review of contemporary cinema providing in-depth analyses and developing a radical film criticism. P.O. Box 865, Berkeley, CA 94701. $6/year.

New Day Films, a distribution cooperative for feminist films on a broad range of subjects. P.O. Box 315, Franklin Lakes, NJ 07417. (201) 891-8240.

Newsreel, a distributor with an extensive listing of films and videotapes exclusively on socio-political issues. Offers production facilities, services and training programs. Encourages community participation. Has a sliding rental scale. 630 Natoma, San Francisco, CA 94103. (415) 626-6196.

Tricontinental Films, an impressive selection of socially conscious features, documentaries and shorts from and about the Third World. 419 Park Ave. South, 19th Floor, New York, NY 10016. (212) 989-3330. Also: 1550 Bryant St., 6th Floor, San Francisco, CA 94103. (415) 864-7755.

PERIODICALS

The following is a select list of progressive Christian publications and magazines and journals of the independent Left. Together they can aid in the development of social analysis by providing a broad range of substantive discussion on a variety of practical and theoretical issues which face us today:

Akwesasne Notes, "largest authentic Native publication in the Western world." Published five times a year by the Mohawk Nation, via Rooseveltown, NY 13683. $6/year.

Coalition Close-up, newsletter of the Coalition for a New Foreign and Military Policy (43 national religious, labor, peace and social action organizations). 120 Maryland Ave. N.E., Washington, D.C. 20002. $10/year.

Dollars and Sense, "a monthly bulletin offering interpretation of current economic events from a socialist perspective to be of use to people working for progressive change." Economic Affairs Bureau, 38 Union Square, Room 14, Somerville, MA 02143. $9/year.

Monthly Review, "an independent socialist magazine." In-depth current and historical analysis published by Paul Sweezy and Harry Magdoff, eds. 62 W. 14th St., New York, NY 10011. $13/year.

Mother Jones, "a magazine for the rest of us." Features investigative reports on corporations and white collar crime. Published monthly by the Foundation for National Progress. 1886 Haymarket Sq., Marion, OH 43302. $12/year.

NACLA Report on the Americas, a bi-monthly magazine of well-researched and documented studies. Each report focuses on a major issue, industry or country in the Americas. 151 W. 19th St., 9th floor, New York, NY 10011. $11/year.

Newsfront International, a monthly bulletin of translations and compilations providing a non-sectarian, Left perspective on world events from the progressive foreign press. Published by Peoples Translation Service, 4228 Telegraph Ave., Oakland, CA 94609. $12/year.

New Left Review, a bi-monthly theoretical journal published in London. U.S. distributor: B. de Boer, 188 High St., Nutley, NJ 07110. $18/year.

The Other Side, "an ecumenical monthly magazine with an evangelical slant. Clear, down-to-earth reading on a variety of social and economic issues from a biblical viewpoint, reflecting a commitment to justice rooted in discipleship." Box 12236, Philadelphia, PA 19144. $15/year.

The Progressive, a monthly publication founded in 1909 by Robert M. La Follette, Sr. Recently led the fight against government censorship and "prior restraint" on the "H-Bomb Secret." Features articles on the military, energy and the environment. 408 W. Gorham St., Madison, WI 53703. $17/year.

Race and Class, "a journal for black and Third World liberation." Published quarterly in London by the Institute of Race Relations and the Transnational Institute. U.S. distributor: Expediters of the Printed Word, 527 Madison Ave., Suite 1217, New York, NY 10022. $10/year.

Radical America, "an independent Marxist journal, featuring the history and current developments in the working class, the role of women and Third World people." Published bi-monthly by Alternative Education Project, 324 Somerville Ave., Somerville, MA 02143. $10/year.

Radical Religion, a quarterly publication serving the progressive religious community and committed to the global development of liberation theology and the international movement for socialism. P.O. Box 9164, Berkeley, CA 94709. $9/year.

Review of Radical Political Economics, a quarterly journal "devoted to the study, development, and application of radical political economics as a tool for building socialism in the United States." Published by the Union for Radical Political Economics, 41 Union Square West, Room 901, New York, NY 10003 $15/year.

Science for the People, a bi-monthly magazine published by the national organization of the same name, which activities are directed at "exposing the class control of science and technology and organizing campaigns that propose alternatives." 897 Main St., Cambridge, MA 02139. $7/year.

Social Questions Bulletin, a bi-monthly newsletter published since 1911, which reports on crucial social and denominational issues for the Methodist Federation for Social Action. 76 Clinton Ave., Staten Island, NY 10301. $5/year.

Socialist Review, "a journal of American politics and culture in their international setting." Issues feature a wide range of articles on politics, social movements, and important theoretical questions. Published bi-monthly by New Fronts Publishing Co., 4228 Telegraph Ave., Oakland, CA 94609 $15/year.

Sojourners, a monthly evangelical journal concerned with the Christian witness in society. 1029 Vermont Ave. N.W., Washington, D.C. 20005. $12/year.

Southern Exposure, news and analysis of current conditions in the South. An excellent regional quarterly published by the Institute for Southern Studies, P.O. Box 531, Durham, NC 27702. $10/year.

Third World, an English edition of *Cuadernos del Tercer Mundo.* Based in Mexico City, it is published by Third World Journalists, an independent non-profit association of professional journalists from over 40 countries. Periodistas del Tercer Mundo, Apartado 20, Mexico D.F., Mexico. $22/year.

Union W.A.G.E., a bi-monthly publication of Union Women's Alliance to Gain Equality "for equal rights, equal pay and equal opportunity." P.O. Box 40904, San Francisco, CA 94140. $4/year.

The Witness, an independent, ecumenical advocacy journal for social issues. It is published monthly by the Episcopal Church Publishing Co., P.O. Box 359, Ambler, PA 19002. $9/year.

The Workbook, "a fully indexed catalog of sources of information about environmental, social and consumer problems. It is aimed at helping people in small towns and cities across America gain access to vital information that can help them assert control over their own lives." Published eight times a year by Southwest Research and Information Center, P.O. Box 4524, Albuquerque, NM 87106. $7/year.

Working Papers for a New Society, a bi-monthly journal published by the Center for the Study of Public Policy. Features concrete ideas and proposals for social change. 4 Nutting Road, Cambridge, MA 02138. $15/year.

POLITICAL NEWSPAPERS

A prelude to coalition work and united front activity is the identification of potential allies. A good first step for progressive religious activists to take is to examine the political newspapers of the organized Left and become familiar with their social theory and practice. Lenin called the publication of a political newspaper "the main line by which we may unswervingly develop, deepen and expand revolutionary organization. . . . A newspaper is not only a collective propagandist and a collective agitator, it is also a collective organizer." The Left in the United States today is going through a period of much fragmentation; several new political parties have been formed in recent years. No doubt the list that follows will first appear to be quite confusing. Even though it is not entirely complete, it does reflect a full spectrum of Left positions in the United States today including dogmatist and revisionist Marxist-Leninist, nationalist, social democratic and Trotskyist tendencies. Several political newspapers (which represent the views of a national organization) will list addresses and telephone numbers so readers can contact local organizing committees. They will also report on the political struggles of other groups whose activities will go unreported by the mass media.

Black Panther
Black Panther Party bi-weekly.
8501 E. 14th St., Oakland, CA 94621. $6.50/year.

The Burning Spear
"Voice of the International Black Revolution."
African People's Socialist Party monthly.
P.O. Box 11097, Louisville, KY 40211. $7.50/year.

The Call — el Clarin
Communist Party (Marxist-Leninist) weekly.
P.O. Box 5597, Chicago, IL 60680. $12/year.

CED News
Campaign for Economic Democracy (Tom Hayden & Jane Fonda) monthly.
304 S. Broadway, Room 501, Los Angeles, CA 90013. $15/year.

Challenge — Desafio
"The Revolutionary Communist Newspaper."
Progressive Labor Party weekly.
220 E. 23rd St., New York, NY 10010. $7.50/year.

Claridad
Puerto Rican Socialist Party weekly.
Betances Publishers, Inc.
P.O. Box 318 Cooper Station, New York, NY 10003. $15/year.

Daily World (see also People's World)
"Continuing the Daily Worker founded in 1924."
Longview Publishing Co. (Communist Party USA).
239 W. 23rd St., New York, NY 10011. $12/year.

Democratic Left
Democratic Socialist Organizing Committee monthly.
853 Broadway, Room 801, New York, NY 10003. $10/year.

The Guardian
"Independent Radical Newsweekly," published by the Institute for Independent Social Journalism.
33 W. 17th Street, New York, NY 10011. $17/year.

In These Times
"The Independent Socialist Newspaper."
Institute for Policy Studies weekly.
1509 N. Milwaukee Ave., Chicago, IL 60622. $19/year.

The Militant

"A socialist weekly published in the interests of the working people."
(Socialist Workers Party)
14 Charles Lane, New York, NY 10014. $20/year.

Obreros en Marcha

"Political Organ of the Puerto Rican Left Movement."
M.I.N.P. — El Comite monthly.
577 Columbus Ave., New York, NY 10024. $6/year.

The Organizer

"The Newspaper of the Philadelphia Workers Organizing Committee."
Published monthly by PWOC, Box 11768, Philadelphia, PA 19101. $10/year.

The People

"Established April 5, 1891."
Socialist Labor Party bi-weekly.
914 Industrial Ave., Palo Alto, CA 94303. $4/year

People's Tribune (also Western Worker)

"The communists' ideal should not be a trade-union secretary, but a tribune of the people." (V.I. Lenin)
Communist Labor Party bi-monthly.
P.O. Box 3774, Chicago, IL 60654. $10/year.

People's World (see also Daily World)

"Voice of the Left for over 40 years."
Pacific Publishing Foundation (Communist Party, USA), weekly.
1819 Tenth St., Berkeley, CA 94710. $10/year.

The Rebel Worker

"News Journal of the Workers Party."
Synthesis Publications monthly.
131 Townsend St., San Francisco, CA 94107. $4/year.

Revolutionary Worker

"Voice of the Revolutionary Communist Party, USA."
RCP Publications weekly.
P.O. Box 3486 Merchandise Mart, Chicago, IL 60654. $12/year.

Socialist Worker

"Paper of the International Socialist Organization."
P.O. Box 10837, Cleveland, OH 44118. Monthly, $5/year.

Unite! (Workers of the world,)

Communist Party U.S.A./Marxist-Leninist semi-monthly.
P.O. Box 6206, Chicago, IL 60680. $8/year.

Workers' Viewpoint

"Political organ of the Communist Workers Party, U.S.A."
G.P.O. Box 2256, New York, NY 10001. $13/year.

Workers' World

World View Publishers (Workers World Party), weekly.
46 W. 21st St., New York, NY 10010. $10/year.

PROGRESSIVE CHRISTIAN ORGANIZATIONS

American Friends Service Committee (AFSC), the Quaker organization for social action and mission work which has been active for many years in movements of peace and justice. For information about the various projects of AFSC write to 1501 Cherry St., Philadelphia, PA 19102. (215) 241-7000.

Catholic Committee on Urban Ministry, a network of Catholic priests, religious and laity bound by the commitment to work for justice within church and society. It provides workshops and training sessions at the local level on urban affairs; resource to diocesan offices on urban questions and problems; communication through bulletins and reports on current issues. It promotes the formation of regional networks of social ministers as sources of support, mutual assistance, analysis and reflection. 1112 Memorial Library, University of Notre Dame, Notre Dame, IN 46556. (219) 283-3293.

Christians for Socialism (formerly American Christians Toward Socialism—ACTS). CFS was formed in the United States in 1974 as part of the international movement of CFS. Its locally-based chapters provide for regular theoretical study, praxis reflection and celebration of faith within their groups. CFS is a movement, not a party or a church, committed to a class option in support of the interests of the poor and working people of the United States. CFS is committed to liberate the churches from the economic and cultural bonds of capitalism and to building socialism rooted in the U.S democratic traditions. For further information on the movement of CFS or for chapter-forming information and papers from the U.S. groups, call or write CFS National Office, 3540 14th St., Detroit, MI 48208. (313) 833-3987.

Church & Society Network, an informal association of Episcopalians and others working at the social mission of the church. For more information about group formation and program, write P.O. Box 359, Ambler, PA 19002. (215) 643-7067.

Clergy and Laity Concerned (CALC) is an inter-faith peace and justice network with 40 chapters nationwide. The national office in New York City publishes CALC Report eight times yearly in addition to a variety of program resources. Program areas include human security (anti-nuke, anti-war), human rights, politics of food and Vietnam. For more information on membership, literature list or chapter formation contact: CALC, 198 Broadway, New York, NY 10038. (212) 964-6730.

Interfaith Center for Corporate Responsibility, monitors the social effects of corporations' policies and works to influence corporate policy through dialogue and stockholder resolutions. Publishes the *Corporate Examiner* monthly. 475 Riverside Drive, Room 566, New York, NY 10027. (212) 870-2295.

Lutheran New Wine Exchange is an informational network for "edge of the church" Lutherans involved in justice work in the United States with the primary goal of building international consciousness and political-economic analysis in order to question the effect of these two things on domestic justice. It publishes a newsletter and conducts two theology conferences a year. 437 E. 140th St., New York, NY 10454. (212) 585-6084.

Methodist Federation For Social Action is an independent movement working within the United Methodist Church since 1907 to promote social action in the church and work for a society not based on the struggle for profit. The Federation has eight area chapters and publishes the bi-monthly *Social Questions Bulletin*. It is giving special attention to combatting politically reactionary tendencies in the denomination. 76 Clinton Ave., Staten Island, NY 10301. (212) 273-4941.

National Convergence of Justice and Peace Centers is a predominantly Catholic network of centers, offices, commissions and organizations joined together for communication and joint action. The Convergence includes groups with a national constituency, some oriented to specific constituencies or locales, as well as some diocesan offices of Justice & Peace. Member groups share in special projects proposed by participating groups; ongoing legislative efforts; clearing house for organizations and committees desiring contacts in the initial period of establishing justice and peace efforts. Institute for Education in Justice and Peace, 2747 Rutger, St. Louis, MO 63104. (314) 773-8884.

Theology in the Americas is a five-year ecumenical program for the contextualization of theology in the Americas. Books, documents, film strips, newsletters and models for theological reflection are available from the nine projects working toward a synthesis to overcome racism, sexism, classism and imperialism. The nine projects are: The Black Theology Project; The Hispanic Theology Project; Women, Work and the Economy; The Asian-American Project; The Native American Project; Theologians Task Force; Church and Labor Dialogue; Alternative Theology Project; Ecumenical Dialogue of Third World Theologians. For more information: 475 Riverside Dr., Room 1268, New York, NY 10027. (212) 870-2078.

World Student Christian Federation is a worldwide coalition of student Christian movements committed to progressive political activity as motivated by a radical faith perspective. The North American Region publishes a quarterly newspaper, *Press On!*, and works through programs and projects of movements throughout Canada and the United States. WSCF encourages participation of all students who are interested in issues of education, students and labor, and international solidarity. Write WSCF-NA, 427 Bloor St. W., Toronto, Ontario, Canada M5S 1X7. (416) 922-8597 or (415) 548-8312.

RESEARCH AND INFORMATION CENTERS

Investigative Resource Center is a tax-exempt organization founded to meet the information needs of labor and community activists, organizers and researchers engaged in educating and mobilizing constituencies around vital public policy issues. It has two major projects: *The Data Center* is an independent, non-profit library focusing on the global political economy. The Data Center collection is organized to reflect the struggle between capital and labor. It provides information services on major corporations, banks, industries, and the struggle to resist these dominant forces of capitalism by labor and liberation movements. The staff will conduct file searches on the subject of your inquiry and send photo copies by mail. Fees vary according to the amount of time spent and the ability to pay. *Information Services on Latin America* (ISLA) has been a valuable resource for 10 years for anyone who needs to know about socio-economic and political developments in Latin America. ISLA provides monthly mailings of articles on Latin America from nine major newspapers of the English language press. Write for subscription rates. Investigative Resource Center, 464 19th Street, Oakland, CA 94612. Data Center (415) 835-4692. ISLA (415) 835-0678.

New York CIRCUS is a specialized ministry based in New York City, working within the progressive Latin American community. It develops, primarily through the work of exiles, a packet of materials and translations of articles designed to build solidarity between Christians struggling for liberation. N.Y. CIRCUS also conducts seminars on liberation theology. P.O. Box 37, Times Square Station, New York, NY 10036. Phone (212) 663-5012. ∎

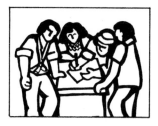